THE MOORS MURDERERS

THE FULL STORY OF IAN BRADY AND MYRA HINDLEY

C.G.C. COOK

PEN & SWORD
HISTORY

AN IMPRINT OF PEN & SWORD BOOKS LTD.
YORKSHIRE - PHILADELPHIA

First published in Great Britain in 2022 by
PEN AND SWORD HISTORY
An imprint of
Pen & Sword Books Ltd
Yorkshire – Philadelphia

ISBN 978 1 39909 875 5

A CIP catalogue record for this book is available from the British Library.

Typeset in Times New Roman 10.5/13 by
SJmagic DESIGN SERVICES, India.
Printed and bound in the UK by CPI Group (UK) Ltd.

Pen & Sword Books Limited incorporates the imprints of Atlas, Archaeology,
Aviation, Discovery, Family History, Fiction, History, Maritime, Military,
Military Classics, Politics, Select, Transport, True Crime, Air World,
Frontline Publishing, Leo Cooper, Remember When, Seaforth Publishing,
The Praetorian Press, Wharncliffe Local History, Wharncliffe Transport,
Wharncliffe True Crime and White Owl.

For a complete list of Pen & Sword titles please contact
PEN & SWORD BOOKS LIMITED
47 Church Street, Barnsley, South Yorkshire, S70 2AS, England
E-mail: enquiries@pen-and-sword.co.uk
Website: www.pen-and-sword.co.uk

Or
PEN AND SWORD BOOKS
1950 Lawrence Rd, Havertown, PA 19083, USA
E-mail: Uspen-and-sword@casematepublishers.com
Website: www.penandswordbooks.com

Contents

Acknowledgements

This book wouldn't have been possible without the close support and encouragement of my friends and family, in particular: Adrian Rodgers for giving me the encouragement to start writing, Rob Wittwer for all of his understanding over the years, and Nick Dexter for his help at the National Archives.

Thanks must also go to my sister Nicola, and her partner Dan, for all of their encouragement over the years, and to my mother Christine and late father George, to whom this book is dedicated, for their unconditional love.

Introduction

During the 1960s Ian Brady and Myra Hindley committed five murders against children that still shock to this day. While Brady had shown signs of disturbed behaviour from a young age, Hindley seemed to have a relatively normal upbringing, was good at sports and enjoyed poetry. She admitted to falling in love with Ian Brady almost at first sight, but it took Brady nearly a year even to notice her, let alone ask her out. From that moment on they became almost inseparable and went on to carry out some of the most heinous acts of murder ever committed anywhere in the world.

This was the first case of a woman being convicted of the murder of children on such a scale in the UK and it shocked the nation so much that the name 'Myra' has become almost obsolete.

This is the true story of their childhoods, how they met, the depravity of their crimes and how they were caught.

Chapter 1

Ian Brady – The Early Years

On 2 January 1938, Maggie 'Peggy' Stewart gave birth to a baby boy in Rotten Row Maternity Hospital, in a tough district in Glasgow. The boy was named Ian Duncan Stewart.

His 19-year-old mother was a waitress in a tea room and his father was a journalist who died three months before Ian's birth. They were never married. On leaving hospital with her new baby, Peggy took him home to the flat she shared with a friend of hers at 8 Huntingdon Place. Three months later Peggy was struggling to work and look after her new-born son; she placed an advert in the window of a local shop for someone to look after Ian for £1 a week – a third of her weekly wage. The advert was answered by Margaret Reilly, better known as Jeannie Sloan, and so Peggy and her son moved to Caledonia Road in the south side of Glasgow and Brady came under the guardianship of Jeannie.

Jeannie was married to John Sloan and they already had two daughters, Jean and May, and a son called Robert, so one more mouth to feed was no hardship and they were glad of the extra weekly income; room was made in the crowded tenement flat at 56 Camden Street. The baby was never officially adopted.

Able to go back to work full-time, Peggy paid for her son's clothes and upkeep, went to see him every night after work and took him out every weekend. She moved several times over the coming months but never lost contact with him.

By 1942 Peggy had changed jobs and became a capstan operator at Albion Motors, but still visited her son in the evenings and at the weekends. She would take Ian out to the cinema and he quickly developed a love of film. He remembered that the first film he ever saw was *The Road to Morocco* starring Bob Hope and Bing Crosby.

The Sloans then had another child, John, and much of the attention Ian had enjoyed as the baby of the family quickly disappeared. In later years Ian would say that this had no effect on him: 'I was popular at school and so I was hardly likely to have feelings of inferiority, but, of course, I still wanted to be accepted and loved by those I loved.'

On 16 August, Ian went to school at Househillwood Primary, about a quarter of a mile from his home. Soon though, he had his first encounter with death when he was playing a game with his friends called 'Catch a Hudgie'. The game involved jumping on to the back of a van or lorry and holding on to the spare tyre or whatever you could get a grip of for as long as possible. One boy jumped but couldn't get a proper grip, slipped off and rolled under the wheels of a lorry that was following. Ian recalled many years later that he ran through the legs of the adults who had gathered around but could see nothing apart from a brown child's shoe filled to the brim with blood.

By 1944 Peggy had met a man named Peter and they had the chance to emigrate to Australia under a government aided scheme for just £10. They asked Ian if he wanted to go but it meant nothing to him and he was more than happy living with the Sloans; they were more of a family to him than his birth mother. Peggy refused to leave her son behind and Peter soon faded into the distance. Another reason Ian didn't want to leave was because he had also begun to thieve. He took the housekeeping money out of Mrs Sloan's purse and hid it in a mouse hole on the landing.

In his later life Ian would tell of a few instances of death during this period of his childhood. En route to his school, for example, there was a children's play area in Hutchestown Square and he was playing on the swing one day when the back of the wooden seat hit a small child walking by. Ian could see the boy was bleeding profusely from a head wound but Ian then panicked and ran away. He assumed that he had killed the boy; although there was never any record of a boy being killed in the area at that time, Ian believed he had killed him right up until the day of his own death.

Another incident that stayed with him involved a Clydesdale horse. He would later recall:

> Ma sent me every morning for hot rolls and milk from a dairy in Florence Street. One morning – very frosty in the Gorbals under the leaden hue of the Glasgow sky – I was holding hot rolls to my chest on my way back and saw a crowd of people huddled in a circle on the corner of Cumberland Street and Crown Street. I was inquisitive and pushed through the mass of gawking heads to discover the cause of the commotion. I was within touching distance of a huge Clydesdale horse lying flat on its side in the road. It was still tethered to the cart.
>
> It had slipped on the icy road and was badly injured. It lay there with its massive sides heaving and its breath steaming in the frosty air. I was near enough to touch the large head. I can still see the great liquid eyes rolling in terror, looking up to the grey Glasgow morning sky. Its great fetlocks raked the air, bedraggled and wet. A man appeared from nowhere to erect a canvas screen around the Clydesdale.
>
> They were going to kill the horse. Even I knew it. My chest was bursting and I began to cry. I fought my way through the mass of bodies and ran to Camden Street, trying to hold on to the bag of hot

rolls with my hands clapped over my ears. I sat on the tenement stairs until the tears dried up before taking the rolls in to Ma. I was afraid to wander near the spot where the horse had died. I couldn't bear to see the remains of bloodstains and hairs. I couldn't rid the event and scene from my mind.

Many years later I saw something in a dark railway arch that triggered the image of the wet, straggling fetlocks of the Clydesdale, suddenly changing my relaxed mood to one of ice-cold fury and leading to a frenzied knife attack on a man in the street. I didn't hang around to check whether it was fatal. It was enough for me to feel that the Clydesdale had been avenged.

In the summer of 1946, the Sloans and Ian went on holiday by bus to Loch Lomond. He later recalled this as his first spiritual experience and said that when they got to Balloch the family walked along the southern shoreline before he left them and climbed through the trees and bushes to get a better view of the loch and mountains.

He said that he couldn't believe the vastness and it felt like he had entered a different dimension. He found the new sense of reality intoxicating and believed he had encountered the essence of life itself. Later the same day, however, he had a very contrasting experience when he went out on a boat with the family; gazing down into the crystal clear water of the loch he could see straight down to the bottom and this sight terrified him. It was then, he said, that he learned that in the beauty of life he could not be spared the dark side of it too.

When Peggy had fallen pregnant with Ian she was in disgrace with her family and as a result Ian hardly knew them. He did, however, later recall during his prison years that when he was around 8 years old he was introduced to a topless man having a shave and later learned that this was his uncle, Murdoch. He also met his grandmother for the first time, but neither were happy to see him or Peggy. He instantly felt that he was not welcome and never saw them again.

New housing was being built after the end of the Second World War and the Sloans were high up on the list for a new council home. At the end of 1946 they moved to 21 Templeland Road, Pollok, a street of new four-apartment, semi-detached houses with deep gardens to front and back.

They were among the first families on an estate that was to be developed into a vast housing project and as such Ian was forced into changing schools. He now went to Carnwadric Primary School on Crebar Street on the school bus, which came and picked up the children from the estate every day for the three mile journey.

Ian was tall for his age and was teased by the other children because of this. He was known by most of the other boys as 'The Big Lassie'. He did, however, have a small group of friends and his best friend at the time, John Cameron, remembered being tied to a steel washing post one day by Ian. Paper was piled at his feet and then lit. 'People tell me that by the time I was cut free I had blacked out. Mind you, we were all rough lads in those days, but Ian was the toughest of the lot.'

He had already developed other disturbing behaviour and began hanging around an old graveyard carrying out some bizarre experiments with animals. He would use a razor to slice open caterpillars to see if they bled and would build cairns in which he would encase cats to see how long it took them to starve to death.

He also had his own pets, including at one point three rabbits and a dog called Sheila, but within a year the dog was dead. He recalled knowing that the dog was unwell, but he had plans to go out to the cinema, so he wrapped it up and left it by the warmth of the open fire. He remembered praying to God and asking him to make sure his dog would recover, but when he got home she had died from distemper.

He recalled that this was when he felt anger and contempt for religion and all it stood for, and that when the mood finally lifted it left him feeling empty, but calm. He felt a kind of energy and power that he had not known before and loved every second of it. He felt that it was the pure contempt that had left him with this feeling and he now felt free of any morals and laws. He felt that God did not exist and, as such, there was no afterlife. He felt there were no limits and no restraints. He felt reborn.

Peggy, started to date an Irishman named Patrick Brady in late 1947. In 1949 Patrick would move to Manchester for work and a year later Peggy would follow him south. They married at All Saints Registry Office, Manchester, on 16 May 1950 and then moved in together at 9 Brammar Street, Ancoats. Nine-year-old Ian committed his first break-in soon after his mother started to see Patrick. It was a ground floor tenement apartment and Ian remembered moving silently through the two rooms, realising it was the home of a sailor. He opened the sideboard drawer which was full of packets of foreign cigarettes. He stole nothing and left the apartment.

The reason he gave for his later break-ins, mostly involving the friends he referred to as the 'Pollok gang', was because they needed cash, but first they stole bags of workmen's tools, which had been stored in the houses still being constructed on the estate, and hid them near the river. The Pollok gang consisted of Ian and five friends. They were brothers John and Tam, Willie T., Bressie and Frankie Fraser. Ian reached puberty early aged 10 in 1948 and it wasn't long before he got his first girlfriend. She had strawberry-blonde hair, high cheek bones and almond shaped eyes. It was these eyes that he looked for in all subsequent girlfriends. He would kiss her so hard that both of their mouths would bleed.

His next girlfriend was called Evelyn Grant. She had a pert figure, honey-blonde hair, high cheekbones – and almond-shaped eyes.

In 1950 Ian passed the Scottish equivalent of the eleven-plus and went to Shawlands Academy. The Academy took the more intelligent children from the district, despite his school records describing him as being slightly below average intelligence. Evelyn also went to the academy, and although the boys were separated from the girls during lessons, they still managed to see each other during the day and in the evenings.

Ian soon started smoking in the toilets at school and playing around with a flick-knife. He also started to watch horror films over-and-over again and talking about them to his friends at school, earning him the nickname Dracula.

A classmate recalled: 'He read all kinds of books about the Nazis and never stopped talking about them. Even when we were playing war-games, he made a great point of being a German…. When Ian used to shout 'Sieg Heil!' and give the Nazi salute, people would laugh.' None of the other boys knew what

Ian Brady aged 12.

to make of Ian. He didn't like football and always preferred to be alone reading books. He was taller than most and had hair that always needed cutting.

In 1950 the annual Sloan summer holiday took them to St Monans, fourteen miles south of St Andrew's. He had the strongest feelings of belonging there and would later take Myra Hindley when they got together. He even recalled it in his first letter to her in HMP Holloway immediately after their trial.

When he returned from the holiday he went back to his usual vice of breaking and entering, but it didn't take long for him and his gang to get caught by the police; they were breaking into up to three properties a night and had spread their ill-gotten gains equally between them. It was only when they were showing off the stolen property at school that one of the other pupils informed on them. Aged 13, he appeared at the Juvenile Court in Glasgow on 5 May 1951 accused of housebreaking and attempted theft. He was found guilty, as were the others on the same charge, but because none of them had any previous convictions and all the families were of 'good character', they were all placed on probation for two years.

On one occasion later in 1950 Ian went to stay with his mother for two weeks in Manchester. Ian called her Peggy, because to him the Sloans were his 'Ma' and 'Da', even though he had figured out that Peggy was his real mother. Ian spent the whole journey taking in the sights and smells through the train window.

One day he visited Moss Side, and later recalled: 'Moss Side became one of my favourite haunts at a future date, particularly after dark. Decades later I was to exchange stories with the Yorkshire Ripper, Peter Sutcliffe, who also knew the area

Ian Brady as
a teenager
(second left).

well, it being rich in prostitutes, two of whom he murdered.' He also visited Ashton-Under-Lyne market with his mother and later recalled:

> I could not have known that, at a time not far into the future, late on
> a November Saturday afternoon, as the fog descended like a shroud
> on the market, Myra Hindley and I would provide a corpse for the
> shroud and take a stranger with us to the high barren wilderness of
> Saddleworth Moor.

It was only once Ian was back from his holiday that he decided to take revenge on the boy who had informed on him and his gang. He and the boy were alone after a PE lesson at school when the boy, sensing something was coming, started to cry. Brady grabbed hold of him and raped him.

In July 1952, a year after his first court case and while still on probation, Ian was caught stealing again. The gang's latest recruit had taken a stolen, crafted cutthroat razor home with him after a burglary and hidden it under the cushion of a chair in his bedroom. His father had found it and made him confess to everything. He took his son to the police and made him tell them the names of everyone in the gang. On 16 July Ian appeared in Govan Juvenile Court accused of housebreaking and was admonished. The record did not even show that he had broken his probation.

He was still seeing Evelyn Grant at this time, but also started to see another girl because Evelyn would not sleep with him. This girl had a reputation with the other boys he hung around with and Brady slept with her. Occasionally, they would mutually seduce a boy or a girl, to deepen an intrigue that began when they confided to each other their early forbidden longings for 'irregular' sex.

Ian left school in 1953 and was employed as an errand boy with R. Wallace and Sons, butchers, of 1583 Paisley Road West, Glasgow, and he remained employed there as both an errand boy and then a Junior Assistant until January 1954. Apart from pocket money, he used the job to find vulnerable properties in the neighbourhood.

He was still seeing Evelyn Grant but met a girl on his rounds and took her to the cinema on a first date. On the way back they snuck into Queen's Park and had sex. They continued to meet there for sex and also had sex on the rug in front of the living room fire at her parents' house when her parents were out. Evelyn soon found out and she and Ian broke up.

After leaving his job at R. Wallace and Sons, Ian worked for a week (25–29 January) as an engine cleaner for British Railways at the Corker Hill Railway Sidings at Glasgow, but they didn't employ anyone with a criminal record, so once their checks were completed, Ian was sacked.

He then went without a job – no doubt stealing to get by – until the 6 September 1954 when he was employed by Messrs Harland and Wolff Limited, shipbuilders of Govan, Glasgow, as an apprentice plater, where he was described as a 'satisfactory worker'.

On 29 November, 16-year-old Ian was in court again. This time, with his probationary period over, he was charged with housebreaking before Glasgow's Sheriff Court. After he was found guilty, he had nine other cases of housebreaking taken into consideration in his sentence. He was placed on probation for another two years on the proviso that he left Scotland and went to live with his birth mother and stepfather in Manchester.

Mrs Sloan had written to Mrs Brady telling her that Ian was in trouble with the police and Mrs Brady had made the train journey up to Glasgow to attend the court session.

Ian moved south to Manchester and lived with Peggy and Patrick Brady in Denmark Road, Moss Side. Peggy was delighted to have her son staying with her and it was at this time that she confirmed Ian's suspicions that she was his birth mother.

Ian soon developed a taste for the horses and he learned from Patrick Brady, the 45-year-old man whose surname he was now to take, what to look out for. They would listen together to the radio commentary and results.

Peggy took the opportunity to spoil her son; her friend and next door neighbour Alma Singleton would recall: 'Anyone could tell Ian was Mrs Brady's son. When he was about the house her eyes followed him everywhere. She thought the world of him.'

The three of them soon moved to Cuttle Street near Manchester's Grey Mare Lane Market. They had little more than the essential furniture, but Peggy Brady kept the house spotlessly clean and Patrick Brady got Ian a job as a porter at the Smithfield Market, working for Messrs Howarth Limited; the two of them used to go off to start work together in the early hours of the morning. He used to bring home apples, oranges and fresh vegetables from the wholesalers' warehouses where his job was unloading the crates from the lorries. It was here that he made a friend, a man called Chas, who was on the delivery run from London. Of Ian at this time, Alma Singleton recalled:

> He didn't want to be noticed, but you couldn't help feeling sorry for him. There were at least half a dozen lads of his age in the street, but he never spoke to any of them. He didn't seem to have any friends and he never brought anyone to the house.

The women in the area were a different prospect, however. Alma's daughter, Carol, said that Ian was considered a bit of a heart-throb by the local teenagers. When he went out in the evenings he was always smartly dressed and clean shaven. He paid a great deal of attention to his appearance. The neighbours had no idea where he went, but it was not to any of the local pubs. As always, he was keeping what social life he had strictly separate from his home life, but he was certainly going to other pubs. Quite possibly homosexual pubs.

In June he was again in court, this time charged with being drunk and disorderly and was fined £1. Alma's daughter recalled seeing him stagger up Cuttle Street one night and later heard him stumbling about and singing in his bedroom next door. Her father saw him one night hanging around a lamp post in the street unable to stand.

What Ian was up to on some of his evenings out alone was soon revealed. In September 1955 he appeared at Manchester City Magistrates' Court where he was found guilty of 'petty larceny as a servant', this time it was the lead from banana boxes (worth £44.10s.0d.) and he was remanded to Quarter Sessions.

A delivery driver to the market had told him that there was a sack of lead seals lying discarded in the warehouse. He asked Ian to load the sack on to his lorry so that he could sell it as scrap and he would split the proceeds with him.

The driver pulled into the yard of a local scrap merchants and offered the lead for cash. Howarth's Fruiterers was painted on the side of the lorry and the scrap dealer made a note of it. When he saw the sack's contents he contacted the local police. Ian was arrested shortly afterwards. When in court the following morning, the driver pleaded guilty immediately and was given a fine because he had a family to support. Ian, thinking that he too would just get a fine, pleaded guilty but said that he preferred to be tried at the Quarter Sessions and was remanded back into custody. The Quarter Sessions had sat only a few days before and would not sit again for around another three months, so Ian was sent to HMP Strangeways. As he had pleaded 'guilty' he was not allowed privileges and was treated as a regular prisoner who had been found guilty.

He later recalled that the prison smelled of urine and body odour. He was given his own cell that consisted of a low bed, wooden table, a chair and a metal chamber pot.

After breakfast he was made to shovel coke into the furnaces underneath Strangeways' towering chimney stack and before long he had made his first acquaintance – a fellow Glaswegian called Wallace.

Brady had already decided that he wanted to be a 'somebody' and was determined to get rich and not work for the rest of his life. At 'association' Brady met other inmates and spoke to safecrackers, fencers etc. He made mental notes of how they did things and also of who to contact upon his release.

To help pass the time, and to understand how to handle money on the 'outside', he began to study accountancy. He also took up a tool-making course.

On 9 November 1955 Ian Brady was back in Manchester City Magistrates' Court for sentencing. He did nothing to help his situation by offering no plea of mitigation and even refused to say a few words of contrition. He had already decided that it was him versus the system and was indifferent to court proceedings. As such, he was found guilty of 'petty larceny as a servant' and the court ordered him to undergo Borstal training. He was sent back to HMP Strangeways until a place could be found for him at a Borstal. Brady would later say: '…I vowed vengeance and that I would never again take risks for anything trivial … I said to myself that if they wanted me to be a criminal, I'll be a *proper* one!'

A fellow inmate at the time recalled:

> We were in there about two months together before he was moved. I was very friendly with him in the nick and he told me on one occasion that he had had sexual connections with queers and that he used to get money off men for doing this. He used to work in the pantry on the Y.P. Wing with another queer.

A later psychiatric report reflected:

> He felt that this was a time of deep crisis in his life and that in some way a decision had been made. He felt increasingly cut off from other people in the emotional sense – he could no longer feel concern for them or feel warmly towards them. He retained affection for his foster family.

On 10 January 1956 Ian Brady was handcuffed and put onto a bus destined for the south of England. Later that evening the bus reached Latchmere House, a former POW camp for Germans. The following morning the newcomers were given an introductory talk and in the evening they were allowed to mix with the other inmates in the gym hall. His luck was in, as he saw a face he recognised. Chas, the man who used to deliver to Smithfield's Market, recognised him too and was able to pass on the local knowledge needed to survive in there.

Their supervisors realised that Brady was showing signs of above average intelligence so both he and Chas were soon sent to Hatfield, near Doncaster. The two were sent to shovel coke every day at first, but Brady was sent to work in the kitchen after a couple of weeks. He exploited his new position and began brewing hooch using methylated spirits, surgical spirit, lemon and sugar. He would hide it in a ditch which ran around the edge of the cricket field inside the Borstal and made so much money from selling it to other inmates that he persuaded others to carry some of the money in case he was searched. With the profits he soon began running books on cards, the dogs and horse racing. Anyone who informed on him was dealt with swiftly. According to Brady: 'One was gang-banged in a dark field and fled from the camp the same night.'

During his time in Borstal he made two friends – petty criminals Dougie Woods and Gilbert Deare. Brady would meet these two men later on the outside and commit further small crimes. Brady was mainly remembered as being 'a very quiet sort of fellow but sadistic. If we were wrestling it would start as a joke and end up with Brady putting his hands round his opponent's throat and nearly choking them before he would let go….'

When release dates drew near, the inmates were allowed out at times to get used to normal life again. On 5 June 1957 a group of inmates were taken to Hornsea, just a few miles north of Hull. They were allowed to do pretty much what they wanted unsupervised, provided they behaved themselves and did not enter the Alexandria pub, as this was where the officers drank. They were expected to fend for themselves in terms of food and they camped out in tents in a nearby field.

One evening Brady and his group began drinking early before going to an arcade. Brady had been drinking from a whisky bottle and he and his group got into an altercation with some of the locals. He and his group were heading back to their tent but decided to go into the Alexandria pub and were seen by two of the Borstal staff. The boys left without incident and crossed a railway line on the way back to their tents. Brady insisted on walking along the rails and was dragged back to camp by the rest of the group. He was still drunk when the two Borstal staff returned and Brady came to blows with one of them; the Governor was informed.

The following morning Brady woke up hungover in a cell and couldn't remember what had happened the night before. It was only when the Governor later visited him that he was told what he had done. Brady was handcuffed and taken to Hull Prison, part of which had been adapted as a Borstal. As a punishment he was given the task of scrubbing the stone floor of the punishment block and then sent to break bricks into rubble.

Brady was released on licence on 14 November 1957, having first been psychoanalysed, and went straight back to Manchester to live with his mother and step-father in Grey Mare Lane. He spent many days and evenings watching banks, department stores, electricity and gas works for the days and times when large deposits were made. He did this mainly in Manchester but also further afield. He would write everything down in a notebook and contacted people he had met in Borstal about doing a job.

He had to report to his probation officer every couple of days, but sabotaged the various job interviews that were set up for him and acted completely uninterested. He had already made his mind up that he would not work a 'normal 9-5 job', and decided that the only way to get rich was to do a 'big job'. One worth running the risk of going to prison for. After a few weeks planning, Brady and his associates carried out a test run which proved to be more lucrative than first thought and they split the £250 proceeds equally among themselves.

By 28 April 1958, no doubt as a result of having to explain to his mother where his money was coming from, Brady got a job as a labourer at Boddington's Brewery. On 9 June, he was fined by the company for being drunk and disorderly. Employees were allowed free beer but were not permitted to be unable to carry out their duties.

His step-father, Patrick, still worked in Manchester's Smithfield Market as a porter and both he and Ian were home from work in the early afternoons. Peggy worked in an engineering works and on her lunchbreak she would go home and prepare dinner for them. In the late afternoon Alma Singleton, Peggy's friend, would usually pop into the house and light the fire so the house was warm in the evenings. Ian and Patrick were mostly asleep when she was there, but occasionally she saw Ian around the house. He would be relaxing in a chair, wearing his bright, checked work shirts, reading a book. 'Ian was a quiet lad', she recalled. 'When I went in he would look up and nod, and then he would blush. He always seemed to be embarrassed when he met anyone. Maybe he was a bit awkward with his mother's friends because no one knew she had a grown up son until he appeared.'

It wasn't long before the Bradys were on the move again. In late 1958 they moved to 18 Westmoreland Street, which was a dingy street off the Stockport Road. It was poorly lit and the road had many uneven and broken cobbles. The house wasn't in the best condition, despite Peggy scrubbing it as best she could. Newspaper was often on the floor as it was easier to throw away the dirty newspaper than constantly wash the floor, and plaster hung down from the ceiling. Brady took to wallpapering and painting where he could and also going to the local library and studying book-keeping. It was at this time that he also began saving for a motorbike.

Alma visited the Bradys in their new home and she took her baby daughter Lesley with her. He was still shy and muttered that the baby was 'bonnie' before hurrying back indoors. Peggy explained this away by saying that his cat had had kittens but the mother was refusing to feed them so he was nursing them by feeding them from an eye-dropper.

Brady had spent some of his ill-gotten gains on a new camera and enjoyed taking photographs of his family, himself and the new house.

Above left: Ian Brady while living at his mum's house, which was just around the corner from Keith Bennett's house.

Above right: Ian Brady while living at his mum's house, around the corner from Keith Bennett's house.

Left: Ian Brady's birth mother, Peggy Stewart.

On 16 February 1959, Brady got himself a job as a Stock Clerk at Millwards Merchandise Ltd on Levenshulme Road. His job was in the stock control department, which maintained and ordered stocks of chemicals in the Manchester railway stations, and supervised deliveries from the stations and warehouse to customers. Most of his time was spent dictating orders and letters.

He would play Bridge on his lunch-break with three of the storemen, and it progressed into a once-a-fortnight bridge party at the home of one of the players, David Greig, but after a short time they gave up because of Brady's furious temper. He would fly into a rage if his team didn't win and spoil the game for everybody.

He also began to buy records by mail order from Anthony Marsh of the Deroy Sound Service, at Hest Bank, near Lancaster; rather than buying pop tunes however,

Ian ordered records of German marching songs, Adolf Hitler's speeches and the Nuremberg Trials. He also sent tape recordings of German broadcasts for Mr Marsh to make in to LP records. When he received them, he would play them as loudly as he could and one of his neighbours, James Spilsbury, recalled:

> The marching songs were bad enough. But what really got me was hearing the Nazi leaders screaming at their troops. I thought Brady must be a very peculiar chap. But he was always so quiet on the street. He rarely spoke to anyone and acted as though he was too good to live in the neighbourhood.

One of the friends Brady had made in Borstal went to visit him in Westmoreland Street. He later gave a statement to the police confirming that Brady was still looking to commit armed robberies at this time. He told the police that Brady wanted him to act as the getaway driver and that Brady and another man, whom he hardly knew but was also present, were to commit the robbery. The target was a woman who deposited money into a night safe near to Piccadilly. Brady told him that he was going to steal revolvers and shotguns (which would have the barrels sawn off) from a display cabinet in a nearby gunsmiths and use them in the robbery.

> He had planned the job to the last detail but I told him that I had no intention of being involved in any job where violence was to be used and I left Manchester.
>
> When I last saw Brady we were good pals and there was no ill feeling because I refused to go on the job with him.

Chapter 2

Myra Hindley – The Early Years

At just before 3.00 am on 23 July 1942, Myra Hindley was born at Crumpsall Hospital, Manchester. Her mother Nellie, a 22-year-old factory machinist, had travelled six miles by bus from her home in Gorton along with her mother, Ellen Maybury, when she felt herself going into labour. Myra's father, Bob, was a labourer by trade but had been called up to fight in the war and was now a paratrooper. Private Hindley 3853894 won the regimental boxing championship and his battered nose would let people know he was a fighter for the rest of his life.

Nellie took Myra home to 24 Beesley Street, which she shared with her brother Bert and his wife Kath, and Myra's grandmother, Ellen Maybury. Ellen had been born illegitimately in Newbury, Berkshire in 1888. She had been 'in service' as a chamber maid since she the age of 11 and had worked in a vicarage for a time before moving to Lancashire and finding work in the cotton mills. At the time of Myra's birth Ellen was working as a chamber maid and would bring home any leftovers for the family to eat. She had been married twice and had suffered ten miscarriages, but had three children of adult age at the time of Myra's birth.

Despite being away fighting for his country, Bob Hindley was insistent that his daughter Myra be baptised a Catholic at St Francis' Monastery. Nellie was not religious but agreed, providing Bob accepted that their daughter would not go to a Catholic school. On 16 August 1942, Myra was baptised and Bert's wife, Kath, agreed to be her godmother.

Bob Hindley returned home from war in 1945 and was an almost completely changed man. He had seen action in North Africa, Cyprus and Italy, and struggled to adapt to both married and civilian life. He went back to his pre-war job, labouring at Beyer Peacock's. Soon afterwards, Myra and her parents moved to 20 Eaton Street, just around the corner from Myra's gran. The house had electricity and a tiled fireplace but was otherwise in a shocking state. It was a two-up two-down property with cockroaches in most rooms. Of the two rooms on the ground floor, the front room opened on to the street, and the rear room opened on to the yard with a damp toilet. The house was in such a poor state of repair that the back bedroom, which was Myra's, had been condemned before they moved in. The ceiling leaked and the floorboards were unsafe to walk on, so Myra had to sleep in the same room as her parents. Myra hated this and later recalled: 'I hated him for forcing us to move away from gran's … having to listen to him snoring and blowing off was a nightmare.'

On 21 August 1946, Nellie gave birth to another girl, who they named Maureen. She was put in a cot and slept in the same small room as Myra and their parents. Unlike Myra, Maureen was not a quiet baby and cried through the night which made Nellie extremely tired and anxious and so she often shouted at 4-year-old Myra for doing next to nothing or going near her father's chair, which was the only decent bit of furniture in the house.

Bob was still struggling with domesticity and rarely spent time at home. He would go to one of the many local pubs and get blind drunk. At around 10.00 pm most nights a neighbour would burst through the Hindley's front door and shout that Bob was 'fighting again' and that Nellie had best 'come and bring him home'. At the beginning she would go to the pub and drag him home, usually covered in blood, and listen to how Bob had bested his foe. Eventually, she grew tired of dragging her husband home and simply shrugged when she was told that Bob was fighting again. Myra was sent instead to retrieve his coat from the pub, which he always took off before getting into a fight.

Nellie would have a go at her husband about the amount of money he was spending in the pubs and Bob would take his frustrations out on his wife, often beating her – and he wasn't afraid of taking his anger out on Myra either. If Myra's grandmother was visiting and an argument broke out she would take Myra outside and wait. If Nellie started to yelp then Ellen would run in and hit Bob around his body with a rolled-up newspaper while Myra grabbed his legs to try to stop him kicking out.

Patricia Cairns, who would become Myra's lover in prison in years to come, once recalled how Myra had told her that both of her parents weren't afraid of hitting her. 'Her mum was cruel to her when she was little. She didn't protect her, and beat her herself. She hit her about her head. I remember Myra telling me that she made her ears bleed.'

Myra soon began misbehaving and answering her father back, which drove him mad and usually led to her receiving a slap. He hardly ever hit Maureen though, and according to Myra, that was because 'she was a lot softer, and, frankly, not as intelligent.'

Now that her parents had a new baby to raise and Myra was causing problems, she was sent to live back at her gran's. She recalled: 'I wanted to go back to Gran's but Dad wouldn't let me … eventually he said I could but had to come home for meals.' She would still go and play with her younger sister, who she nicknamed 'Moby', as well as doing her fair share of the house chores, but she would spend the nights sleeping at her grandmother's and it was her grandmother who took her to school in the mornings. It was at this time that her father took a new job as a labourer at Gorton Foundry.

Myra Hindley (right) as a bridesmaid at her Uncle Bert and Auntie Kath's wedding.

Patricia Cairns had spoken to Myra about this time in her life and later recalled:

> She always said in public that being sent to live with her gran was a good thing. While she was happy to criticise her father she did not want to upset her mother. In reality, it was the most hurtful thing that could have happened to her. It was the first time in her life that she was made to feel the outsider. That lasted for the rest of her life.

In 1947 Myra and her gran moved to 22 Beasley Street, Gorton, just around the corner from her parents. She attended Peacock Street Primary School and became a member of the Catholic congregation at St Francis' Monastery on Gorton Lane.

In 1950 Myra was still going home to her parents' house for meals and it was at the dinner table on one of these occasions that Bob told his daughter she needed to learn to stick up for herself. He taught her how to throw punches and how best to protect her head and stomach. She used his advice when one day a local lad, Kenny Holden, raked his finger nails down Myra's face leaving eight bloody scratch marks. Frightened and upset, she ran home crying and told her father what had happened. She thought he would either go and sort the boy out himself or pay a visit to the boy's mother, but instead he grabbed Myra by the wrist, led her outside and told her: 'Go and punch him, because if you don't, I'll leather you. It's either him or you!' He then shut the door on her.

Myra saw the boy walking down the street, waited until he got within range and then threw a punch at his head. He saw it coming and covered up, allowing Myra to punch him in the stomach, which winded him. Dropping his guard, Myra then punched him again in the head, on his right temple, and he fell to the floor. She recalled: 'I stood looking down at him triumphantly. At 8 years old I'd scored my first victory.'

She also recalled other emotional moments in her childhood, such as the rare occasions that her father showed her some affection:

> I was sitting in front of the fire in my nightie, and Dad picked me up and sat me on his lap. He suddenly kissed my forehead. I was so shocked it made me jump and I knocked the fag out of his hand. It

burnt my shoulder and I ran out of the house screaming that he had burnt me with a fag end.... Poor man, he was only trying to be nice to me, which wasn't often, and I accused him of child abuse. Mam had a go at him for hurting me, so he gave her and me a beating for causing such a fuss.

She didn't want to be the cause of any more distress to her parents, so she developed,

a strength of character that protected me a lot from emotional harm ... from a very early age I learned to keep [emotions] under control, to refuse to cry when being chastised, except in the privacy of my bedroom at Gran's house, to never let my feelings show, to build up layers of protective buffers, to tremble, rage, cry and grieve inwardly.

By 1952, Hindley had grown into a tomboy. She was tall and skinny and the boys would call her 'beanstalk'. She would join in when the boys wrestled and was also reportedly quite good at football. Some of the mothers of Hindley's school friends recalled her as 'a mischievous one.... She was always up to something and her so clean and tidy when her mother sent her out! Nellie thought the world of her.... She was a proper little picture when she was small.'

Another recalled:

Myra thought a lot of young children herself. I remember that little lad in Railway View that was poorly. His mother used to have to give him special foods, you know, and Myra was always round there asking after him and taking him little presents she bought out of her pocket money. She was a good lass.

After school Myra would mess around on Gorton Lane with her friend Joyce Hardy, who lived on Peacock Street. They would go to the local shop and buy sweets and sarsaparilla before going home for her dinner.

Myra's tomboy behaviour continued and she got in to various fights and scrapes, usually with boys. After she had been treated for a case of nits one of the local lads, Eddie Hogan, starting tormenting her and calling her 'Nitty Nora'. Myra jumped on him and after some rolling about she managed to sit on top of him and she lashed out with her fists. Myra's gran heard the commotion and ran out to separate the two, dragging Myra off with one hand and hitting Eddie with a newspaper in the other.

Myra Hindley as a child.

She began to steal coal from the local railway for her grandma and on one occasion was caught by the police. The officer took her home and her grandmother promised to take appropriate action, but when the officer left simply told her to be more careful in future.

Every Sunday Myra went to Mass at Gorton Monastery with her Aunt Kath. She would sit at the aisle end of the pew so that she would be sprinkled with incense from the passing Priest. She didn't understand a lot of what was going on as the service was conducted in Latin, but she enjoyed the sights and smells.

Father Roderick, a priest who would go to Myra's house and her parents' house to collect donations for the church, began to abuse Bob Hindley after he had decided to become an atheist. Because Bob and Nellie had wed at a registry office the priest would tell Bob that in the eyes of God they were not married, and as such his daughters were nothing more than 'bastards'. He would tell Bob that he would go to Hell, and Bob would reply that he had already been there too many times to care and would then threaten to hit him – man of the cloth or not.

Bob, known in the area as a hard man and former boxer in the army, would sometimes add to his drinking money by boxing in the local halls after work or at the weekends. Nellie would not attend and the children were not allowed to either.

In November 1954 Myra failed her eleven-plus exam and as a consequence ended up at Ryder Brow Secondary School. Despite her exam result, she was a bright pupil and had an IQ of 109 – above average. She was placed in the highest stream which gave her a chance of taking General Certificate 'A' Levels, or do a commercial course in shorthand and typing. She loved English and especially poetry. She was an enthusiastic student who was also noted as being good at sports.

As much as she liked school, she was soon playing truant. She was always telling her mother and grandmother that she had headaches, flu and even bad periods. At first they would write a note to her teachers, but when they suspected she was faking it and sent her off to school, she would write the notes herself and bunk off.

She would go off with her best friend, Pat Jepson, and wait in Sunny Brow Park before looping back to Beesly Street and entering the house via the back door when they were sure Nellie would be out. Pat Jepson, who lived on nearby Taylor Street, recalled:

> We didn't have television in those days. We got rid of our energy by playing a lot of running games. It was good clean fun. I don't ever remember Myra crying or being a bad sport. Myra would not let herself be pushed around by any of the boys. She was so tough she frightened some of them off. She would batter them in playground fights. She was so much a tomboy that I sometimes thought she wanted to be a boy. On the other hand, she was in the top class for five years. She was very intelligent and could hold her own on any subject.

Linda Maguirk, Head Girl at Ryder Brow, remembered Myra as 'funny and always singing, with long, lanky hair.' Some of the boys also gave her a new nickname – 'Square Arse' – on account of her broad hips.

Myra herself recalled this time later in life:

> I felt like a fish out of water at first. All of the other kids seemed to have big smart houses and smart clothes, but I still lived in the same house, with a loo down the back yard. This had quite an effect on me at the time and I remember thinking: one day, I'll have all of that.

She soon moved again – to another house on the same street – now renamed Bannock Street; the family moved in to number 7. She remembered that the house was 'old and decrepit, shabby but tidy, and comfortable. I lived there until I was 15 and loved it as a home but hated it for its lack of almost everything.' Her gran's sister, Hannah, lived on one side and on the other were two 'old men' and their mother. There was no electricity, just gas and a big old-fashioned black fireplace. You had to go through the kitchen and out the back door, mostly taken up by a large air-raid shelter, to access the toilet which was at the bottom of the yard.

Myra's grandmother, Ellen, had an operation to remove cataracts from both of her eyes in 1955 and Myra found this tough for a while, having to do more around

Myra Hindley at Ryder Brow School - She is 2nd row from the top and third from the left.

the house until her grandmother fully recovered. She listed this in her unpublished autobiography alongside various incidents of death in her youth, such as a Jack Russell called Timmy that she had found by the railway line which had been decapitated, a boy she saw bleed to death having been crushed by a lorry on the Hyde Road and a cat she saw torn in half by two dogs.

She also writes of her first experience with a corpse when she was 13 years old. A friend of her gran's died without any money to pay for his funeral so Ellen cashed in part of her own funeral insurance so she could buy a coffin for him. His body was then 'laid out' in the coffin in Myra's house in the front room prior to the funeral.

When Myra arrived home from school that day and opened the door, the odour of embalming fluid hit her nostrils. Ellen and her friend Hettie Rafferty were sitting with the coffin and immediately noticed Myra's alarm, so Ellen suggested that Myra see for herself that there was nothing to be frightened of. Myra remembered peering in to the coffin and touching his hand, but then quickly recoiling at the sensation.

Although Maureen would grow into a fierce street fighter herself, when she was younger Myra would always beat up anyone who picked on her little sister or called her names. In a letter written by Myra in 1977, she gave an account of what happened one day when she found out about a girl who had been tormenting Maureen for a couple of weeks. Myra saw the girl and chased her across a field.

> She glimpsed me pelting across and started running like the clappers, but I grabbed her before she had time to lock herself in her backyard and pasted hell out of her. Her big brother, who was in my class, came out and, scared though I was of him, for he was the bigger bully, I went for him before he came for me. To my amazement – to say nothing of relief – he threw his sister and himself into the backyard and bolted the door…. Returning home, filthy and scruffy, I got yelled at by Gran and clouted by Mam, who, when Maureen explained, was full of contrition, but, bristling with indignation, I stole without compunction two of my mother's Park Drives [cigarettes] and decided to run away from home – until about 10, when I returned because I was starving hungry.

Allan Grafton lived on Casson Street and knew Myra from playing football with her at Ryder Brow. He recalled how he liked her father, Bob, who used to sponsor his Sunday League football team at the Steelworks Tavern:

> He was a really super guy, and what happened to his daughter later killed him…. He was a kind, generous man. Myra's mother on the other hand – she was a bawler and a shouter. You'd hear her yelling every day, 'Maureeeeen! Come in for yer tea!' She was tall and slim, and always used to walk about with her arms folded. Myra did the same, and Maureen.

He remembered that Myra was,

> one of the lads. We used to practice football on Ryder Brow Field and she'd hang about with us. Afterwards we'd pile into a pub just off Ryder Brow called 'The Haxby' for pints of Shandy. We were under age, but the landlord never bothered because we didn't cause any trouble. Myra always came in with us. Because she was such a tomboy the lads never took much interest in her. She could look after herself anyway; she was good company, but she said what she thought and didn't hold anything back.

Myra was very good at sports. Pauline Clapton knew her in late 1955 and recalled:

> Myra was in 4A and I was in 4B, but we used to be together for cooking and gym. Myra was only fair as a cook, but she could run very fast and she would have a go at any game. She was always the best in the gym class. She was in the school Rounders team.'

Myra was also on the school's netball, tennis and swimming teams and was learning Judo.

Myra Hindley's netball team. She is back row, 2nd from the right.

She was well liked by her teachers and her teammates, but was also disliked by a lot of her classmates. She took up smoking and would smoke on the way to and from school, as well as on the bus that took the children to the public baths for their swimming lessons – if she thought she could get away with it.

Myra and Pat Jepson would often go and babysit for neighbours and family friends and one of their neighbours, Mrs Phillips, later recalled:

> They were a grand pair of lasses; they were often around the house drinking tea and talking about clothes and boys. They never used to take a penny for baby-sitting – they wouldn't hear of it – but I used to take the two of them to the pictures now and again as a treat.

Myra's temper was still getting the better of her at times as she entered her teens and she got into a fight with a boy called Albert Goodwin. She was walking down Taylor Street one day when he purposely stood in her way, so she grabbed him and tripped him backwards. She then jumped on top of him, grabbed his hair and slammed his head into a puddle repeatedly. The attack only stopped because two of his friends dragged her off of him. On the face of it, this seems like an overreaction, but it is possibly indicative of how her personality was being shaped by the increasing violence between her parents.

Pat Jepson later recalled: 'Myra was a strong character. If we were going anywhere, she picked the place to go. We went baby-sitting together, and she got on with kids. She was not a violent person, but if she said something, it was taken that it was done.'

Pat Jepson wasn't her only close friend; Myra had become good friends with a boy two years younger than her called Michael Higgins. He lived on Taylor Street but was small for his age and Myra protected him from bullies.

They would spend hours together walking around West Gorton and getting into trouble. They both enjoyed swimming and during the summer evenings they would go to Mellands Field Reservoir in Station Road to cool down and splash around. The days were spent playing games and getting into trouble. They would go with their friend, Eddie Hogan, to the sweetshop and Myra would go in first, buy some sweets and talk to the shopkeeper while the two boys loaded as many sweets as they could into their pockets before running away. They would meet up in Gorton Tank Railway Yard and, having broken in, split everything between them.

They stole various other things in addition to sweets, including potatoes from a local greengrocer 'to roast on a bonfire we had made, and on another occasion I ran off with some Christmas cards. I was waiting to pay for them, but I kept getting ignored, so I ran off. I also remember stealing some alleys [marbles] from Woolworths', Myra later claimed. On one occasion they heard some shouting as they were playing around in the train driver's cab in the railway yard. They looked around and saw two men in boiler suits running towards them. They jumped down onto the tracks and ran away as fast as their legs would carry them. They jumped over the boards and headed for the allotments, but something was wrong. Myra's leg stopped moving and an incredible pain shot up from her ankle. She fell to the floor and saw blood trickling into the teeth of a 'man-trap'. She tried to get up to run again but collapsed with the pain. Michael Higgins saw what had happened and ran for help. A short time later, Myra's Uncle Bert and a neighbour called Mr Richards arrived and carried Myra home. They put her on the sofa and tried to prise the jaws of the man trap open but couldn't, so they sent Michael Higgins to fetch Dr Chadwick. Between them, they managed to free Myra's leg and she went on to make a full recovery.

The first death of someone close to her that Myra encountered was one that always stayed with her and happened on 14 June 1957. Michael Higgins had asked Myra if she wanted to go with him, Eddie Hogan and another friend called Walter King to the Mellands Field Reservoir for a swim but Myra already had plans with Pat Jepson. They were going to catch a bus to Reddish for afternoon tea with Pat's Aunt.

The three boys went off for a swim; after resting on the grassy banks for a while, Michael and Walter dived back in but then Walter noticed that Michael was thrashing around and appeared to be in difficulty. He shouted over to Michael to stop mucking around but then Michael grabbed his arm and pulled him under the surface. Walter struggled free and resurfaced but Michael never did. Eddie Hogan had been watching it all unfold from the bank and an older boy, whose attention had been drawn by the commotion, realised what had happened and dived into the reservoir to look for Michael. Someone else alerted the police.

Within a few minutes uniformed officers from the fire brigade and police were wading into the water to look for the boy. At its deepest points the reservoir was 25ft deep and they couldn't get to him.

At 6.50 that evening, a Lancashire County Police frogman finally broke the surface of the reservoir with Michael's body in his arms. Laurence Jordan, who was on the bank at the time, recalled: 'I saw them bringing out this chalk-white body. You could see the whiteness of the body against the blue uniform of the police. His arms were outstretched…. They hurriedly put him in the mortuary van.'

Myra and Pat returned that evening and were told by a mutual friend what had happened. Feeling guilty because, being such a strong swimmer, Myra believed she could have saved him if she had been there, the two girls ran to the reservoir as fast as they could. By the time they reached the reservoir they were just pulling Michael's body from the water. He was given the kiss of life and had his chest pumped but all to no avail. Pat Jepson later confirmed that it was the only time she ever saw Myra cry.

The inquest later heard that 'It [the body] was just lying on the bottom face downwards. The water was dark and clouded with mud. The deeper he went down, the colder it got.' It was concluded that he had drowned after getting cramp in the cold water. The verdict was given as accidental death.

Myra Hindley and a friend.

Michael's mother gave Myra his Speedway programmes and a comb to remember him by. Myra went door-to-door collecting money for a wreath. The day before the funeral Michael's body was laid out in his front room wearing his alter boy outfit. Myra was then handed the rosary from his hands by his mother before the lid on the coffin was closed for the final time.

Myra couldn't face going to the funeral but she did attend the requiem mass. Pat Jepson recalled: 'She started going to church, and she took the Catholic vows. I used to go with her to the monastery, although I was Church of England.'

One month later, on 19 July 1957, Myra's name first appeared in the press. The local newspaper, the *Gorton & Openshaw Reporter*, printed Ryder Brow's school sports day results and she had won the 'Individual Championships' for senior girls and taken home ten awards. She was the overall winner in her year group and finished first in high jump, second in javelin and third in the 220-yard run.

She was now 15 years old and loved to babysit. Joan Phillips, who lived just around the corner, recalled:

> She was a real treat with the kids. When she was about 15 she used to babysit a lot for us. My husband used to say he liked Myra to babysit because we could go out in peace, knowing everything would be all right…. The boys loved her because she spoiled them; she used to bring them chocolate and let them stay up late and, when it was light in the evenings, she used to play football with them on the little bit of waste ground near the house.
>
> In her last year at school she and her friend Pat Jepson used to play wag [truant] and come round to our house to hide. They used to say it was time they had a holiday. She was wonderful with our Denis – he was only a year old then. She used to turn a kitchen chair on its side and put him in between the legs to teach him to stand up and then to walk. She used to take Gordon, who was about 6 or 7, to see the cowboys at the children's matinee on a Saturday at the Cosmo or the Essoldo. Often I would come in and find she had Gordon all scrubbed clean and in his pyjamas ready for bed – I think it was the only time Gordon liked being washed because Myra made such a game of it. She was like that, Myra, always full of fun and if she wasn't chattering on about boys or records she would be singing the latest tune. You never saw her depressed.

On leaving school, Hindley got her first paying job on 26 July 1957, working as a junior clerk with Messrs Laurence Scott & Electro Motors, an electrical engineering factory, in Higher Openshaw, before leaving of her own accord on 26 March 1959. She later recalled:

> I couldn't wait to leave school and start work … [They] were the happiest days of my life, except for those of my childhood when I didn't have to go to school. I had a wide circle of friends with whom I went dancing, swimming and roller-skating and also spent a lot of time in local libraries, where I could browse and read in peace and quiet.

She had been given a good reference and took a test to assess her suitability for a College of Further Education. 'I was delighted when I passed because I wanted to learn secretarial skills. I didn't want to end up in a dead-end job like most women seemed to', she later recalled. To top up her earnings she sometimes took on evening work too, such as working in a local jam factory, topping strawberries.

When she mislaid her first week's wages the other girls all felt sorry for her, so they organised a whip-round and actually gave her more money than she'd lost. She used the extra she'd been given to help pay towards a holiday to Butlin's in Ayr, Scotland. She then pulled the same stunt again a few weeks later and the other girls realised what she was up to and none of them helped her out.

There was a table tennis set at work and being sporty, she was eager to give it a go. One of the men showed her how to play and she was so good that she was asked to join the factory team. They would travel across Manchester and play against other companies and afterwards go out for a few drinks. It was during these drinks that she got to know a welder called Ray at her factory. They went out a couple of times on the back of his motorbike and he introduced her to his friends, but the relationship soon soured when she refused to sleep with him.

She also fancied a gypsy called Johnny, who stayed for a short time at the Rafferty's who lived across the road. They flirted openly but before anything could happen the police turned up looking for him and he managed to escape through the back window before he could be captured. Myra never saw him again.

By 1958 Myra and Pat would go dancing at the 'Alhambra Ballroom' twice a week. Pat recalled:

> Myra liked jiving. It was the only kind of dancing she would do. She never bothered much with boys. Of course she used to go out with them, but not a lot. Myra looked very grown up; she always wore straight skirts and blouses. You would never see her in a flared skirt or a dress, and I think she thought the boys round our way were too young for her.

Myra aged 18, on holiday in Blackpool.

On one occasion the two girls went to Ashton-under-Lyne for a dance, but they missed the last bus home and had to spend the night at a friend's house. Pat recalled: 'I got a clout, but Myra's mother battered her in the street and she wasn't allowed out for a week.'

When Myra's punishment was over she was allowed to go on holiday for a few days with Pat and her family to Blackpool.

Upon her return the 16-year-old Myra was taken out by a young man called Ronnie Sinclair, who Myra had known since she was 11 years old. Myra wore a tight black skirt and blouse, high heels and her hair was dark and flowing. Ronnie later recalled that Myra was trying to look 18 and that she'd pulled it off well. They went to various pubs around Gorton and Myra was drinking light ales. When the pubs had all closed they went for a coffee in Sivori's milk bar before he walked Myra home. As they approached Myra's grandmother's house she grabbed him by the hand and led him into an alleyway where she undid the top buttons on her blouse and made it clear that she wanted to be petted. Ronnie, however, was aware that Myra was underage and didn't want to get into trouble so he made his excuses and left. They continued dating and Myra would see him most evenings when she was not busy doing something with Pat.

It was around this time that Myra's father suffered an injury at work and was forced into early retirement. In 1995 she recalled:

> My father, who was working on a building site, broke his leg so badly
> that he was made disabled, and quite soon after he had the first of his

strokes. For the first time in my life I saw him almost helpless, unable to walk, sitting almost constantly in his, the only, armchair in the house or lying in his bed in the living room, and all of my fear of him left me. In spite of all he'd done to make our family life unbearable, I felt sorry for him, compassionate and even tender toward him. I could never love him, but seeing this strong, brutal man, reduced to the helplessness of a baby made me feel strong and almost maternal towards him. I waited on him, fetched and carried for him, because I wanted to and not because I had to, as in the past.

On 16 November 1958, Myra decided to become a practising Catholic. She took instruction from the Franciscan Friars at St Francis' Monastery in Gorton and was given the name Veronica. She became a devout and regular worshipper at the church and on her first communion her Uncle Bert and Aunt Kath gave her a prayer book. This prayer book would go on to be a significant piece of evidence at the Moors Murders trial.

At the beginning of 1959 Myra was made redundant at Laurence Scott's due to cutbacks but she soon got a new job, along with three friends Irene, Maggie and Pauline, with the Belle Vue catering department. They worked on the mobile food trolleys every Saturday night from 5–10.00 pm. After just a couple of weeks the catering manager said that Myra and Irene were 'wasted' on the food trolleys and asked them if they wanted to help out in the German-themed 'beer cellar'. They enjoyed it more down there and Myra was soon pouring short measures to the customers. She got herself a new day job at the end of March and worked as a junior typist with a firm called Clydesdale Supply Co. Ltd, Cross Street, Gorton.

In her spare time she rekindled her fondness for Judo and went once a week to classes at Gresham Street School for Girls, but soon gained a reputation as someone who was slow to release her holds and the other girls soon refused to take part with her.

When Myra turned 17 on 23 July 1959 she got engaged to Ronnie Sinclair. He was working as a tea blender at the Co-op and lived nearby in Dalkeith Street. Ronnie was a year older than Myra and in full-time employment – this was the best that the local girls could hope for. Myra knew she would soon be expected to settle down and have children, but something inside her wanted more. She tried hard to suppress those feelings.

In a letter written to the *Guardian* on 18 December 1995, Myra recalled:

> I didn't have a grudge against society or a chip on my shoulder. The things I wanted in life were not unusual. I got engaged at 17 to a boy I first met when I was 11 and pulled the ribbon out of my hair at the pictures.

But when I began to witness many of my friends and neighbours, some of whom 'had to get married', having baby after baby, almost tied to the kitchen sink and struggling to make ends meet while their husbands went out every night drinking and betting away their wages just as my father had done, I began to feel uncomfortable and restless.

I wanted a career, to better myself, to travel and struggle to break free of the confines of what was expected of me. Although so much was unattainable, I still dreamed and made plans and kept everything to myself. I didn't want to leave home, because I loved my family, but I wanted more scope and space, and they would think I was 'getting above myself' if I confided in them.

On 15 February 1960, Myra started another new job as a junior typist with Messrs Bratby & Hinchcliffe Limited, Engineers and Automatic Bottling Manufacturers. She hated the job because the manager was a bully who shouted at the typists when he found a mistake. She did make two friends though, Mary and Anita.

By the time Myra turned 18 she had decided she wanted her life to change. She started to dye her hair and paid 10s 6d a time to have it tinted at 'Maison Laurette'.

In 1998 she would describe her years before meeting Ian Brady:

I was an attractive, confident and sociable teenager, never short of dates. I had a particularly close bond with five friends, and we went everywhere together; dancing, skating, swimming, to newly opened sporting clubs and cabarets, shopping together for clothes when there was bargains offered. They were the happiest three years of my life, the only times I never felt imprisoned. I'd felt imprisoned at school, at home because of my father, and then I walked into Brady's prison.

Myra Hindley (back) with friends.

Chapter 3

Hindley Meets Brady

On 13 January 1961, Myra saw a job advertised in the local newspaper for a typist at Millwards Merchandise Limited. Millwards Merchandise supplied heavy chemicals, mainly to the cotton industry.

Her friend, Mary, told her that she used to work there and that the pay was fair and the manager was a good man. Myra recalled: 'She told me something about the firm and mentioned some of the people I'd be working with, if I got the job. She told me about … a tall and good-looking, very quiet and shy, smartly dressed 'intriguing man' who had appealed to her.'

Without asking permission, she walked out of her job and telephoned the number on the advertisement. She was in luck – the job was still available so she jumped on a bus and headed there straight away for an interview.

As soon as she arrived she had a 'good feeling' about the place. Her interview consisted of typing a small, handwritten letter – which she did with consummate ease and she was offered the job on the spot. Upon acceptance, she was taken to meet

For Service and Satisfaction !

Millwards Merchandise Limited

LEVENSHULME ROAD WORKS
GORTON (P.O. Box No. 2
Gorton), MANCHESTER, 18

CHEMICALS & OILS of all descriptions.

Gums, Rosin, Turpentine, Waxes, etc., etc., for all Industrial purposes.

ESTABLISHED 1810

Telegrams : "Dyestuff, Manchester"   Telephones : East 1261/1263

Advert for Millwards Merchandise Ltd.

the rest of the staff by the manager, Tommy Craig, and vividly recalled meeting Bert Matthews, who was sitting at his desk and stood up to shake her hand. Tommy told her that she would be 'taking quite a lot of dictation from him'. Tommy then turned and introduced her to the man standing by the filing cabinet. 'Myra, this is Ian. Ian, this is Myra.'

Myra herself recalled: 'I can only describe my reaction to him as an immediate and fatal attraction, although I had no inkling then of just how fatal it would turn out to be.' She was struck by his 'dark hair, deep blue eyes and fresh complexion', as well as the 'well-manicured fingers' that were 'in stark contrast to my boyfriend's, which were always greasy.' She later told journalist Duncan Staff:

> I'd always been a romantic dreamer falling in love with film stars – I was crazy about James Dean and Elvis – and had read and heard the phrase 'falling head over heels in love' but never thought it would happen to me. But as soon as Ian Brady looked at me and smiled shyly, that's exactly what happened.

That evening Myra went out with five friends and couldn't stop talking about Ian Brady. She told them how he reminded her of Elvis and James Dean.

She started work three days later and was earning £10 a week. She was really happy when told she would be taking a lot of dictation from the stock clerk, Ian Brady, who would dictate stock lists, order forms and letters to her. She was somewhat disappointed that he didn't make a fuss of her, or even really notice her or on her first

Millward Merchandise.

day. 'He gave no indication that he noticed me, appearing to be the strong silent type. I was determined I would make him notice me.'

Six months later, on Myra's 19th birthday, her fascination with Ian became clear as she wrote in her diary: 'Wonder if Ian is courting. Still feel the same.' It was obvious that this man, who she still knew hardly anything about, was on her mind constantly and she realised that she wanted to be with him, rather than her fiancé Ronnie Sinclair. Myra recalled that Ronnie 'cared a lot about me, which mattered, but he didn't like dancing and we spent most our time at stock car races, which was his hobby.' She broke off the engagement not long after her birthday.

Ronnie was distraught and rang her at work every day begging her to reconsider. She didn't mind at first, as it brought the fact that she was now single to the fore, but before long she grew annoyed and asked her boss, Tommy Craig, if he would answer the phone the next time Ronnie called, and to tell him to stop calling otherwise he would get the police involved. According to Ronnie's mother, he took it badly and tore up all the photographs he had of Myra and threw away all the mementos he had been saving. Myra's mother, however, was happy about the broken engagement because she hadn't really liked Ronnie, whom she thought too immature.

Another reason Myra broke the engagement off was because her best friend Pat had just got married and she felt that her friends had been 'trapped into family life, with no money and no freedom'.

She was absolutely infatuated with Ian but he was not forthcoming with any information about himself so discreetly she asked around their colleagues to see if anyone knew of his background, but no one did. The only bit of information she managed to gain was where he lived so in order to talk to him outside of work, she 'borrowed' her baby cousin and took him for walks along the surrounding streets hoping to 'bump into' Ian.

A few weeks passed and Myra had still not bumped into Ian so she decided on a new tack. She persuaded another of her friends, May Hill, to go for a drink with her in the pub on Ian's street in case he used it as his local. Again, this went on for a couple of weeks but they soon gave up when it became obvious that Ian didn't drink in there.

Years later, when she was in HMP Holloway, she told a fellow inmate: 'My feelings for him ranged from loving him desperately to almost hating him, from the total despair and hopelessness of unrequited love to wild, passionate hopes and prayers that he would somehow begin to share and return my feelings for him.'

Ian, however, just wasn't interested:

> Myra had been working in the office for several months, but she was simply the new typist as far as I was concerned. I paid no more attention to her than I did the rest of the females on the staff – that is to say, very little. She worked in a small room close to mine. She typed the letters I dictated to her. I can't recall having any memorable conversations

with her. It was just standard, routine office dialogue. I didn't go for her peroxide hairstyle. She had obviously been standing or sitting too close to the fire at home – she had heat marks on her calves.

A couple of colleagues told me that Myra had been asking questions about me. She was intrigued to know why I lowered my voice when I answered the phone to certain callers. Who were they? After hearing about this, I was careful, about what I said and kept an eye on her. Her curiosity made me curter with her. Much later, I was told that she had written down her feelings for me in her shorthand notebook. It was only puerile romantic tosh.

The following is what Myra wrote in her notebook and was found after she was arrested:

25 July 1961: Haven't spoken to him yet.

27 July 1961: Spoken to him. He smiles as though embarrassed. I'm going to change; you'll notice that in the way I write.

30 July 1961: Ian and Graham (a colleague) aren't interested in girls.

1 August 1961: Ian's taking sly looks at me.

2 August 1961: Not sure if he likes me, they say he gambles on horses.

3 August 1961: Ian likes Boddingtons Bitter Beer.

6 August 1961: Irene Eccles has clicked with a lad she met in April.

8 August 1961: Gone off Ian a bit.

The reason for Myra's change in feelings, as she told DCS Peter Topping in 1987, was because there had been an altercation in the office in which she was inadvertently involved and Ian had stopped talking to her. She said he went out of his way to insult her and she felt belittled and humiliated, as well as angry. He would be in a mood with her which would last a week and then he would talk to her again, usually after she had apologised. This is apparent in her diary and the pattern would carry on once they became a couple too.

10 August 1961: Tommy is scared of Ian.

11 August 1961: Been to Friendship pub (not with Ian).

13 August 1961: Wonder what 'Misery' will be like tomorrow?

14 August 1961: I love Ian all over again. He has a cold and I would love to mother him. Going to a club.

<u>19 August 1961</u>: Visited Belle Vue. Tony Prendergast and Eddie were there.

<u>24 August 1961</u>: I am in a bad mood because he hasn't spoken to me. He still has not made any approach.

<u>29 August 1961</u>: I hope Ian loves me and will marry me some day.

Myra later told her prison therapist that she would,

daydream about what life would be like with a man like Ian. He was so different to the men I had known before … I wanted him badly…. Some of my friends would feel this way about pop idols or film stars, but my idol was sitting in my office behind his desk.

I'm not sure that Ian knew how much I wanted to be with him, but I can accept that perhaps he knew what effect he was having on me and baited me until the time was right … I didn't know of any of his activities but even if I did I would have ignored them. All that mattered was that I was with him.

<u>30 August 1961</u>: Ian and Bert have had a row. Tommy sided with Bert and said Ian loses his temper too soon.

<u>2 September 1961</u>: Sivori Milk Bar in Clowes St.

<u>9 September 1961</u>: Ian mentioned Hadfield to George, I suppose near Glossop. Ian wearing a black shirt today.

<u>10 September 1961</u>: In Siv's Tony and Eddie were arguing about a girl.

<u>14 September 1961</u>: Marge went in to see Eddie about his tape recorder.

<u>16 September 1961</u>: Irene's 21st Birthday Party. Hodge, Tony P and Eddie. I could fall for Eddie.

<u>20 September 1961</u>: Still hoping for date with Ian.

<u>23 September 1961</u>: Saw Eddie drunk (Sportsman's pub, where we go every Sat).

<u>2 October 1961</u>: Ian has been to Glasgow.

<u>8 October 1961</u>: Ian never talks about his family.

<u>9 October 1961</u>: Eddie lives in the next street to Ian.

<u>13 October 1961</u>: Ian hasn't spoken to me for several days.

<u>18 October 1961</u>: Ian still ignores me. Fed up. I still love him.

19 October 1961: Ian lives with his mam and dad and hardly ever goes out.

21 October 1961: Malcolm phoned Ian at work and Ian arranged to go to him for drinks.

23 October 1961: I fancy Eddie. I could fall for Ed.

25 October 1961: Ian and Tommy had a row. Ian nearly hit Tommy. Ian was swearing. He is uncouth. I thought he was going to hit Nellie. [Nellie Egerton was the cleaner at Millwards].

28 October 1961: Royal Oak Pub in Wythenshawe.

1 November 1961: Months now since Ian and I spoke.

2 November 1961: Met Bob, pub crawl, went up to Ashton-under-Lyne, Dukinfield, Denton. Quite a good night

3 November 1961: Ian swearing at work, using crude words.

4 November 1961: Rodney had drinks at Plough. Rodney said, 'All Ian is interested in is making money.'

6 November 1961: Ian still not speaking. I called him a big-headed pig.

7 November 1961: Have finished with Eddie. He is courting another girl

28 November 1961: I've given up with Ian. He goes out of his way to annoy me, he insults me and deliberately walks in front of me. I have seen the other side of him and that convinces me that he is no good.

2 December 1961: I hate Ian, he has killed all the love I had for him.

11 December 1961: Visited Empress Club, Stockport, with Joan, Irene and Dave.

13 December 1961: Pauline's party.

15 December 1961: I'm in love with Ian all over again.

She tried one last tactic to get Ian interested in her. She knew that at lunchtime he would sit by himself and read books by Dostoevsky and others, so she went to Gorton Library and picked out *The Collected Works of William Wordsworth* as she had enjoyed poetry at school and so knew she could hold a conversation about it.

At lunchtime the following day she sat by the office door to the yard and Ian was already there playing chess. He glanced up and looked at Myra's book. Mildly impressed, he asked her if it was any good, to which she replied 'marvellous'. He skimmed through it and said he might get himself a copy. She later said that at that moment she almost 'died from bliss'.

She tried that same tactic again a couple of days later and took in William Blake's *Songs of Innocence and Experience*. Again, he took it from her and read a few lines. He asked her about which type of music she enjoyed and, not wanting to put him off by saying the wrong thing, she told him a bit of pop, classical, big band etc. Ian said he didn't really like that and that he preferred something a bit more intelligent. He told her that he had a tape recorder which he used to copy things from the library and off the TV. He then offered her an olive branch and told her that she could borrow it if she liked.

The following weekend she put down a deposit on a Phillips machine, the same as Ian's. She signed an agreement to pay it off in weekly instalments and took it home the same day and practiced on it with her friends.

Myra Hindley.

Back at work, Ian brought Myra various tapes for her to copy, including jazz and classical music and on some of these tapes she recalled hearing the voices of Ian's mother and stepfather in the background.

More than thirty years later, when Myra was in Highpoint Prison, she told Father Michael Teader what had drawn her to Ian Brady:

> She had never met anyone like him. He was completely different. Well read, intelligent, with a more sophisticated view of the world than any of the people she had encountered before. He seemed to offer her the chance of escape. It was what she'd looked for in the Catholic Church, and she thought she'd found it in him.

Unknown to her at the time, Ian was spending his time after work at home blasting out German marching songs along with the speeches of Nazi leaders Hitler, Goebbels and Himmler on his record player. He would also spend the occasional evening going off to the homosexual bars around Manchester.

A few days before Christmas 1961, the staff from Millwards went out for a few drinks at lunchtime and returned to the factory slightly worse for wear. Sandwiches were laid on for them, as was a record player and plenty of wine, rum and more beer. Myra later recalled to journalist Duncan Staff:

> Someone put the record player on. I was too drunk to remember what was playing, but to my utter amazement Ian suddenly pulled me off my chair and began staggering around dancing with me. I thought I would die from being held in his arms; even though he was a lousy dancer and trampled all over my feet.

Ian then asked Myra if he could walk her home after the party. When they reached her street he then asked her if she would go out with him later that evening, to which she immediately said that she would.

When she got through the front door she found her sister Maureen and cousin Glenys talking to her gran. She told them all about her first dance with Ian and that she had a date with him in a couple of hours. Maureen and Glenys went down to the chemist to get some perfume and mascara for her while she tried to sober herself up by making a bacon sandwich, cup of tea and laying down on her bed for a while.

Myra met Ian at the Three Arrows pub on the corner of Church Lane and Hyde Road before going on a pub crawl around the centre of Manchester. Ian then got Myra back to her home safely and they shared their first kiss. Ian then wanted to go inside with her, but she refused as they were both very drunk and she didn't want things to go too far. They stood on her doorstep kissing for a while and Myra always remembered the pain of their kisses. He pulled her in close, crushing her and kissed her so hard that it hurt her. He then left, telling her that he would see her back at work.

On 22 December, Myra wrote in her diary: 'Eureka! Today we have our first date. We are going to the cinema.' They went to watch *King of Kings* and then on to the Thatched House pub. The film was about the life of Jesus and Ian had noticed how Myra had become upset when Jesus was nailed to the cross. He didn't understand why and told her that the sole purpose of religion was 'to keep working people in their place', and as such, religious people were weak. She had already told him about the tragic death of her friend Michael Higgins and rather than show compassion he told her that if God was good, why did he let Michael drown? Where was the good in that? Myra had no answer for him. She later told Duncan Staff: 'He scorned me for believing all the crap in the Bible, for going to church, Mass, with its mumbo jumbo and incense and confession.'

Two days later, on Christmas Eve, Myra and Ian went out again. When Ian was walking Myra home, they heard church bells ringing. Myra told him that it was the call for midnight mass. Brady was curious and when Myra offered to take him to the monastery on Gorton Lane he outright refused to enter a Roman Catholic church, but she managed to persuade him to go with her into St James' Protestant Church and they sat on the back row.

As they left the church, Ian told Myra to hang on. He walked round to the side of the building and urinated against the wall of the church, showing his contempt for all it stood for. He then took a flask out of his inside coat pocket, had a swig of whiskey and told her 'That's what I think of Christianity!'

They walked back to her gran's at Bannock Street and kissed as they stood outside her front door. Myra then invited him in, knowing that her gran would be upstairs asleep. They were greeted by Myra's dog, Lassie, and went into the living room. They sat by the fire talking and drank two more bottles of wine before they kissed passionately. Ian gave her a series of bites down her neck and 'with the heady wine and the flush of a possible romance, we were sexually inventive through the small hours', according to Brady. Myra confirmed that it was this occasion when she lost her virginity. Brady later wrote:

> It was nearly eight in the morning when I put my clothes on, feeling invigorated in every sense as I invariably did after a night of acrobatic fornication. Our farewells seemed tame and casual in the light of what had happened between us through the night. We were both sexually replete by morning. I stepped into the Christmas early morning air, drawing Gorton into my lungs. It was sheer pleasure to walk the three miles across the city. All was right with the world.

In the mid-1980s, Myra wrote about this period in her life:

> When I met Ian I was 18-and-a-half. He was cultured, listened to classical music, he read classical literature. They were things that interested me too, but I had no one to share them with. And he was good-looking. I was very impressionable. I thought I loved him, but I realise now with twenty years' hindsight that I was infatuated, and that infatuation grew into an obsession. He was God. It was as if there was a part of me that didn't belong to me, that hadn't been there before and wasn't there afterwards I'm not saying that he took over my mind or anything, or that I wasn't responsible for what I did, but I just couldn't say 'no' to him. He decided everything; where we would go for our holidays, everything.

On New Year's Eve, Myra told Maureen that she and Ian were together. They went to the cinema to see *El Cid* before Myra took Ian to her parents' house for the celebrations and Ian took them a bottle of whisky as a gift. Myra later wrote in her diary: 'Dad and Ian spoke as if they'd known each other for years. Ian is so gentle he makes me want to cry.' Myra's mother, however, disliked Ian at first sight and told Myra: 'No good can come of that Ian Brady, you know.' She could see that Ian thought he was better than them.

Just two days later Myra wrote in her diary: 'I have been at Millwards for twelve months and only just gone out with him. I hope Ian and I love each other all our lives and get married and are happy ever after.' Ian, however, thought otherwise:

> I behaved as though nothing had occurred between us. This wasn't difficult. From my point of view, nothing had. Myra should accept that fact or find some loser in pastures new, she could do whatever she wanted; I intended to. There was no chance of my walking blindly into the death trap of marriage and respectability. I had other things on my

mind. I was too busy to bother. I made the real money at night. My job at Millwards was a necessary inconvenience.

He continued to see Myra but only on Saturday nights. Myra remembered:

> Although I saw him almost every day at work and every Saturday, with just an occasional week-night thrown in at first, for most of my free time he just wasn't available. He didn't volunteer much information about his private life….
>
> Because our relationship was new and very unsure, I was afraid to do or say anything which might jeopardise it, so I stifled my curiosity and accepted what little information he volunteered.
>
> When our relationship first began, I was stupid and naïve enough to believe it would eventually lead to marriage. But I soon learned that marriage was foremost among the things that Ian didn't believe in, and I resigned myself to nothing more than an affair.
>
> Although it was the first and only affair I had ever had, and I knew that my family were unhappy with the situation, I clung to what little Ian offered me, for I simply could not envisage life without him anymore, even though I could hardly describe myself as happy or contented. It was, at best, a tenuous, unsettled relationship, but I cannot deny that I didn't prefer it to an existence from which he was absent.

Ian Brady was still spending his evenings planning robberies and listening to his Nazi speeches. He was also travelling into the centre of Manchester to visit various homosexual bars and meeting men for brief encounters. It later came out, mostly at the trial, that Ian would go to the Rembrandt pub. It was a pub where men with respectable jobs went to meet other men for sex, both with each other and with rent boys.

The change in Myra was noticed almost straight away by her best friends Pat Jepson and May Hill. They wanted to meet Ian and asked Myra to bring him along to the Ashton Palais, but Myra told them that it wasn't somewhere that would interest him. They also asked her out on evenings when she had no plans to meet Ian but Myra refused to leave the house in case Ian decided to pop over. Over time they simply stopped asking her.

Ian and Myra often went to the cinema and Myra remembered him taking her to see a film about the Nuremberg Trials on the back of his newly bought motorbike, despite him not having a full licence and so not legally permitted to carry a passenger.

He soon started to turn up randomly at Myra's during the evening and leave early the following morning. The neighbours complained about the noise of his motorbike leaving during the early hours and this added to Myra's mother's distaste for him. Myra recalled:

When he bought a motorbike, he came one weeknight unexpectedly and we went for a ride. After that, because he never made a date, I began staying in every night, terrified that I might be out when – if – he came round. I became estranged from most of my friends, who had become disgusted with me for 'letting him tread all over me' … I'd become totally besotted with him, always trying to fathom out the mystery he'd become to me, the aura that emanated from him.

Many a time Ian had arranged to meet Myra but failed to appear:

I asked where he was going or where he had been [and] he would answer: never mind. Some women might ask why I stayed with such a self-centred man, but at least when he was with me he made me feel good, when he wasn't I was content to stay in and wash my hair or babysit.

It was from this moment onwards that Myra admitted that she began to absorb many of Ian's beliefs and opinions, such as his opposition to marriage. Ian later commented about this stage of their relationship:

It wasn't master and slave. It was more like teacher and student Bit by bit we were moving towards an almost telepathic relationship. I was never conscious of having to exert myself to coerce Myra into accepting my belief in relativist morality. I aired my views for open discussion, nothing more. They were on the table to be rejected or accepted … Myra was surprisingly in tune with me from the very beginning. She was as ruthless as I was. I had no need to force her intellectually, and she didn't have to pretend she was being forced.

He showed her how to use books for inspiration, such as *The Carpetbaggers* which tells of rape, incest and paedophilia as ways to enjoy adventures, and that if an opportunity presented itself to a man then he should take it. He and Hindley soon began to incorporate and act out parts from such books in their sexual fantasies. He also introduced Myra to the works of his favourite philosopher, Friedrich Nietzsche.

On one occasion Ian began to play tapes of Hitler's speeches to Myra and told her how much he admired him and Myra agreed that his passion and force of conviction was admirable. He told her how right Hitler was in regards to his views on 'Jews' and 'blacks', and offered her proof of his views by telling her to look at how the Jamaicans in Moss Side 'sponge off our taxes'.

As Patricia Cairns, Myra's prison lover, would later say: 'What you have to understand about Myra is that when she falls in love with somebody, turns her beam on them, she becomes like them. She must have been getting some pleasure from it as well.'

Ian and Myra would often go for a drink in The Waggon and Horses pub as it was close to his bus stop and it was easy for her to find her way home from there. It was here, under the influence of alcohol, that he would occasionally drop a hint about his past, but he would soon realise and clam up again. He told her that he used to hurt animals when he was a child, and about putting cats in cairns', but he had realised that it was far more pleasurable hurting people.

He soon told her about his past criminal life and being sent to both Borstal and HMP Strangeways by the 'corrupt system' and how he planned to better himself. He told her about his humble beginnings back in Scotland and how he wanted to become a 'somebody'.

He told her how he thought he and Hitler had both come from similar backgrounds and that he admired how Nazi Germany had risen from the ruins of the First World War to become one of the richest countries in the world.

He then gave her a copy of the Marquis de Sade's biography to read and later Myra said that she agreed with much of what Ian was offering to her and that at the time she accepted them too. She soon believed that

Left: Myra Hindley.

Below left: Myra Hindley at home.

Below right: Myra Hindley.

she had no soul and that there was no religion. She believed Ian held all of the answers.

Ian told Myra of his sexual fantasies. He was bisexual and certainly didn't lack desire, but what he wanted was hard to obtain. He shared his violent sexual fantasies with her and told her that when he'd first read de Sade he felt like he was looking in the mirror. He told Myra she was the first person he'd told about this and it greatly excited her. He later commented:

> I made sure Myra understood that we were both still individuals, free to indulge as we wished. Extra-sexual activity wouldn't sap the strength of our personal relationship, no more than would the whimsical preference for a different kind of wine. We laughed together as we exchanged details of our excursions into irregular sex.

Ian Brady pictured here posing at his desk for his firm's cameraman - George Clitheroe, a keen amateur photographer who took portraits of the staff on the occasion of retirement. Circa 1962.

Myra recalled: '[Ian] took the lead most times. He enjoyed rough sex and light spankings became whippings…. He excited me in a way that no other man had before.' She also told how she would have to drink to lower her inhibitions:

> I needed to drink to perform for him or to do the things Ian wanted to do. He liked me to dress up like a tart, for us both to wear hoods. He enjoyed anal sex the most…. He also enjoyed having a candle inserted up his backside. It gave us both pleasure, especially me, because then I was in the dominant role.

They sometimes used pornography which wasn't always of interest to her, but she 'went along with it for Ian's sake. I didn't reach orgasm, but I was very excited by seeing him satisfied.' She denied that some of this pornography was of children, but due to the later nature of their crimes it cannot be ruled out.

Ian still went home most evenings straight from work for his dinner before going out again in the evenings. He told Myra of his 'dark room' at home where he developed all of his own photographs. He suggested they make pictures of their own, to which she was agreeable. He bit her before, during and after sex. He gave her whisky to help numb the pain but bit her hard enough that the marks would show up on his camera.

Myra and Ian had started to build their 'World Above'.

Chapter 4

The Twisted World of Brady & Hindley

Ian and Myra soon turned their fantasies into reality. They began looking through the court reports in the local newspapers for any mention of cases involving cruelty to animals. The address of a person convicted of crime was, in those days, printed in the newspapers and Ian and Myra decided to hand out their own punishments. They would often go to the individual's address and give them 'what they deserved'. Their brand of punishment was usually a brick through the window, but on the rare occasion that the person concerned was out walking alone, then Ian and Myra would attack them from behind and give them a good beating.

Myra's friends and family had noticed how her behaviour had changed. Her friends saw less and less of her and when they did bump into her in the street Myra would just make small talk or ignore them completely. They often felt that Myra thought that she was 'above' them. Maureen also felt that they were growing apart as sisters because of Ian's influence and that Myra was hiding things from her. At the trial she told the court:

> Myra used to go to church. She liked dancing and swimming. She liked the normal way of life. She had many girl friends. She liked children. After she met Brady she stopped going to church; she said she didn't believe in it anymore. She didn't believe in marriage. She said she hated babies and children. And she hated people. Then she started keeping her things under lock and key.

Instead of going home for lunch Myra started to bring sandwiches into the office and she joined Ian at his desk where they read aloud to each other from his books on Nazism and he also started to teach her German. Years later, Myra herself admitted:

> One important aspect of our relationship was that we shared equally the ability to shut down our feelings and our emotions. Ian talked of controlling the subconscious urges or presenting a cold exterior. This ability, plus the use of alcohol, influenced our sexual experience and would eventually influence everything in our lives…. We had to be able

to blend into our surroundings like chameleons. To exist on two different planes, convincing others that we were normal, not capable of committing crimes…. He taught me how to conquer my emotions, to do things on autopilot and disregard the consequences. I was a willing apprentice.

The following account was given by Myra – as with almost everything she said, there was a portion of truth in it but she always painted herself as the victim caught up in Ian's world. This account was given at a time when she was trying to excuse her later crimes.

Ian continued to make his own wine, as he had done since his days in Borstal, and Myra recalled that one evening he took a bottle of Cinzano filled with his homemade wine round to her house. She recalled that it had a gritty sediment in it and he told her it just hadn't matured too well. She said that she got quite drunk on it, couldn't remember anything that happened for the rest of the night and then slipped into semi-unconsciousness. All she could remember was pain and flashing lights. Myra later claimed that Ian showed her photographs he had taken of her naked which explained the flashing lights, and that Ian had also raped her anally while she was semi-conscious which explained the pain. This is the first recorded incident of Ian's fascination of having sex with dead, or unconscious bodies. During the police investigation in 1965 they found many pornographic photographs of Myra and Ian, but obviously couldn't tell whether Myra was drugged or not.

Myra then claimed that she woke up the following morning feeling very ill. She phoned in sick at work and went out for some fresh air. She got on a bicycle and went for a ride but crashed into the back of a bus which was stationary at a set of traffic lights. Somehow she was uninjured and walked the bike back to Bannock Street. That evening, Ian went round to see why she hadn't turned up for work, she told him how she felt and apparently he told her that he had drugged her with her gran's Nembutol sleeping pills. She was apparently shocked and demanded an explanation and he told her that his old dog was going blind and didn't want to take it to the vets to be put down, wanting instead to do it himself. He told her he'd emptied a couple of capsules to see how much would be needed to kill the dog, that he'd had no intention of killing her and that it would never happen again.

There are questions that need to be asked about her account here. How did Ian get hold of her gran's sleeping tablets when they were kept in her bedroom? Why didn't her gran notice that tablets were missing? If she was too ill to go to work, why did she go for a bike ride? Especially as she had never mentioned having a bike before? If your partner had admitted drugging you, why would you not end the relationship?

A possible answer for that last question is that Myra also claimed that Ian had threatened to kill her grandmother, Ellen. He told her that he would push her down the stairs, and because of her old age people would just assume she had fallen. One morning Myra was unable to wake her grandmother when she took her a cup of tea. She fetched her mother who also could not wake Ellen, so the doctor was sent for.

The doctor told them that Ellen was in a drugged sleep and must have taken double her amount of sleeping tablets by mistake and that she would soon wake. Myra said that later, Ian told her that it was he who had drugged Ellen:

> He had made a pot of tea that evening, and put Nembutol in my gran's cup (which meant that he'd crept upstairs to her bedroom again to get them. Gran always took her tablets before she got in to bed, with water), and if she thought the tea tasted bitter, he knew she was too polite to say so. I asked him why, why my gran, and he said unless he convinced me he was serious about murder it would be my 14-year-old sister Maureen next, and then my mother.

She claimed that she realised he needed professional help by this point, but was scared of what he would do to her grandmother.

Ian denied that this had happened, claiming that it was at this point in the relationship he had told Myra that he wanted to commit a murder. He asked Myra who she thought of as a 'special enemy', and she had replied Ronnie Sinclair. He then asked her: 'If someone volunteered to remove him for good, and you complied, how would you feel about your role in his death?' According to him, Myra replied: 'I'd feel nothing. I'd be relieved.' Ian was pleased with this response and said to her:

> Good, we're talking about the fundamentals now. The average person is on a slow conveyor-belt from complete obscurity to total oblivion. With a bit of luck, they might have one opportunity to step off it. You are at that point. In itself, the crime is nothing to be perturbed about, only the sentence and the odds of being arrested. Some of the cards are on the table. How do you feel now, Kiddo?

Myra told him that he dare not exclude her and so he put her to the test. He told her:

> Tomorrow night I want you to see a film – *Tunes of Glory* – and retain the ticket stub. Remember what's shown on the Pathé newsreel and anything else that's on the bill. Tell me if anything unusual occurs – an incident in the audience or a break in the film, any exception to the routine. I'll meet you outside the cinema when it's finished to collect the ticket stub.

Myra's version was that Ian talked to her about a book called 'Compulsion'. It is a story of two boys from wealthy backgrounds who wanted to commit the perfect murder, and who had kidnapped and killed a 12-year-old boy. They only escaped the death penalty because of their young age.

He gave Myra a copy to read and told her that he couldn't believe the mistakes Leopold and Loeb had made. They had made a mess of the pick-up and were seen by people who knew them; they beat the boy to death in the car so there was blood and forensic evidence everywhere; then they hid the body in a drainage pipe but left a foot sticking out. Finally, they rang the victim's father to try to extract a ransom.

Ian told her that the way to commit the perfect murder was to plan it properly. You had to make sure that the body was never discovered. He told her that she would help him pick up a child, wearing a disguise; they would drive to the moor where he would rape, kill and bury the child. Everything would be carefully prepared: the grave, the body disposal plan, the clean-up afterwards. Nothing would be left to chance. There was no way they would be caught. He was going to commit the perfect murder and she was going to help.

Myra later said that 'I told him it was a very disturbing book, but why exactly had he wanted me to read it? One night he asked me if I wanted to see anyone I didn't like dead. I said 'No, don't be silly.' Then one evening – and he hadn't been drinking – he told me he wanted to do a perfect murder and I was going to help him: 'I knew by the time he began talking about the perfect murder that I was going to help him, that I had very little choice.'

What certainly did happen was that Myra went to see one of her best friends, May Hill, but did not tell her about Ian drugging her and her gran. They hadn't seen each other in a while so went to the Steelworks pub and drank quite a lot. May told Myra how she had split up with her boyfriend because she had refused to sleep with him, and on the way home May told her that no one liked Ian and she was getting a bad reputation by sleeping with him. When they got back to May's house Myra wrote a letter which said if anything happened to her then her body would be found close to a lay-by on Saddleworth Moor, probably by the rocks. She hid the words from May but made her promise to look after it and she was to take it to the police if she ever disappeared. They then moved the sofa and tucked the envelope beneath the carpet.

If what Myra had written in the letter is true, then it suggests that both Myra and Ian had both discussed murder and where to dispose of bodies. They had also possibly visited the site, as this is a very good description of where the bodies of three of their victims were later found.

The following Saturday Ian went to Myra's house and as she was making a pot of tea he sat down and began spreading out pictures of her on the table. She was naked and in a series of pornographic poses. She said this was another way of Ian exerting his dominance over her. Shortly afterwards, she contacted May again and took the letter back and burned it. This was because Myra had found a way out of her predicament. She responded to an advert for cafeteria and clerical workers for the NAAFI (Navy, Army, and Air Force Institutes). She went to London on the train for the interview and was offered a two-year contract working in Germany.

Myra later recalled: 'Because of Brady's fanaticism about Hitler and the Nazis, I persuaded him that if I got the job and went to Germany, I would be earning good wages, tax-free for two years, and renewable after that, I could save up and send him the fare to come over and spend his holidays there.

> I got the job in spite of feeling that I'd failed the medical, for some weeks earlier, he'd bitten both my breasts so badly, for his sadistic pleasure, that although the teeth marks had faded, there were still bruises. I explained them away by telling a half-truth, that I'd recently been in a motor-bike crash, which I had, and that was how I got the bruises and others that were on my body, where he'd bitten me or hit me.

When she got off the train back at Manchester's Piccadilly station at 11.00 pm, Ian was waiting for her with his motorbike, which she was not expecting. He asked her if she had got the job and she told him that she had. He drove her home where she was met by her mother, grandmother, sister, aunt and cousin who were all anxious to hear how she had got on. When she told them that she was moving to Germany they were all shocked. According to Myra they all started to cry, including her, 'because I didn't want to leave either, but how could I stay, knowing they were in danger? Then Brady, who was standing behind me, put his hand on my shoulder (he never touched me in any way when others were around....) and said: 'You've still got two weeks to make your mind up', and I knew exactly what he meant: 'anything could happen in two weeks'.

This made her realise that by getting away from Ian she would be leaving her family behind and so decided not to take the job.

> I couldn't go to the police about him for there was no proof of anything, and while I feared and often hated him, I was so emotionally obsessed with him I just couldn't change my feelings for him.... When everyone had gone home and gran had gone to bed, he stripped me, gagged me and beat me with a cane, raped me anally, which he often did because he knew I cried with the pain and hated him doing that to me. Before leaving, he warned me that if I ever tried to get away again I'd be the sorriest person alive.

It is far more likely that Myra applied for the job so that Ian could visit her and they could possibly commit more crimes over there, where the police would more likely suspect a local. As it turned out, she chose to stay in Manchester as she was 'emotionally obsessed with him', as she stated above.

Myra's sister, Maureen, had met Ian many times when he used to stay at Bannock Street. She said it was around August 1962 when Myra would go to the market at

Ashton-under-Lyne every Saturday to buy her diamond-pattern stockings because the market was much cheaper than anywhere else. This was in stark contrast to Myra's defence in the later court case. Maureen also recalled that Myra used to get tinned food at the market, as well as matting for the front door 'and things like that', but stopped going when she later moved.

Things were not great between Myra and Ian at this point, and she recalled:

> He stopped talking to me at work, except to tell me to take dictation, and didn't come near the house. He would never argue with me or explain whatever I'd done; he just stopped talking to me, which I thought of as his 'silences'. For a whole week he ignored me, then on the Friday afternoon not long before we all finished work, he came through to my small office and dropped a note on my desk before going upstairs to the bathroom. It said that he would come for me at seven that evening.
>
> When he arrived, he said we were going to Whitefield, to a country pub we'd been to before. When we reached the car park he drove by and down the small winding country lane. By then it was dusk. We sat on the bike in silence, then he told me to get off, which he did too. When he turned round, he had his sharp-bladed Stanley knife in his hand, which he ran lightly over his fingers. He asked me if I wanted to finish with him. I said no, why, what gave him that idea, and he said he'd ignored me all week because on the Monday morning (he hadn't spent the night with me but had left in the early hours of the morning) he saw me getting a lift in Brian's car (Brian was a married man with a child, happily married, and he was always polite and courteous; he worked in the finance office, a job Brady wanted for himself, he knew he wouldn't get it, and was rude and obnoxious to Brian) and I knew how he felt about Brian and I should have refused the lift because I couldn't have failed to hear his bike coming down the road. I said I didn't hear his bike, and whatever he felt about Brian was his business, but I had no reason to dislike or be nasty to him. All the time we were talking, he was still running the knife across his fingers, and I honestly thought he was going to stab me. Then he laughed, put the knife away, told me never to accept a lift from Brian again, and we drove back to the pub.
>
> Later, as we were driving home, I dreaded what he would do when we got there, for I knew he would do something. He raped me anally and began strangling me until I nearly passed out. Then he bit me on the cheekbone, just below my right eye, until my face began to bleed. I'd tried to fight him off strangling and biting me, but the more I did the more the pressure increased.

Before he left, when he'd seen the state of my face, he told me to stay off work the next day and tell people I'd been in a pub when a fight broke out and was accidentally hit in the face by a thrown beer bottle. And wear a polo neck jumper to hide the strangle mark bruises.

My face, the next morning, was an absolute mess; an eye was black and bruised and my cheek bone swollen; my neck was red and swollen, and the pain was terrible. I tried to hide as much as possible with make-up, but it still looked as bad. My gran almost fainted when she saw me, and went to get my mother, who asked me if 'he' had done this to me (my mother disliked him intensely and kept telling me he was no good for me; she'd been telling me that since I'd met him at 18½, but what girl of that age listens to her mother when she is wholly infatuated and in love).

I told them what he'd told me to say, but I knew they didn't believe me. She said there were teeth marks on my cheek; I told her there weren't, the marks were obviously from the bottle top. I decided to go to work because the marks and bruising would take ages to go down. Brady had the nerve to ask me if I'd been in a pub fight, and everyone made comments of sympathy tinged with suspicion. He strangled me so often, to this day I can't bear anything tight around my neck....

I used to ask him why he kept strangling me so much, so many times – this was before the offences took place – and he told me he was 'practising' on me. I said one of these days he was going to go too far and kill me, but he just laughed and said he wouldn't – he needed me. This wasn't an affectionate remark; I knew what he needed me for.

Ian agreed with the incident where they talked about whether or not Myra wanted to end things but made no mention of him holding a knife at the time, and also made no mention of them having sex that evening. Instead, he recalled that the following day: 'We made up for lost time. The office was empty at lunchtime and I made love to Myra on her desk, my own desk and then the director's; in that order.' After they had made up, Myra recalled:

We often drove up to Saddleworth Moor on his bike, during the day at the weekends, and sometimes at night.... We used to climb up to and over the big rocks, where he would tell me he was going to practice carrying a body, tell me to make myself as limp as possible, then he'd hoist me up over his shoulder, with my arms and head hanging over one side and my lower body and legs over the other side. The blood used to rush to my head until I thought I was going to faint.

Sometimes he would stumble over a small rock or large tuft of grass and we'd both fall and I often hurt myself. He'd pick me up again and walk up and down and round in circles; it was a horrible feeling, and when I saw the old movie Great Expectations, where Magwitch, the convict, picked up Pip and held him upside down and round and round, that was exactly how I had felt, seeing the sky and the ground whirl round until I was faint and dizzy. I don't know why he did that to me, because the only victim not killed and buried on the moor was little Lesley Ann Downey.

One evening in early January 1963, Ian and Myra went out for a few drinks. On the way home on Ian's motorbike they were overtaking a bus when it suddenly turned in to them. Ian took avoiding action and swerved onto the other side of the road, avoiding the oncoming traffic, but they then mounted the pavement and ran into a fence that ran around Belle Vue car park. The motorbike came to a rest near two uniformed policemen.

Ian had hit his head and was unconscious for a short time before he got up and picked his bike up. He wasn't drunk but had certainly been drinking and the police may have thought he was drunk from the smell of alcohol on his breath. Ian thought he was uninjured but one of the policemen pointed out the blood streaming from his right leg while the other policeman had gone to call for an ambulance.

Until she climbed into the ambulance with him, Ian hadn't realised that during the crash he had hit a woman. His goggles were smashed into pieces and the right side of his crash helmet was torn. He had a V-shaped cut under his nose and received five stitches in his knee. Myra had barely a scratch on her.

Above left: Ian Brady on his motorbike.

Above right: Myra Hindley on her sofa.

Myra reading a letter. Photograph taken by Ian Brady.

Following the crash, Ian and Myra both went to Manchester City Magistrate's Court on 9 January, where Myra was found guilty of 'Aiding and abetting – No 'L' Plates on motorcycle', and for 'Aiding and abetting – Access by passenger not qualified'. She was fined £2 for each charge. Ian was charged with the same offences and also fined £2 for each offence. He was then fined £5 for 'Driving a motorcycle in a dangerous manner' and told to pay the witnesses expenses.

On 16 April Ian sent a letter to Myra. He had sprained his ankle and told her that he wouldn't be at work. He said he would use the opportunity to stake out an establishment for a robbery. 'However, let us capitalise on the situation. I shall grasp the opportunity to review the investment establishment in Stockport Road. I will contact you before then to go over details.'

This is the first evidence that Ian and Myra were planning robberies together. At the trial, Myra denied this and stated: 'I thought it related to the buying of a car.' She went on at the trial to say that the first she knew of any possible robbery was when Ian told her the night before their final victim, Edward Evans, was murdered.

From around May onwards, Ian stayed most nights with Myra at 7 Bannock Street. Myra's grandmother would go up to bed at around 8.00 pm every night to get away from Ian, whom she did not like. When she went upstairs to bed Myra and Ian would drink as much as a bottle of wine each while they waited until Mrs Maybury had taken her sleeping pills and fallen asleep before Ian would get his expensive camera out. He had his own lighting equipment too, which was stored at Myra's, and they turned the living room into their own studio. Myra would pose for crude, pornographic pictures for Ian and sometimes he joined in. Police recovered thirty photographs in all. Thirteen of them show Ian and Myra having sex. Myra appears in various poses in twelve of the prints. In some she is kneeling, in others she is lighting a cigarette. One shows her lying face down with lines across her buttocks. Part of a knotted whip appears in one picture and was presumably there to show that it had been used to make the marks on her buttocks.

There were also photographs of Myra penetrating herself with various household implements such as broom handles and ones of her wearing crotchless black knickers. Ian appears alone on the remaining five photographs and seems to be urinating against a curtain on one of them. In 1998, Myra seemed to suggest that she was forced into it:

He used to take pornographic photographs of me, telling me to smile and pose and look as though I was enjoying it…. Sometimes, using the timer on his camera, he took some of both of us and told me to take some of just him. Once he cut some material he'd brought from work, sack-like material, and made it into hoods with just eye holes in them. The photographs he took with both of us wearing them he said he was going to sell.

She also admitted that the rape and murder of children was something that they talked about during sex. She admitted: 'Sex with children was an interest he had that influenced his offending behaviour, but it was a sadistic trait, gaining excitement from their suffering.' She denied sharing his paedophilia, but admitted that it was a part of their sex lives and they watched children at play with a view to the crimes they would eventually commit.

Ian was soon raising the idea of killing Ronnie Sinclair with Myra again. Now that they were back on track (relationship wise) he asked her if she still wanted him dead, to which (according to him many years later) she did. She told Ian that she wanted him humiliated before he was killed and said she'd 'love to see him treated like a woman'. Ian asked her if she wanted to kill him herself, and she apparently replied that she wouldn't mind, but would prefer to watch and savour the scene.

That evening they drove up to Saddleworth Moor on his motorbike to watch the sun set. He asked her: 'Do you think Ronnie would like to spend eternity up here?' to which Myra replied: 'We agree on everything these days, Neddie.'

The conversation continued on the way home, with them both shouting above the noise of the engine, and Myra apparently told him that she wanted Ronnie to be terrified and to know that he was going to die just before he was murdered, but Ian later told her that it would have to look like an accident, unless they could get a third party to do it as they would both be obvious suspects otherwise. Besides, he had a criminal record and would go to the hangman if he were caught. He dropped her at her door and said that he needed to get an early night as he would be up first thing in the morning to take a closer look at Myra's ex-fiancé.

He duly woke at 5.00 am and had breakfast, then went to stand at the end of Ronnie's road. When Ronnie left his house, Ian 'vaulted the fence and followed him, keeping my distance'. He followed him on to a bus which took them into the centre of Manchester and out to the Cheetham area. They then both disembarked and Ian followed him into a side street. At the end of the street he crossed a broad expanse of waste ground and Ian watched him walk into a building but did not follow. He said that he turned around and saw a row of pre-fabricated concrete lock-up garages and recalled that 'this open ground would be an ideal place to commit murder'.

He then retraced his steps, went home and, knowing that his house would be empty, thought through his plan to murder Ronnie Sinclair. 'I felt no hatred towards him. He was simply the target in an exercise, a problem to be solved.'

Ian believed that one of his 'acquaintances' could commit the murder by using a stolen car and driving at speed on to the waste area and hit Ronnie Sinclair from behind before he was aware of any danger. Ian said that he would arrange it for a time when both he and Myra were at work so that they had a cast-iron alibi.

He then went in late to work and dictated letters to Myra. He took her into the small typing office and gave her a brief account of what he had learned about Ronnie's movements and a possible plan for his murder, but did not tell her about the possible involvement of his 'acquaintance'. The plan, fortunately, was never carried out. Brady was just showing Myra that he was serious and wanted to show her the lengths to which he was willing to go.

At around the same time as this, Ian and Myra also started to visit the library together. Barbara Hughes, a trainee librarian at the time, recalled seeing Myra in Mount Road while queueing for her bus to the Levenshulme branch. Myra would pass the spot on her way to work.

> She wore quite short skirts, even before the mini-skirt was in fashion, so the first impression was that she was tarty, a bit common. That's why I thought they weren't suited.
>
> When he returned his books at the Longsight branch, he never said 'Please' or 'Thank you'. He always walked straight to the True Crime shelves, crash hat under his arm. They frequently came into Levenshulme Library, chatting together, but they never spoke to the staff.

In 1998, Myra recalled:

> When we went to the central library in Manchester and upstairs is the reference library, he'd give me a list of books to pick out, such as 'The Cradle of Erotica', which was pornographic, 'Havelock Ellis', 'Kinsey' etc.; and show my library card to get them and casually leave all but one at the desk he'd chosen to sit at, some distance away from mine. There was one book, 'Sexual Murders', which could only be taken out on a special ticket. I had to go to the main desk and ask for it, and get it stamped out on my card and give my name and address.

Myra also visited 'dubious' bookshops on Ian's behalf. She was to ask the bookkeeper if he had any books by de Sade, and in one particular bookshop she remembered being watched by the owner, Eric. He told her that he did have some, 'Justine', 'Juliet' and a book 'with a title similar to a hundred nights of sodomy'.

He told her that he didn't keep such titles in the shop in case they were raided, but he did have them in his flat and if she went with him a couple of nights later then she could borrow them. Myra didn't want to go to his flat and said she would think about it. She left the shop and met Ian around the corner. She told him what Eric had said and Ian told her to go back in the shop and say that she'd like to go ahead. A couple of nights later Eric picked her up in his new Jaguar and drove her back to his flat while Ian told Myra that he would follow discreetly behind.

Eric tried it on with her when she was in the flat but Myra told him that she was there only for the books (although she did give a very vivid description of his bedroom), so he gave her the books, wrapped in brown paper, and drove her home. Myra didn't want him to know where she lived so asked him to drop her off somewhere close to home. He gave her a date when he wanted the books back and told her to phone his shop and he would come back and collect them.

She said that when she got out of the car, she cut across a playing field and down some alleys and back streets so that Eric couldn't follow her. When she got home, she saw that Ian's bike was parked outside and he was waiting for her inside. He hadn't followed her as he had promised.

> He'd already been drinking and opened up the bed settee. He took the books off me and began reading one of them. I was so exhausted and traumatised by my experiences, I got into bed, drank half a bottle of wine and fell asleep. Sometime later, he began shaking me to wake me up, and I said leave me alone, I need to sleep. He was enraged – I knew the book had 'turned him on' and I just couldn't bear to be touched by him – and said he'd soon wake me up. He went to the kitchen and came back with a sweeping brush and using handle and head in turns, beat me until I was a bleeding bruised mess. I'd learned not to cry out when he was hitting me, for my gran had been wakened several times and shouted down the stairs, 'What's going on? What are you doing?' Either Brady or I, to prevent her coming down the stairs, had to make up some excuse – we were moving the furniture and something had fallen on me; all kind of excuses.

She later told David Astor, one of her supporters (both financially and morally while she was in prison): 'He did many other things to me, such as forcing my mouth open and urinating in it, or urinating all over my body, in my ears, up my nose, everywhere he could think of. I was so humiliated....'

As well as the library, Ian and Myra spent most of the weekends and evenings after tea going out. They would head out on his motorbike to the moors and hills around Glossop, Woodhead, or Whaley Bridge in Derbyshire as well as Ramshaw Rocks and, to their favourite spot, Saddleworth Moor.

Above left: Ian Brady on his Triumph Tiger Cub 200cc.

Above right: Myra Hindley on one of their trips out on Brady's motorbike.

Ian Brady on one of the couple's outings. Photo taken by Myra Hindley.

Myra sunbathing.

Myra sitting on Ian
Brady's motorbike.

Right: Myra Hindley on
one of her and Brady's
excursions.

Below left: Unseen
photograph of Myra
Hindley found in their
'Tartan Album'.

Below right: Brady and
Hindley on the Serpent
Stone.

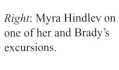

It was these times when they were alone up on the moor that they discussed crimes. Myra later said that she admitted finding it 'exciting to swim against the tide, to do things that others would never dream of ... I just don't know how much, but I have always wanted something different, more exciting. I have never been satisfied with any situation for long.' They discussed 'not killing people initially, but criminal activities – the perfect robbery, its planning and execution.'

By June, Ian had permanently moved in with Myra at her gran's at 7 Bannock Street. He had almost completely indoctrinated Myra by now and had her believing everything that he believed. His favourite book was 'Justine' by the Marquis de Sade. It tells of a robbery, and the woman leading the gang states:

> Why shouldn't we kill to cover up our job? We should never value things except how they concern ourselves ... therefore if we got the slightest gain doing away with them we ought to be glad. The only feelings that may be involved are moral ones and moral feelings are always false; the only real feelings worth bothering about are the physical ones. The weakness of our bodies, lack of reason, the stupid prejudices in which we are brought up, the vain promises of religion and the laws are what stop fools from becoming criminals and doing great deeds. But a man, strong and vigorous, knows where his interests lie and he mocks God and man, braves death, despises the law and is thoroughly convinced that he alone is the measure of all things.

He soon had Myra believing that:

> Remorse is just an illusion, merely the whining of a cowardly soul – too cowardly to stifle and kill it ... If you have remorse for anything you do, do it again and again, and you'll see how easily you forget about your conscience. And, anyway, who said that remorse is a crime – it simply shows a weak soul, easily subdued.... Crime is the most meaningless thing in the world though sometimes necessary.

Myra later recalled that she believed Ian was anti-social and had a chip on his shoulder. To quantify this, she recalled an incident where they were walking along a footpath together and Myra stepped into the road to allow a middle-aged woman and a girl to walk past. Ian berated her for this and barged ahead, pushing the woman and child out of the way.

At work, Ian and Myra kept their private life separate and didn't tell anyone that they were a couple, although a few had already guessed. It hadn't gone unnoticed that Myra no longer went home for lunch, choosing instead to sit and read books on Nazi Germany and sexual horrors with Ian. They developed a catchphrase with which they used to greet each other: 'Money and food is all I want – all I want is money and food.' Myra had even written it on a wall behind a picture on her desk.

George Clitheroe, the Foreman at Millwards, recalled shortly after their arrest: 'I have seen Myra point out a particularly gruesome page of horror to Brady and watched them both laugh at the contents. At the same time, she became very over-bearing and started wearing kinky clothes.'

Myra had started to imitate Irma Grese, the infamous 'Beast of Belsen'. Grese was an SS guard at the Nazi concentration camps of Ravensbrück and Auschwitz and served as a warden of the women's section of Bergen-Belsen. Myra would dress like her and even carried a photograph of her in her handbag.

Ian wasn't a fan of Myra's peroxide blonde hairstyle though. He thought that it brought too much attention to her, and therefore to him too. Because of this, Myra went to the hairdresser who told her that a new colour would have to be done in stages, and after the first stage Myra emerged with a pink rinse, cut in an urchin style.

She hated the temporary look and made sure that she had her crash helmet on when Ian called to take her out after visiting his mother. When plucked up the courage to show him her hair, Ian remembered that he liked it. According to him, they then had the wildest sex that they ever had when they returned home. 'A woman should change her hairstyle occasionally to seduce her partner into thinking that she is being unfaithful or committing adultery', he later said.

The following day Ian and Myra went to Bollington, Cheshire, and sunbathed in the meadows. Ian wanted some photographs of Myra's new hairstyle. She recalled

Above left: Myra sunbathing.

Above right: Ian Brady.

Unseen photograph of a topless Ian Brady from their 'Tartan album'. (Photograph taken by Myra Hindley)

laying with her eyes closed, listening to The Beatles singing 'From Me to You' on the radio. She then took a photo of Ian balancing a beer mug on his head.

That summer, Myra's sister, Maureen, asked Ian if he would take some photographs of her so that she could give them to her boyfriend, David Smith. Over the next few days he openly flirted with Maureen as he took the photographs, much to Myra's annoyance.

According to Ian, when he had finished taking the photos of Maureen and she had left, he and Myra finished off a bottle of wine that had been opened. Myra then wondered aloud if David Smith could be of any use to them in their future crimes. Ian agreed, but said there was no rush and they should discreetly ask around about him. Myra then said: 'I've just remembered something Mo mentioned. Dave Smith was seen with another girl. She lives next door to him in Wiles Street. A right dump. Her name's Pauline Reade.' Ian then asked Myra if she knew her, and Myra replied that she only knew her to say hello to and that she was aged about sixteen. Pauline would go on to become the couple's first known killing.

Above left: Maureen Hindley.

Above right: Unseen photograph of Maureen Hindley from the 'Tartan album'.

Above left: Maureen and Myra Hindley. Photograph from the 'Tartan album'.

Above right: Maureen Hindley. Photograph from the 'Tartan album'.

Not long afterwards, Maureen and David Smith had a huge argument. Myra's mother disliked David just as much as she disliked Ian Brady and she called Smith a 'dirty bugger'. Nellie went around to Myra's and told her that Smith had been hanging around and waiting for Maureen and she had chased him away. Myra assured her that she would go and find Maureen and that she would sort out David. Ian went with Myra but was warned: 'Don't get involved, Neddie, the little toad isn't worth it.'

They found David Smith first, standing in the entrance to an alley with his back against a wall. Ian remembered: 'He didn't look promising on first viewing. It's a pity I didn't heed my own first impressions. I would still be a free man.'

Myra went over to speak to Smith while Ian waited. When she went back to Ian she was angry and told him that 'Smith wants to marry Mo!' Ian managed to calm her down and told her:

> Find out what Mo wants before we decide what to do. If Smith married Mo, we could exploit the relationship. A blood relationship would be a safeguard against grassing, Kiddo, if we decide to use him. If we don't, and you don't want Mo to marry him, you can have him gift-wrapped.

The following day, Ian asked Myra if she had seen her sister, to which Myra said she had and that she was determined to marry David Smith. Ian then told her that the marriage would work to their advantage, but that Maureen would be kept out of any criminal activities.

That evening, Ian was starting to fall asleep when Myra said something that woke him up. Not sure if he heard her correctly, he asked her to repeat it. She said that Ronnie Sinclair had been reprieved and now so had David Smith. Ian took this to mean that she thought he was going soft.

Ian said he sprung awake and told Myra that there must first be a written plan. They sat on the floor surrounded by hand-written sheets while drinking wine that had been cooled by mixing it with water as it was a very warm evening. By the end of the evening they had produced the master list.

Ian, who was very forensically aware for the times, later said: 'The first principle was absolutely fundamental. There must be no thread connecting our starting point with our destination, and vice versa. All surfaces had to be free of tyre and footmarks, hairs, fibres and fingerprints.' There must be duplicates of all clothing including shoes. The set used on the day would be burned and the ashes thrown into a river. Buttons should be carefully counted and cleaned. The vehicle used must be thoroughly cleaned and polished before and after the event.

Both the inner workings and outer surfaces of guns must be free of fingerprints. Bullet heads must be scored to turn them into a shapeless mass, destroying all ballistic markings on impact. Disposable plastic sheets must cover the interior of the vehicle.

The house had to be cleared of anything that might arouse police suspicions. These items would be placed into left-luggage at a railway station. In the target area itself, the vehicle must not be parked where it could be spotted through overlooking windows. False number plates must be used. All weapons, guns excepted, must be broken up and disposed of over a wide area after use.

Alibis must be established and remain valid for fourteen days. Then it would be relegated to 'vague' status. Few people can remember where they were a fortnight before, unless there was something special about the day. Normal, daily routine behaviour must be adhered to, on or after the day in question. Verifiable records would show no break in the regular schedule.

The master list would apply to any criminal activity, ranging from theft to murder. There were very detailed cross-references, modifications, sub-procedures and divisions, and footnotes for each category of crime, making up a comprehensive list of detailed procedures to select from. Red and green colours were used to pinpoint cross-references and details germane to a particular activity.

When everything was transferred to the columns in thirty pages of foolscap, all other sheets were torn up and burned, as well as any blank pages that might have served as pressure copies. The complete master list was finally put into a large brown envelope with other items such as lists of contacts, maps of projects and photographs, address books, tapes and other incriminating material. A working list for each particular crime would be written by drawing from the master list.

The following day they hid the envelope among piles of redundant files in a locked room in the warehouse at Millwards. When the pair were arrested, and a hastily written list was found in Brady's wallet, the police wrongly deciphered two abbreviations – WH and REC – to mean Woodhead and Reconnaissance. It was only during the reinvestigation in 1986 that the police figured out that they actually stood for 'Warehouse' and 'Records'.

Myra backed this up to journalist Duncan Staff many years later: 'He'd told me what to wear and had counted the buttons on my coat.... He'd counted the buttons on his coat and jacket and shirt and made a list of everything.... He was so methodical and precise, he thought of everything, every possibility, absolutely everything.'

Chapter 5

David Smith

David Smith was born on 9 January 1948, in Withington Hospital, Manchester. He was the only child of 28-year-old engineer John Smith and 19-year-old Joyce Hull. John Smith travelled the length of the country in his job and rarely saw his partner and son. Joyce found it incredibly hard raising their son on her own at 39 Aked Street, Ardwick, and on St Valentine's Day 1949, baby David was legally adopted by his father's parents. When he was older he was told that his mother had passed away.

Annie Smith, his adopted mother and actual grandmother, was a cleaner at the Royal Infirmary, but her husband, John, had an addiction to gambling. The relationship between the two was always strained and John would disappear at times to Blackpool where he would use household goods and clothes instead of money for a stake in a game and this caused many arguments. At home, he would sleep in one of the two bedrooms while Annie and David would have to sleep in the attic.

Annie also ate alone in the back kitchen and David never recalled any intimacy between his adoptive mother and father.

From a young age David would steal coins from his grandfather, but he never stole anything from Annie. His grandfather, noticing that his coins were missing, started to count them before he went to sleep at night, and if he discovered any were missing then he would beat David.

David had no memory of the woman who gave birth to him. He always considered Annie as his mother and recalled: 'The only Mum I ever knew showered me with love and spoiled me rotten. Anything I ever needed or wanted was mine, I didn't even have to ask.'

In 1953, aged 5, David began school at Ross Place Infants in Ardwick, Manchester, where he stayed until he was 9, when he transferred to Stanley Road Junior School, Gorton; he remained there until he was 11 years old.

When he was 7, David's biological father began visiting him on Sundays after the pubs had closed and he was usually drunk. John hated women and used to tell everybody who would listen that a woman's fortune was to be found between her legs. He wasn't fond of children either, but did take David out to the zoo at Belle Vue.

It was in 1956 that David learnt that his mother, Joyce, was not dead. He asked his grandmother why he was getting free school dinners when they could afford to give him a packed lunch. Joyce explained that as far as the education authorities were concerned, David came from a one parent family, which entitled him to free meals.

Angered by this, David kicked his grandmother's shins as hard as he could. He cried and screamed for over two hours. Annie retaliated by dragging him into the kitchen and whipping him with a strip of rubber from an old pram wheel, which had two steel threads running through it. This changed David's attitude and from then on he called his grandmother 'Mrs Smith'. He was rude and hostile towards her for months and refused to eat his free school dinners, so Annie relented and gave him money to buy fish and chips. Any left-over change was used to buy cigarettes.

His father was still trying to form a relationship with him and would buy him comics when he'd been working away in Belgium. The only problem was that they were not written in English so David couldn't read them. He was seeing more and more of David, but one night David remembered being woken up by loud shouting and thuds from downstairs. He crept down to see what was going on and saw his father, who was steaming drunk, being beaten by his grandfather with a poker.

One night not too long after the beating, David's father took him out of his bed in the middle of the night and put him into a taxi; they went to a house that would become his home until he turned seventeen – 13 Wiles Street, Gorton. David was never given a full explanation as to why he was moved. He remembered not being allowed to see Annie, and being kept home for a couple of weeks so that she would not be able to take him from school.

The house in Wiles Street was owned by a lady named Elizabeth Jones, whom David was scared of as she had a large purple cyst on her forehead, and David's father rented a room where he and David shared the same bed.

During the two weeks David was kept off of school his father still went out to work and Mrs Jones also worked, so David was home alone. He grew bored quickly and one day opened the front door to see who was around. He noticed a boy and girl leaving for school a couple of doors down. The girl was a couple of years older than him and she smiled at him. The girl was called Pauline Reade. Little did he know that his name would forever be linked to her murder in just a few years' time.

Having forgiven his grandmother for the whipping, David was eventually allowed to see her again and would go there for an hour or two after school each night. His home was always locked when he got back, and he had to wait on the step, no matter the weather, for Mrs Jones to come home drunk from the pub to let him in.

Pauline Reade would sometimes be sent out by her mother, Joan, to sit with him and she would take jam sandwiches and a cup of tea. He recalled that initially they used to just talk, but then they would hold hands and eventually kiss.

David started arguing at home with his dad and the arguments nearly always became physical. He was also struggling at school and by November 1957 he was fighting at school too. 'I was rebelling by then and saw myself as the cock of the school', he recalled years later.

He had a fight with a boy called Tony Jackson on the cricket field but they were caught by the teachers, who broke it up and told them that if they wanted to fight then they would do it properly after school. A lot of the children in their class stayed behind after school and formed a ring around the two fighters. Just then, one of the teachers put a pair of boxing gloves on the two boys, a move that David was not expecting. He recalled:

> It was like putting clown shoes on a long-distance runner – a real handicap. Tony Jackson was twice my size anyway, and I wanted to gouge my nails into him, pull his hair and stick my fingers in his eyes. That to me was fighting. But Jackson was used to boxing, so he threw me all over the place that afternoon and was declared the winner in front of the whole school. I was gutted, but it didn't take me long to bounce back.

In 1958, David changed school and was now attending St James' Secondary Modern School. His behaviour didn't improve.

It didn't help that things were getting worse at home. In 1959, when he was just 11 years old, he was sexually assaulted. Mrs Jones's adult nephew had come to stay for a while, but as there were only two bedrooms in the house, for some reason it was decided that he would share David's bed. One night he recalled that he froze in terror as the man began to touch him. He pretended to be asleep through the experience and kept it a secret.

This had a detrimental effect on him and on 2 October 1959, aged 11 years and 9 months, he was charged with 'wounding with intent to do grievous bodily harm' at Manchester City Juvenile Court and was given a conditional discharge for twelve months. He had taken offence to being called a 'bastard' by a 15-year-old boy; he then got into an argument with one of the boy's friends and when the boy's younger brother tried to intervene, the argument turned physical and David stabbed the boy with a sheath knife. Luckily, the wound was not serious.

One morning he woke up to find he didn't have a clean shirt. He complained to his father, who was drunk, and his father waited until David had turned his back before hitting him with a dog chain. David lost his temper and punched his father square in the face. They got into a scrap and the 11-year-old David beat his father. Years later he regretted hitting his father and recalled: 'I should not have won that fight. I never lost one after that.'

The headmaster of his secondary school – Stanley Grove School in Longsight – ran a boxing school and saw an unpolished talent in the young David. He won many bouts, including the final of the school championships which were held at the Kings Hall, Belle Vue. His reward was a brand new pair of boxing gloves from his father.

Soon, though, he was persuaded to give up boxing by Annie. She scared him with tales of cauliflower ears and broken noses. David wasn't too upset though as he preferred fighting to boxing. 'I just wanted to hammer my opponents with my right fist.'

Aged 12, he was now the local hard case and everyone knew who he was. He paid attention to how he looked too, styling himself on James Dean with tight jeans, black t-shirt or shirt and winkle pickers. He was often sent home from school for not wearing acceptable attire and his father would send him back wearing baggy trousers.

As a result, David was sent to the headmaster's office; he listened to what the head had to say but as the man rose out of his chair, David punched him and was immediately expelled. He was then taken on at All Saints' School, opposite Gorton Monastery – the school Myra attended.

In the summer of 1962 David got into a playground fight with a boy called Percy Waddington, who had called him a bastard. They had been playing cricket when the name-calling had begun and David hit Percy's hand with a cricket bat, breaking his thumb. On 27 August, 14-year-old David was charged with 'assault occasioning actual bodily harm' and was put on probation for two years at Manchester City Juvenile Court. He was also sent to Rose Hill Remand Home.

When his time in Rose Hill was done he began to hang around with two brothers, Chris and Arthur Hamnett, who lived just a few doors away from Myra and her gran in Bannock Street. The boys' mother Patricia hated David, especially when he got hold of an air pistol, and would shoot at her son Chris in the sort of stupid but consensual games boys of that era played. She recalled: 'I used to go to Dave Smith's house with a knife to threaten him but he just swore at me. It was a waste of my time mithering over him.'

David was always looking for his next fight and recalled seeing a friend of his being touched inappropriately by an old man in the Essoldo cinema. 'I leathered him, butted him with my head and in the end the management had to be called to stop us. My friend went out and told his friends that I had helped him. That protected me for a few weeks.' He didn't always win his fights, but he did always have the last say.

> There was no point in being beaten, because you lost everything, in them days. You might get the best hiding, but the other boy would not be able to claim he was walking at the end of it. If he was walking away, you had to get up and use a brick on him. Otherwise, other boys would come looking for you.

Bricks weren't the only weapon he would use.

> You didn't carry weapons to use as tooth-picks. I carried knives to use
> them. It didn't matter if you met a hard man; he just would not win.
> I used the weapon properly on him. I was not 'into' guys who carried
> weapons and wouldn't use them. I carried a weapon because I knew
> I was going to be beaten up. But sure as hell that did not mean I was
> going to lose the fight….

Aged 14, he became sexually active. His first was Valerie, the local greengrocer's
daughter, who David remembered would loudly eat an orange as they had sex, then a
girl called Pat who let him go 'all the way' and a girl called Maureen Verity. He also
dated the girl from two doors down – Pauline Reade – for a couple of weeks, she used
to bring him jam sandwiches, but nothing sexual happened between them.

David became serious about a girl named Gloria. She was highly sought after by
all the boys but there were only really two contenders for her affections. Him, and a
local lad named Tony Latham.

They were soon sleeping together in his bedroom at Wiles Street while his father
was out getting drunk, but she wasn't enough for David and he started to see another
girl on the side. Gloria soon moved out of the area, and David used to visit her
occasionally on the back of his friend Sammy Jepson's motorbike. Sammy was the
brother of Myra's best friend Pat. He recalled: 'Little did I know, but after Sammy
dropped me home he would roar off back to the nursery alone to spend a bit of
quality time with Gloria himself…. In the meantime, my relationship with the other
girl became serious….'

That other girl was called Maureen Hindley.

Pauline Reade, aged 14.

David had known Maureen at school and she
also lived near him. He recalled in his memoirs
how he saw Maureen standing on a street corner
with her friends. She had her hair in rollers under
a headscarf and a cigarette hanging from the side
of her mouth. Someone had brought a transistor
radio out and they were listening to Radio
Luxembourg. The girls were dancing while the
boys were leaning against the wall – until Elvis
came on the radio. The boys all moved in on the
girls and he made a beeline for Maureen. He put
his hands around her waist and she gave him a
love bite on his neck.

Later that day the group met up in Sivori's
Milk Bar; they talked about dating and he

recalled saying that it was her he turned whenever he argued and fought with his father, and that it was her he had sex with in the back alleys and on the sofa at her parents' house while listening to Elvis on the record player.

He said that he could tell fairly early on that Maureen loathed her father, Bob, and worshipped her mother, Nellie. He also noted that Maureen copied many of her mother's mannerisms and could see that she got on well with the other members of her family, such as her gran, aunts and cousins, especially Glenys. He was aware of Myra, but as she was older and with Ian, had very little to do with her.

> She didn't hang around the streets like the rest of us. The only time I ever saw her out and about was when she was 'in transit' between Eaton Street and Bannock Street. She'd either be walking very fast and purposefully with her arms folded or clicking in her high heels down the street carrying two plates balanced on top of each other. Nellie cooked tea for daughter and Granny Maybury every night….
>
> The only other time I'd see Myra was when she was in a temper, heading home to sort out her drunken father.

He recalled that one Saturday evening he went to Eaton Street to see Maureen and her parents were out at the local pub, the Steelworks Tavern. They were listening to Elvis records when Myra burst in, she asked Maureen not to go out that evening and begged her to do her hair for her. Maureen agreed and Myra put a couple of bottles of cider on the table for them all to drink. According to David, Myra was 'the mannish female with nice legs, great tits and the punch of a heavyweight boxer'.

A couple of weeks later Maureen asked him to go to her house and talk to her father, Bob. He knew that Bob would be drunk and that Maureen only asked him to go around because she was scared of telling Myra as it would come to blows. When he got there, Bob was sitting in his chair by the fireplace and Nellie was in the kitchen. Maureen went into the kitchen to talk to her mum and shortly after, Nellie appeared holding two plates of dinner for Myra and her gran.

David knew that Bob hit Nellie but was shocked by what he saw. Nellie was a battered mess. One eye was completely closed and her top lip was so swollen that it almost touched her nose. She looked at Bob and said: 'Fuck you, Bob Hindley, fuck you to hell and back.' Bob retaliated, shouting at Nellie to 'Fuck off', before throwing his glass of whisky across the room. Nellie then left to deliver the food to Myra and her mother and David waited for the real violence to erupt.

A few minutes later, with Myra having seen the state of her mother's face, she burst into the house and started swearing at her father. He was so drunk that he struggled to get up out of his chair, all the while Myra was in his face, shaking with rage. She screamed at him: 'Come on, you bastard! Get up, fucking stand up, you fucking useless piece of shit!'

When he was almost to his feet Myra started to lay into him with her fists and was punching him full in the face. There was blood pouring from his nose and mouth which covered his shirt. Myra was still shouting and screaming at him, 'Fucking bastard, fucking big man … fucking come on!' She grabbed Bob by his hair and dragged him up from his chair. He tried to get Myra by the throat, but she saw it coming and threw him on the floor. She then picked up his walking stick and began beating him with that.

At that point Nellie came home but made no attempt to intervene. Myra soon stopped the beating, and Bob told everyone to 'Fuck off' again. Myra then threw his walking stick on the floor, walked over and gave her mother and sister a hug. She told them that if Bob even looked at them the wrong way ever again, they were to tell her and she'd sort him out. She then warned her father: 'And you, not one word. If there's a next time, you end up in hospital or the fucking cemetery.'

Spitting blood from his mouth, Bob told her to 'Fuck off' – and with that Myra ran across the room and slapped him hard across the face. 'I said not one word. That was two. Now keep your fucking mouth shut!'

David left the house and the three women followed after him. Myra told them she wasn't going out for the rest of the evening and that if they needed her again, they weren't to hesitate to come and get her.

Chapter 6

Reconnaissance & Pauline Reade

Ian and Myra began looking for potential targets in order to commit the 'perfect murder'. Myra had babysat for a friend of hers, Ben Boyce, on a couple of occasions and although Myra never took payment, Ben did give her the use of his old black Ford Prefect van from which he ran his mobile greengrocery business. He knew that Myra didn't have a driver's licence, but he also knew that she was having lessons.

It was in early July 1963 that they began scouting. Ian thought it was perfect that they now had a vehicle with which a victim could be abducted, especially as no paperwork could link the vehicle back to them. He would sit and pick out a 'victim' and describe to Myra what he'd do with 'it'. Myra later admitted: 'We were of one mind, not troubled by our consciences.' Getting as low as he possibly could in his seat, so as not to be seen, Ian then took photographs of children from the van.

Professor Malcolm MacCulloch, the former medical director of Ashworth Hospital on Merseyside who interviewed and treated Ian Brady, later commented: 'He is planning what to do, and at the same time transferring the script in his head to her. But she is not fighting it. She is a willing participant.'

Above left: Unseen photograph taken by Ian Brady at Old Hall Drive School on Levenshulme Road.

Above right: Photograph taken by Ian Brady at Old Hall Drive School on Levenshulme Road.

Unseen photograph taken by Ian Brady at Old Hall Drive School on Levenshulme Road.

Myra also drove around Gorton on her own. Ian wanted to know if she had the bottle to abduct a child on her own and so he sent her out on trial runs. She recalled how, when she had been sent out by Ian, she wrestled with her conscience: 'I was considered to be good with children, an excellent babysitter and able to put children at ease. Could I therefore be considered capable of child abduction or violence towards children?'

Myra always returned empty-handed and told Ian that the area in which she had been looking had been too crowded and she would have been seen; Ian told her he had been following her on his motorbike and had seen that she had simply 'bottled it', and would then give her a slap.

In July 1963 Myra got Maureen a job at Millwards as a Filing Clerk. This was on the proviso that she was not to tell anyone that Myra and Ian were seeing each other. Myra told her that because it was such a small firm, gossips would ruin their working conditions and she and Ian preferred to keep their private and work life separate. It was at this time that Maureen started to notice that Myra was keeping lots of things under lock and key, both at home and at work. She also noted that Myra was beginning to object to anyone calling at the house unannounced.

At lunch times Ian and Myra began to disappear. One would leave, followed a minute or two later by the other. They would go to the local shops and Ian would wait outside while Myra bought some bits and pieces, then they would go to the bookmakers so Ian could place a few bets. Afterwards, they would eat fish & chips. The bookmaker, Mr Gibson, remembered:

> In four years he came in to my shop every day. I never saw him smile and he never answered to 'Good morning'. He always argued about his bets and he lost his temper and swore violently when his horses lost. And I've never known a meaner punter. One day he thought he had been underpaid twopence and he sent Myra Hindley all the way round here [about three hundred yards] in the car to collect it. I gave her the coppers, but in the meantime he had been working out the odds and decided it was threepence he was underpaid. It's hard to believe, but the next I know he's come all the way round for a penny. He came in and thumped the counter shouting about it – all over a penny. I told him not to come back in the shop again, but of course he did come back and I took his bet.

After work most nights Ian would go back to his mother's house for dinner and then go round to Bannock Street to stay with Myra. He told the police in 1965 that he did this because he liked to 'keep the two environments separate. I like to relax at home and drink at Myra's.' He told DCI Tyrrell that he eventually introduced Myra to his mother in 1964, but that he still preferred Myra to wait outside the house in the car for him to finish his dinner.

Towards the end of 1963 David Smith's mother, Annie, passed away after a long illness. Around the same time the landlady of the property on Wiles Street, Miss Jones, moved away to live with her sister and so David's father took over the tenancy of the whole house.

David and Maureen were growing ever closer but neither of their families were happy about it. David always had trouble getting past Nellie in order to see Maureen, and when Maureen called for David at Wiles Street his father would answer the door to her by saying: 'And what the fuck do you want?' David's father had a strong disliking for women and would often call Maureen, among other things, a 'fucking little bitch'. He would call her far worse at other times, and Maureen would have to drag her boyfriend away before a fight broke out.

David recalled one evening, just after he had finished his dinner, there was an odd knock at the door. David answered the door and discovered Myra stood there. She was dressed as if she were going out for the evening, and she said to him: 'Get inside, this is private.' David prepared himself for a fight, but Myra said to him, in a hard, deliberate monotone: 'Maureen's waiting for you on the corner. I'm here to lay down some fucking ground rules and, for your own good, you'd better mind yourself and listen for once.' As he started to protest, Myra jabbed her finger towards his face.

> Keep your mouth fucking shut! I've tried to explain to our Mobee what an arsehole you are. But for some reason she still wants to be with you, so I'm telling you now – if you ever, *ever*, hurt her in any way you're a dead man. Do you get me? A dead man. This *thing* between you both will be tolerated but you better mind your back because every step of the way I'll be watching you, David Smith. Right? Every fucking step you take. Got it?

Aged just 15, David left school that summer and began to get involved in petty crime with a group of lads known as the Taylor Street Gang. They began to break into people's homes and various stores and take whatever they could carry, but he soon got caught and on 8 July 1963, he appeared at Manchester Crown Court where he was charged with 'house-breaking and larceny', 'store breaking and larceny', and admitted three other offences. It emerged in court that he and his friend Sammy Jepson (brother of Myra's friend Pat), had stolen electrical goods such as kettles and blankets from a shop and had then passed them on to Sammy's contact

(Pat's boyfriend) who had been caught with them. To ease his own sentence he had told the police who had given him the stolen items. David was put on probation for two years. He tried to go straight and got a job as an apprentice electrician at Messrs A.E. Sudlow, Brown Street, Manchester, where he stayed for the next six months before being sacked for poor time keeping.

In the meantime, he recalled that Ian Brady appeared 'as if from out of nowhere' and that he didn't like him from afar. He recalled seeing Ian leaving Bannock Street early in the mornings on his motorbike, and would also see Ian and Myra pass him on the street heading out towards the countryside, with Myra riding pillion. He also backed up Maureen's claims of Myra telling people not to call at her home on Bannock Street unannounced; apparently Myra would tell her sister not to go over on some nights because Ian would be busy recording on his eight-track machine or developing rolls of film.

On the evening of 9 July 1963, Ian and Myra decided to plan an abduction for the following evening. They had decided to clear both Bannock Street and Ian's parents' home of anything incriminating, put the contents into suitcases and deposit them in the 'left luggage' at one of the local railway stations, before going on to find someone to abduct. Myra knew that the abductee would be murdered, and Ian told her to 'pick up anyone you choose – it's of no consequence to me. An existential exercise of sheer will power. A sacrifice.'

While at work the following day, Wednesday 10 July, Ian took the 'Master List' out of the drawer and made a working list from it. Myra had borrowed the black Ford Prefect van from Ben Boyce and after work, while there was still a few hours of light left, drove Ian up to Saddleworth Moor to look for a spot where a parked vehicle wouldn't attract any unwanted attention. They discovered the perfect spot for burying a body – Hollin Brown Knoll. There was a lay-by close by so they parked up, got out and after thirty paces they were invisible from the road. The elevation of the rocks also gave them the advantage of being able to see if anyone was approaching them.

They drove home for some dinner and then Myra drove them both to Manchester Central Station where they deposited the two suitcases that contained evidence of their intent. They then drove back to Bannock Street where Ian deposited the ticket they had been given for the suitcases in Myra's prayer book. They sat on the floor with a map of Manchester and quickly tried to decide on an area that would be best to abduct someone. They soon decided on Gorton because they knew the area, the police would not suspect a woman, and Ian wasn't an official resident in Gorton. Myra was to drive him to his mother's home in Westmoreland Street and then select the victim, as had been rehearsed, and Ian was to follow them both later on his motorbike.

They chose Froxmer Street as an ideal place to pick the victim up as it had no overlooking windows and a parked vehicle would not look out of place. Ian later said about the abduction:

After the van had been parked, Myra would use her discretion in selecting a target. If no one had been chosen by 8.00 pm, the plan would be aborted for that evening. The deadline time was vital. I would stay at home in Westmoreland Street till 7.45 pm to establish an alibi, and then ride over to Gorton. If Myra's van were neither at her house nor Froxmer Street, I would know that she had picked up a target and travelled to Saddleworth Moor. I would follow on my bike.

They had decided that the person selected by Myra should be no younger than 16, because the police wouldn't look as hard for them as they would for someone younger; in order to get the person into the car she was to tell them she had dropped an expensive glove up on Saddleworth Moor during a walk and if they helped her to look for it they would be rewarded with some 78-rpm records that she had placed next to her in the van. The chosen person would be asked to sit in the front and help to stop the records from sliding off the seat and breaking.

If Myra had the least suspicion that she had been seen with the pick-up then she was to stop the operation there and then with a prepared excuse. Luckily that evening, either no 'target' presented itself to Myra, or she simply lost her bottle and drove home to meet Ian.

The following morning Ian had a sudden urge to return to Glasgow, so Myra drove the van back to Ben Boyce's and Ian followed on his motorbike. Myra then jumped on the back of his motorbike and they headed north. They stopped on the steep descent of Shap Fell to light cigarettes and absorb the view. It started to rain as they crossed into Scotland and they booked into the Crescent Hotel in Glasgow. They changed clothes, had some whisky and went out for fish and chips before going back to the hotel for the night.

The next day Ian went to Pollok to visit the Sloans, leaving Myra in the city to entertain herself. He went back to meet Myra and they rode back to Manchester. Ian felt invigorated by the visit and that evening he and Myra decided it was time for a 'sacrifice'.

Sixteen-year-old Pauline Reade lived with her parents Joan and Amos, and her younger brother Paul in Wiles Street, Gorton, just two doors down from David Smith and his father. Amos Reade worked at Sharples Bakery in Cross Lane, Gorton, and Pauline had joined him as a trainee.

She had attended a convent school and her friend Pat Cummings remembered that she was 'very quiet. When she came to our house, she would ask me to walk her home if it was dusk. She was very frightened. She was not the sort to get into a car with a stranger.'

At around 5.00 pm on Friday, 12 July 1963, on her way home from work, Pauline called at her friend Linda Bradshaw's house to see if she would go with her to a dance later that evening at the local Railway Institute on Cornwall Street, less than half a mile away, but Linda's mother said 'no' because there would be alcohol on sale.

Pauline Reade (L) with her brother Paul and their parents Amos and Joan, at Butlins in Yorkshire, shortly before she disappeared.

This didn't help Pauline's anxiety, as her best friend Pat had already been told by her parents that she couldn't go for the same reason. She went home and her mother, Joan, later recalled:

> Pauline was looking forward to this dance. A friend was going with her and then for some reason or another her friend couldn't go. Pauline was very upset. She didn't think she would be able to go because I didn't want her to go on her own. I said let's get you ready and go round to your other friend's and see if they'll go. 'Mum', she said, 'Sandra and Pam said they may be going and they'll see me so I'll be alright'. So with that she convinced me and I let her go or else I wouldn't have let her go on her own.
>
> I got her ready before she went out, done her hair and everything, and she looked beautiful. Even her father commented on it, saying how beautiful she looked.
>
> Before she went out the door, I put my necklace around her neck and she said 'Oh Mum, that's your favourite' and I said 'Well you're my favourite girl aren't you?' and she said 'I will look after it'. I went out with her and stood at the top of the road and I waved to her as she went around the corner.

Pauline was wearing new white shoes and a new pink and gold dress her father had bought her underneath her light, powder blue coat, along with long white dress gloves. The time was now 7.30pm.

Also at 5.00 pm, Myra and Ian left their work at Millwards for the day. As usual, they left separately and Ian picked her up on his motorbike just around the corner, out of sight of any possible co-workers. He dropped her off at Bannock Street and went to have dinner as usual with his mother and Pat Brady. He and Myra had spent the day planning what was to happen that evening. Ian counted all the buttons on their clothing (His shirt, jacket and trousers; her blouse, skirt and coat) and every number was written on a piece of paper that was to be checked again when they got home after the murder. They also listed all the things they would need to do afterwards such as burn their shoes, cut up and burn their clothing and wash the spade, among other things. They both worked three out of every four Saturdays but the next day would be their Saturday off. They had gone over and over the plan for the past few days. This evening would be a prime time to find a 'sacrifice'.

After dinner, in his bedroom at Westmoreland Street, Ian put a 2-inch wide elastic band on his right wrist and put a knife in its sheath under it. He then put on a pair of surgical gloves and covered those with the leather pair he always wore when he took his motorbike out. At 7.45 pm he went downstairs to talk to Peggy and Pat Brady, who were watching TV. He purposefully asked them if the clock on the wall was correct in order to establish an alibi for himself. He then left, telling them that he would be seeing them again tomorrow.

He rode his motorbike to Gorton and went past Bannock Street. The black Ford Prefect van wasn't outside Myra's. So far so good, he must've thought. He later recalled: 'For me it was the beginning of an existential exercise beyond good and evil.... This was the one-off event to which my destiny had been taking me all these years.'

However, on his way to check to see if Myra was on Froxmer Street or on her way up to Saddleworth Moor with the 'sacrifice', he caught up with her on Gorton Lane. Just before he made contact with her, Myra spotted a small girl walking towards her from the direction of Peacock Street but she didn't stop. Instead she slowed down before driving past. Ian had seen this and was enraged. He wanted to know why Myra had driven past the young girl, so he flashed his headlight. Myra saw this in her mirrors and, realising it was Ian, she pulled over. He demanded an explanation as to why Myra had not picked the child up and Myra explained to him that she knew the girl. She was called Marie Ruck and was aged around 8 years old. She lived only two doors away from her mother and as such would be too much of a danger to pick up. Ian accepted the explanation, but told Myra that she had better not let him down again. He told her to carry on with the plan and to wait on Froxmer Street for any potential target. He would wait at a distance to make sure she didn't fail again, and as such they waited longer than the 8.00 pm cut-off time they had originally agreed upon. These events confirm David Smith's suspicions that Myra picked up the victims alone. He said in his later memoirs:

> I don't believe – and I realise I am probably alone in this, but I knew them both well enough to have given it much thought – that Ian and Myra always acted together, posing as a harmless couple, when they abducted the children. Ian's appearance was too conspicuous. In Gorton, everyone talked about his strange manner and old-fashioned attire, and even the adults were wary of him. He had to work hard to make me feel comfortable in his company; I simply cannot picture a child walking away from everything familiar to be with him, or climbing happily into a car where he sat waiting. Far easier if the woman acted alone, and the public far less likely to notice as she and the child disappeared from view. He isn't noticed because he isn't there, but close by, just far enough away to ensure that their desires are realised.

Pauline's best friend, Pat Cummings, who wasn't allowed to go to the dance with her, had instead decided to go to the cinema with her friend Dorothy Slater. On their way to the cinema they saw Pauline in her dress walking along Gorton Lane and couldn't believe that she was going to the dance on her own, so they decided to follow her at a distance of roughly 100 yards. They noted the time was just after 8.00 pm. They watched as Pauline turned into Froxmer Street and walk down towards Railway Street. She had almost reached the end of the road when the two girls decided to cut across the croft and catch Pauline up on Railway Street. By the time the two girls got there Pauline had disappeared.

Myra had done a U-turn and the van was now facing away from Railway Street and back towards Gorton Lane. Ian was waiting on his motorbike in an alleyway next to The Vulcan pub which was on the corner of Froxmer Street and Gorton Lane and Myra knew he must have seen Pauline walking alone towards her. Almost thirty years later, she told her prison therapist: 'I chose to pick Pauline up because it was an easy option, less chance of failure and someone who was known to me. If I could do this without conscience, I could do anything.' She told how the difference between Marie Ruck and Pauline Reade was that Pauline lived a little further away and was a little older. She knew that there would be less fuss if a teenager went missing than a 7 or 8-year-old.

Myra wound down her window and attracted Pauline's attention. She asked where she was off too as she was all dressed up. Pauline replied that she was off to a dance and Myra offered her a lift, which Pauline accepted, having known both her and her sister, Maureen. As Myra pulled away, she asked Pauline if she wouldn't mind helping her to look for a glove that she had dropped while out with her boyfriend. Pauline told Myra that she was happy to do this, especially when Myra offered her the records as a reward.

Myra recalled that part of the conversation they had on the near forty-minute drive up to Saddleworth Moor was her telling Pauline how the van was her friend Ben Boyce's and that he wasn't having much luck as his new van had broken down. She told her that she was to pick him up later that night and take him to tow it, after he had been forced to leave it at the side of the road. Pauline asked Myra where her boyfriend was and Myra told her that he had to sort out an emergency but that he would then join them in the search soon if he could. Little did Pauline know that he was following on his motorbike, not far behind.

The sun was close to setting when they reached the moor and Myra parked up in the layby that she and Ian had previously picked out, just by Hollin Brown Knoll. It was now around 8.45 pm. Myra fell silent for a while, and this was broken by Pauline who asked her if she was OK as she was still gripping the steering wheel tightly. Myra replied that she was, she was just still getting used to the old van.

Ian soon arrived and saw straight away that they were both sitting in the van and Myra had a cigarette between her index and second finger. He parked up, opened the van door and Myra said to him that she thought he'd never get there. Pauline slid across the front seat closer to Myra and Ian got in next to them. He then lit a cigarette and thought through what was to happen next while Pauline and Myra chatted. When he had finished his cigarette they decided that they had better go and look for the glove as the sun was fading. He later recalled: 'I strode as casually as possible up the slope of the moor that led to the knoll at the top. I was about five yards ahead of Myra and the girl.' Pauline was struggling badly with the terrain as she was in her heels, but Myra was walking beside her, helping to steady her as she walked. Ian continued:

> As I approached the knoll I walked further into the moor. Myra and I knew exactly where we were heading for. We had rehearsed it. It was a place on the moor where we would be out of sight from the road … I dawdled and pretended I was scrutinising the grass closely, to allow the girl and Myra to walk past me. Pauline's eyes were also focused on the ground. Myra furtively glanced in my direction and nodded.

Brady then suddenly grabbed Pauline from behind and 'she collapsed on to the ground and stared up at me. I knelt down and said: "Don't make a noise and you'll be all right. It's pointless." She turned to plead with Myra, who was standing looking down at her: "Myra, tell him to stop!" I looked up at Myra … her expression was taunting and pitiless. Myra snapped: "Just keep quiet!"'

Pauline knew that she was about to be raped and told Myra to tell Ian that she was on her period, in the hope that he wouldn't go ahead. 'Myra knelt on the grass to unbutton the girl's coat, disregarding her pleas. I was standing by this time and looked for any movement on the moor. The sun had slipped below the horizon….'

At this point Ian went on to describe how Myra forcibly undressed Pauline practically by herself before they both took part in raping her.

Myra's version of events was that Ian and Pauline went alone on to the moor while she waited in the van. Twenty to thirty minutes later Ian went back to the van and got her to go with him. When she arrived she could see that Pauline's clothes had been tampered with and it was clear to her that Pauline had been raped. She was laying on the ground with her throat cut, the last drops of blood spilling from the wound. Ian then left her alone with the body before going back to the van to collect a spade, and then burying the body while she again waited in the van.

Her versions were always slightly different, depending on to whom she was giving the account. There are also too many unanswered questions regarding her version of events and she was always trying to distance herself from the actual murders in the hope of getting out of prison.

According to Ian's version, Pauline was then told to get dressed and Myra said something that made her realise she was not going to live much longer. Ian slapped Myra for letting the cat out of the bag and has said that he always remembered how 'the uncomprehending look of terror in the girl's eyes – as her fate dawned upon her – has haunted me every day to this day. Myra was staring at me in silence.' Pauline then began to plead for her life and tried to get away, but she was caught and punched in the head and face by Myra. Brady then said:

> Blood was streaming from her nose and had soaked the front of her dress. Her eyes were closed now. She gasped for breath.
>
> I instantaneously withdrew my sheath knife from my wrist and knelt towards the girl to cut her throat. My first attempt was not deep enough to sever the carotid artery. My second attempt was. Blood gushed from her throat. She was dead within seconds.
>
> I pushed the coat collar into the wound to stem the flow. Saddleworth Moor was silent. There were no sounds after the last trickle of blood.

His version is partly backed up by the post-mortem that was carried out by Dr Garrett when Pauline's body was eventually discovered in 1987. He concluded that,

> there were two parallel knife wounds to the neck, one very severe, three inches below the point of the chin, and a second, less deep, two inches below that. In addition there was a swelling on the forehead the diameter of a kitchen mug. Pauline had been hit hard on the head.
>
> Internal examination showed that one of the throat cuts had been delivered with such force that it severed the spinal cord … there was no other sign of injury we could detect and, such was the extent of the

body's deterioration, we were not able to investigate whether there had been any sexual assault.

At the later inquest, the following details were given:

> There are two separate incised wounds running horizontally across the midline, one four inches in length which gapes and one more superficial, two inches in length … the upper incised wound almost completely divides the sternomastoid muscle and appears to involve the anterior surface of the cervical spine.
>
> The swelling in the centre of the forehead appears to be a haematoma and is consistent with the application of blunt force, either with a fist or an instrument.
>
> Post-mortem deterioration of the perineum and anus precludes any examination of sexual assault…. The pushing of the collar of the coat into the wound of the neck appears to have been deliberate rather than accidental during the burial of the body and could well have been carried out in an attempt to reduce the amount of bleeding.

It is highly possible that Ian and Myra took photographs of Pauline Reade's body and put them in the file back in Millwards' warehouse which housed their master lists. It's just as likely that they took photographs of Pauline in the moments before her death too, as would happen in the case of one of their later victims, Lesley Ann Downey. In his description of events right after Pauline had been killed, Ian made constant references to him sending Myra back down to the van in order to put the camera and the knife (which he had wiped clean on the grass) away, and to return to him with a spade which had been put in the back of the van, although he did also say that it was 'too dark to photograph the site by now'.

When her body was discovered, Pauline's knickers were missing and it's probable that Brady and Hindley took these as a memento of the killing. As he waited with Pauline's body, Brady lit a cigarette and stared at her.

> I reflected on the chain of events that had led her to this high barren wilderness on a sunny evening.
>
> I chain smoked, taking the precaution to put the butts in my pocket. When she appeared Myra handed me the spade and held on to the binoculars. I told her to scan Saddleworth for the least sign of movement.
>
> The peat was soft and I was able to dig out a burial spot to a depth of four or five feet in just a few minutes. I held the shoulders and Myra grasped the legs as we lowered the body into the grave. I shovelled

in the peat as Myra pulled up clods of grass by the roots from the surrounding area. Both of us stamped the clods into the surface of the grave so that the plot would show no signs of recent disturbance.

Both of us counted our strides back to the knoll so that we could locate the grave and photograph it periodically to check that there had been no change to the surface of the peat to arouse suspicion.

When they reached the van, they pulled out two planks of wood and pushed Ian's motorbike into the back. They put the spade into a plastic sack and then changed into an almost identical set of clothes and put the dirty, blood-soaked clothes into a bag.

It was 11.00 pm when they got back to Gorton, and as Myra drove past the foundry she saw Pauline's mother and brother out looking for her. Pauline's brother recalled:

It was so unlike our kid to go on her own like that. It was just not in her nature. Nor was it like her to be late. My mam and I got dressed and went out to look for her. We didn't want to wake my dad because he had to be up so early.

They walked swiftly along the route that Pauline would have taken to the dance but there was no sign of her. When they reached the venue they could see that the dance had finished and it was very quiet. Joan knocked on the door and was answered by a man she knew. She asked if Pauline had been there and he told her that he hadn't seen her all night. Panic then set in and they ran home to wake Amos. The three of them then went out searching again.

While Joan and Paul Reade were out searching for Pauline, Myra parked the van on some waste ground at the back of Bannock Street and Ian took his motorbike out from the back. He then insisted that they stick to the plan and go to see Ben Boyce and help him to tow his new truck. He drove the motorbike to the front of the house before putting the bag of their bloodstained clothing inside. Myra's grandmother had banked up the fire to keep the front room warm. Ian carried the knife and spade in through the door and locked them in a cupboard. He and Myra then drove the van to see Ben.

When they arrived Ben was in bed. Myra apologised for being so late, saying that her and Ian had stopped in Whaley Bridge and they hadn't been able to get the van going again. They drove out to where he had had to abandon his van in the Abbey Hey area. They hooked it up and Ben drove the old van while Myra and Ian sat in and steered the new van.

It was around 1.00 am when they got home to Bannock Street. Amos, Joan and Paul had not found a single sign of Pauline so they contacted the police. Meanwhile, Ian and Myra set about clearing up after themselves. They put a large plastic sheet on the ground in front of the fire in the living room and Ian took out the 'Master List'.

They cut their clothing into strips, wrapped it in newspapers and threw the small parcels onto the fire. Ian tried to snap the handle of the knife to separate it from the blade but failed, so he threw the whole knife on to the fire too. Myra scrubbed the spade clean in warm, soapy water in the kitchen sink and it was around 3.00 am by the time they had finished. Myra later stated:

> He'd brought a bottle of Drambuie to celebrate and he sat down next to me on the settee sipping his drink and saying that after all the years of dreaming of it he'd actually done it: he'd committed the perfect murder.... He put his arm round my shoulder and kissed me clumsily on the cheek telling me it was all over now; I'd learn to live with it and he'd try to control his temper and not hit or hurt me. I was so relieved I clung to him, still crying, and promised I'd do everything I could to cope with what had happened and do my best not to antagonise him.... He stroked my hair ... in spite of what had happened this new tenderness touched the core of my heart and flooded it with all the love and emotions I'd felt for him for so long.

They then almost undoubtedly had sex. She later told her prison therapist that their best performances sexually were in the periods immediately after the murders: 'We celebrated our bonding with drink and sex. I would lay myself open to Ian in a physical demonstration of our unity ... Ian and I became further bonded by the blood of our victims.' She denied getting any sexual gratification from the murders, but she did gain, 'a sense of security due to the fact that one could not be safe without the other ... there were times when we would be paranoid about each other, but loyalty was a duty we both respected. There was no room for weakness or treachery.' She said that the secret they now shared 'bound us together more closely than any ties of affection possibly could.'

Professor Malcolm MacCulloch commented on her version of events:

> Her reaction is abnormal. This is one of the most horrendous things that can happen to anybody. A person of a more nervous disposition, or with less fortitude, would disintegrate. They would become distressed, anxious, develop post-traumatic stress disorder. There is no evidence of any of this.

Myra and Ian woke at 6.45 am and upon seeing that the fire had gone out he removed the contents of the grate, wrapped them up and put them in the dustbin. Myra went into the kitchen and came back with a bucket of warm, soapy water, which she took outside for her and Ian to wash the motorbike and van with. Every inch of the vehicles was scrubbed and wiped down with strips of sacking they had stolen from work. They did this as quietly as possible and spoke in whispers so the neighbours didn't hear. Myra shone a torch over the surfaces as Ian worked to make sure that every speck of possible evidence was removed from both the outside and inside of the old van.

Myra then told Ian that she had kept a gold medallion and four half-crowns that had fallen out of Pauline Reade's clothing during the struggle. Ian fumed at this as it would connect them to the murder. They left on Ian's motorbike and headed out towards the River Irwell in order to dispose of the remains of the knife handle and the medallion.

Years later, during the reinvestigation of the case in the mid-1980s, Myra told DSC Peter Topping that she had never even seen Pauline's medallion, but Ian pointed out: 'She's lying. What would I want with it?'

Ian and Myra then went to a shop and spent the half-crowns on chocolates and cigarettes, before heading off along the Stockport Road towards Macclesfield and throwing the ashes into the river and burying the medallion at Alt Hill. They then went to the cinema.

When they got home police were everywhere in the local area searching for Pauline. Ian asked Myra if she was sure that no one had seen Pauline get into her van. She said she was. The living room was full with Myra's gran, mother, sister and cousin Glenys all talking about Pauline's disappearance. They asked Myra what she thought, but she said that she hardly knew her and she was more Maureen's age.

Joan and Paul Reade went out again looking for Pauline, and they saw her friend Linda Bradshaw waiting at a bus stop. Somewhat unfairly, Joan erupted and shouted at her for not going to the dance and blaming her for her daughter's disappearance. David Smith recalled:

> The police knocked on our door a couple of times. They wanted to speak to us as part of their routine inquiries – we weren't suspects; no one was, in fact. Dad and me sat at the table, answering the coppers' questions. They asked about the sort of girl Pauline was, whether I had noticed anyone suspicious in the neighbourhood and when I last saw her. None of us paid any attention to the rumours. Pauline wouldn't have gone off with someone she didn't know and she wasn't the sort to do a flit with a boy, especially not one of those cocky fairground types. It was a strange, unsettling time. Her disappearance became the Great Unspoken Event, quietly simmering under the surface of normal life. There was a big wave of sympathy for the Reade family, even if no one knew what to say to them. I saw Mrs Reade very often, walking up and down Wiles Street, looking left to right, so lost, so alone. A mother in deep, deep distress.

Abduction and murder were not the only crimes that Ian and Myra had been planning. They also wanted to not have to work and Ian had been planning armed robberies for a while. There was just one problem – he couldn't get hold of any guns. Legally, he was ruled out because of his criminal record, so that left only one person – Myra.

George Clitherow, the Millwards' warehouse foreman, was president of Cheadle gun club and Ian told Myra to 'work on' George in order to get an invite to the club. It didn't take long and she soon got her invite so Ian then drove her into town to apply for her firearms certificate which was granted on 17 July 1963, just five days after the murder of Pauline Reade. The certificate was granted by the Chief Constable of Manchester Police at Bootle Street Station and it authorised her to acquire one .22 Target rifle and one .22 Target pistol.

Just a week after Pauline's murder, Myra had her first shooting lessons from George at Cheadle Gun Club. Ian told her that she needed to be as nice and sociable as possible as guns were expensive and he needed her to find out where to pick one up on the black market.

23 July 1963 marked Myra's 21st birthday. Ian bought her a gold-plated Ingersoll wristwatch that was kept in the original crocodile-skin-effect brown cardboard box and which she kept for the rest of her life. Ben Boyce gave her the old Ford Prefect van that had been used to abduct Pauline Reade, which delighted Ian as they now had a permanent vehicle with which to abduct more victims. They spent the weekend painting the whole inside of the van in white gloss in an effort to destroy any lingering forensic evidence and Ian also wanted to get the outside sprayed. The van was neither taxed nor insured and had no MOT but Myra still drove it around using the tax disc from another vehicle; she was soon reported to the police. They went to Bannock Street one morning while Myra and Ian were out and told Myra's gran that they would be coming back in the evening.

Mrs Maybury told Myra about the visit from the police and Ian told her to remain calm. What's a traffic offence compared to what they had already achieved? He told her that to be on the safe side he would go to Longsight and stay out of the way.

That evening the police went back and spoke with Myra. She told them that the van did have a tax disc in the window – Ben Boyce had lent her one. The sergeant told her that he was going to have to charge her as now deception and a third party were involved.

On 2 August 1963, the front page of the *Gorton & Openshaw Reporter* featured a photograph of Pauline Reade standing and laughing with her best friend Pat Cummings and her brother, Paul. The newspaper quoted her mother, Joan, as saying: 'She used to go dancing often. I was not worried at first, but I became alarmed when she failed to return…. There will be no trouble for Pauline when she does come home.' The police were also quoted as saying: 'The search has drawn a complete blank and we are very anxious about the situation.'

Pauline Reade (centre) with her brother, Paul, and friend, Pat Cummings.

A week later the papers arrived which summoned Myra and Ben Boyce to appear at Manchester Magistrates' Court. Myra and Ian were going on holiday up to Scotland and she told the police that she was leaving the untaxed van parked on waste ground at the back of her house. She called in at the local police station to ask them to keep an eye on the van while she was away. The policemen knew her because she was always popping in to get coins for her gas meter in Bannock Street. She then jumped on to the back of Ian's motorbike and drove off for a few days holiday north of the border near Loch Ness.

When they returned from their break, PC Norman Sutton called at Bannock Street on his motorbike. Myra opened the front door and recalled seeing 'the tallest, best-looking man' she had ever seen. He told her that he had heard about her troubles with the van and asked her if she would be interested in selling it as a friend of his needed something just like it for his business. Myra said that they instantly began flirting and

Myra Hindley in Scotland.

Right: Myra Hindley aboard the 'Maid of the Loch' paddle steamer.

Below left: Ian Brady on the shore of Loch Lomond.

Below right: Myra on the shores of Loch Lomond.

she invited him in for a cup of tea. She told him that he could have the van for free, but he insisted on paying for it and they decided on a sum of £25. The only problem they had was that he wasn't allowed to hand money over while he was on duty, so he asked her to meet him for a drink the following week, to which she agreed.

Myra and Ian were in a field having a picnic when she told him about the van. She recalled that Ian found it absolutely hysterical that they had used the van to commit the perfect murder and now she'd sold it to a policeman. Myra admitted that she also found it hilarious.

Ian started to disappear again some evenings, so Myra decided to enrol in evening classes back at Ryder Brow School. She studied English on Wednesdays and Maths on Fridays. After one of her English classes had finished, Myra walked outside and was greeted by PC Sutton standing next to his 650cc motorbike. They rode off to find a pub where no one would recognise Myra and it was in the pub that he told Myra that he had actually first set eyes on her when she worked as a barmaid at Belle Vue and that it was his mum who had been the manageress.

He gave her the £25 for the van and they then went back to Bannock Street, where Myra invited him in for a drink, knowing full well that her grandmother would be in bed, but she told him that if Ian turned up then he would have to say that he was there purely to hand over the money for the van and then leave. As they sat in the living room he made his intentions clear and asked her if her relationship with Ian was serious, to which she told him that it was. They still shared a long and passionate kiss before having sex and arranged to meet again after her next school class.

When they met again Myra discussed with Norman about becoming a police officer. He told her that he thought it was a great idea and would help them to have a future together. She even went to Mill Street Station for an interview with the inspector. They told her that the business with the van wouldn't be a problem and he gave her an application form to fill out.

There is no official record of Myra's attempts to become a policewoman as she never completed the application form, but an officer who worked in the station at the time recalled: 'She was given a number of brochures which outlined the opportunities open to a woman officer. That much is certain, but it's impossible to confirm whether or not she actually went for an interview.'

She told Ian one night what she had done and she recalled that Ian was shocked at first but then encouraged her to join the police as it made him laugh and would make her even less of a suspect. Ian wanted to know if Myra had slept with PC Sutton and she told him that she had. She recalled that her and Ian made love that night, but it was rough, and Ian bit her hard on the shoulder from behind.

When Ian disappeared in the evenings, usually to one of the homosexual bars in central Manchester, Myra would go out with PC Sutton. They went dancing, out for rides on his motorbike and for drinks in the pub. They then usually had sex. Myra knew that the relationship wouldn't go anywhere. She and Ian were too involved with each other.

At weekends Myra and Ian would go back up to where they buried Pauline and relive the last moments of her life. They then took photographs to use as souvenirs and they would look at them when they were at home to remember the events of that evening. According to Professor Malcolm MacCulloch: 'That is the sort of thing that happens with sadists. They review what they've done. Either they remember it in fantasy, and that reinforces them, or they have souvenirs – body parts, hair, pictures – through which they're able to relive what happened.'

On 24 October Ian gave Myra the money to purchase a .22 BSA rifle from T. Stensby & Company Ltd., Registered Firearms Dealers, 12 Withy Grove, Manchester. The couple started to go for rides out across the moor to a lay-by at the head of Hoe Grain stream to practice with the guns. They usually walked along the edge of a narrow stream until it reached Shiny Brook and then turned right. After about twenty minutes they would arrive at a stone sheep pen, in the middle of a large, secluded clearing. The rifle was kept in a canvas bag which Ian had over his shoulder and he wore a leather cartridge belt that Myra had stolen from the gun club. Ian and Myra would then line up some tin cans along a wall and take twenty paces back. Myra then showed Ian how to work the gun and they would practice shooting the cans until they ran out of bullets.

On the 7 November 1963 Myra finally passed her driving test at the fourth attempt. She had been taught by local instructor Harold Rainger, and he remembered that she was an apt and willing pupil but she developed nerves when it came to her tests. After she had passed, she bought a second-hand green Morris.

It was during this month that David Smith first met Ian Brady properly. There had been an officer party at Millwards and he later recalled: 'Maureen told me that one of her co-workers at Millwards had pinned her up against a wall and tried it on.' This enraged him and he went to Millwards, armed with a knife, to sort out the man.

He hid behind some containers in the yard and when everyone was leaving work for the day he waited until the man emerged. He watched as Myra, Ian and Maureen walked past and almost as soon as the man came out he saw David and ran. David gave chase but as they passed Ian and Myra, Myra shouted out to David to 'pack it in and get over here'. He gave up his chase and Myra told him forcefully to get in the car. According to David,

> We sat in the back together. Ian hadn't said a single word. He looked completely deadpan, sitting in the passenger seat next to Myra. She drove us home; it was only a few streets. On the way she asked, 'What the bloody hell was all that about?' I sat there in a filthy temper and Maureen said in a timid little voice, 'Oh, I'll explain to you later, our Myra.' As for Ian, he said nothing again. Not a word. Just that expressionless face, staring straight ahead.

Chapter 7

A Near Miss & John Kilbride

During the second week of November Myra was still seeing PC Sutton, but the affair soon came to a close. After Ian had gone out and Myra had attended one of her English classes, PC Sutton picked Myra up and they went back to Bannock Street. Unbeknown to them, Ian came back early and caught Myra and Sutton having sex. Ian fumed and threatened to kill PC Sutton, who made his excuses and left. He later said that during the affair with Myra he was a married man and so didn't retaliate with Ian for fear of the affair becoming public. Myra later recalled: 'If we'd met before Ian and I did, I knew that the love that had grown between us would have blossomed. I would have had no hesitation in marrying and having children with him.' There is the possibility of some truth in this statement as, when Myra died in 2002, she still had pinned to her bedroom wall a clipping from *The Sun*'s front page where the affair was exposed.

On the evening of Sunday, 10 November 1963, Ian and Myra decided that it was time to 'do another one'. She asked him why he wanted to and he replied that he 'just did', and that it was too late for her to back out now.

The following day at work they retrieved the Master List from the warehouse and spent the evening planning their next move. Once Myra's grandmother had taken her sleeping pills and gone to bed, Ian and Myra spread out a map of Manchester on the table. They agreed that the next 'sacrifice' should be picked up from further afield than Gorton, as the police were already on alert there following Pauline Reade's disappearance and they considered going somewhere like Leeds or Huddersfield, but decided it was too much of a risk to travel so far with someone without being seen.

They quite liked the thought of Ashton-under-Lyne, as Ian had been there once on a visit when he came down from Scotland to see his mother, and Myra knew it as she sometimes went to the market there. Also, it wasn't too far away, being just five miles from Gorton and six miles from Saddleworth. They immediately jumped on Ian's motorbike and decided to go and do some reconnaissance.

When they arrived they went first to the market area and Ian led Myra down a side street. It was long and dark and ran right alongside the market. There were no houses or overlooking windows and they decided that the spot would be perfect.

They drove back to Bannock Street and Ian recalled: 'We carefully planned the procedures for the pick-up, and selected the following Saturday, a busy day for markets everywhere…. We included the new information in selected guidelines from the Master List.'

From the Master List they made a working list which they used abbreviations for, such as TOBAC meaning Tobacconist's, OBV meaning Observation Points and TA meaning Target Area. They planned for Myra's car to be parked in the dark backstreet and for her to walk to the target area via a side street. Ian would then scout the area via various observation points and once a target had been decided upon the signal was given, usually via a facial movement, and Myra would move in.

Once Myra had the target with her, Ian would follow for a short distance and if he noticed anything odd then he would stop the situation with a prepared excuse. If everything was going to plan then he would veer off to a tobacconist's shop and wait for Myra to pick him up from there.

They made a decision regarding the vehicles they would use too. Myra didn't feel so comfortable taking the target by herself in the car, and Ian wanted to make sure that she didn't back out so he decided not to take his motorbike and to get in the car with Myra. They decided that for this purpose they would have to use different vehicles, so they chose to replace the car frequently and would sell it in a part-exchange deal for different cars. But for this operation they decided that instead of using Myra's car, they would use a hire car. They went through the plan and all possible outcomes over and over again. It was almost dawn by the time they finished. After a short sleep, they went off to work and put the Master List back in the warehouse.

The following day Ian and Myra went to Warren's Auto's on London Road, Manchester, on the back of Ian's motorbike in order to hire a car, but Myra only had her green slip and not her actual driver's licence with her so she couldn't hire the car. Ian gave her £10 and told her to put it down as a deposit and they would pick it up the following week. The date they had planned for their next abduction and murder was Saturday 16 November, but an unexpected opportunity would present itself much sooner.

On Friday 15 November Ian and Myra had the house to themselves as Myra's grandmother was visiting her son. Myra's full licence still had not come through and so they had to put off collecting the hire car from Warren's Auto's until the following weekend (23 November). This left them upset and Ian was desperate for another 'sacrifice'. He had spent all day at work coming up with a 'Plan B' and decided that as the house would be free that evening, they could abduct someone local, get them to the house, rape and murder them, and then take the body up to the moor in Myra's car to be buried.

They waited until nightfall, then went out on foot and soon found what they were looking for in a local park – a 7-year-old boy named Tommy Rhattigan. His abduction was originally denied by both Ian and Myra, who said that they had no 'near-misses', but Ian finally admitted, a couple of years before his death, that there had been a few 'close calls'.

Tommy was playing on the swings in the park by himself while he waited for his two younger brothers, Martin and Nabby, to arrive. Out of the corner of his eye he could see Ian and Myra deep in conversation. 'I could see the top half of them standing on the opposite side of the small boundary wall of the park as the man lit a cigarette and had then held the flame to the woman's cigarette before he took a long look across in my direction.'

They slowly made their way towards Tommy, with Myra walking ahead of Ian until she was within talking distance. Ian stayed back, with the collar of his raincoat turned up and with his hands in his pockets. Myra smiled at Tommy and asked if he was waiting for his friends. He told her that he wasn't and she then started to ask him where he was from, in order to gauge how local he was. When he told her that he was from Stamford Street in Hulme, Myra looked back at Ian and told him 'The lad's from Hulme!'

Ian became impatient and told Myra to 'hurry up!' Myra moved closer to Tommy, putting her hands on the chain of the swing, and asked him what his name was. When he told her, she said to him that he looked hungry and asked if he would like to go with them for a 'jam buttie'. If he did, then they would make sure that they took him straight home afterwards.

Tommy agreed and put out his hand for Myra to hold, but she thrust her hands into her coat pockets and told him: 'You mustn't be seen walking with me, or you'll get in trouble. I'll call you when to come', before she walked a little way off, away from both him and Brady.

She soon turned and called for him to follow and Tommy did as he was instructed, but looked behind him and noticed that Ian threw his cigarette to the ground and put his hands back into his pockets. Tommy followed Myra out of the park and they headed towards Gorton. As they were walking along, Tommy noticed that Ian was following him with his head bowed down and half-hidden by his collar.

As they approached a pub on the corner of Taylor Street, a group of lads started to heckle Myra, but she ignored them and carried on walking, with Tommy following behind. At this point, he again looked behind him, but realised that Ian was no longer there. As they reached Bannock Street, Myra opened the front door and called Tommy in with her gloved hand.

As if from out of nowhere, Ian suddenly appeared next to Tommy, put his hand on his shoulder and guided him into the house. Tommy went with Myra into the back room with Ian following; Myra undid her coat and Tommy remembered that she removed two scarves. He sat down at a table and Ian walked off into the kitchen in silence. Myra began to ask him about his siblings and then asked him if his mother would be angry with him for being out so late. Just then, Ian reappeared and hung his coat up in a cupboard under the stairs. Myra then did the same and they walked off together into the kitchen. Tommy could hear them talking quietly but was unable to make out what was being said, and he became unnerved when Myra suddenly spoke sharply to Ian.

Just then, Myra walked into the room with a plate of bread and jam, while she drank red wine from a glass. She told Tommy to: 'Hurry up and get that down you and we'll get you off home', before leaving the room and going upstairs. He felt that Myra was suddenly nervous and that she was shaking as she put the plate on the table in front of him. Being left alone to eat, he felt a sudden wave of panic come over him and he had an urge to leave the house immediately. Something just wasn't right.

Myra soon came back down the stairs and she asked Tommy if he was OK, as he hadn't made a start on his bread and jam. He replied that he was, but could he have a glass of water? Myra went into the kitchen, and again Tommy could hear her and Ian have a muffled conversation, before a smiling Myra then came back with the glass of water and told him to 'get all that down you so we can take you home'. She again left him alone to eat and went back to the kitchen to talk to Ian, but this time she raised her voice and Ian shouted back 'Fucking wait!' They then returned to their whispered conversation.

Tommy realised that now was the time to get out. He tried the window, but it got stuck after just a couple of inches and he quickly began to panic. Fuelled by the adrenaline, he gave it everything he could, and the window shot up with a bang. Myra shouted: 'The little shit's out the window!' as she ran from the kitchen into the living room. Tommy was mostly out of the window, but his foot was caught up in the curtain and he felt a hand grab at it. He wriggled free and dropped to the ground just as he heard the bolt from the back door open and Ian shout 'Bastard!' Tommy jumped on top of Ian's covered motorbike, got over the wall and ran as fast as he could. He ran down various streets and alleyways before he found himself at a row of three bomb-damaged houses. He hid himself under a green toilet door that was propped up against a mound of debris for a while, before making his way home when he felt it was safe.

Not being put off by this close call, the following week Ian and Myra stuck to their original plan of abducting someone when they were able to rent a car. On 22 November 1963, Myra drove Ian out to Manchester Piccadilly station, where they deposited their suitcases containing possible incriminating evidence, as they had the evening before the murder of Pauline Reade. As Ian was walking through the concourse of the station 'I passed two passengers, and I heard one say to the other 'Did you hear about Kennedy?', and then the word 'dead'. The girl [Myra] was in the car park and as soon as I got in, I switched on the radio and found out he was dead.' US President John F. Kennedy had been assassinated.

The following morning, Ian gave Myra a record – Gene Pitney's 'Twenty-Four Hours from Tulsa' – which they listened to as Myra got herself ready. Ian dropped her off at Warren's Auto's and then went immediately round to see his mother.

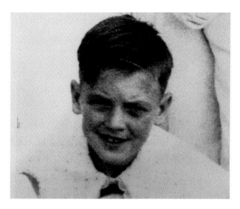

John Kilbride.

When Myra turned up at the garage to collect the car she was wearing black trews, a high-necked sweater and a black leather jacket.

The car given to her at Warren's Auto's was a white Ford Anglia; Myra wasn't happy, she knew it would show every speck of dirt. This car was to prove a crucial piece of evidence for the prosecution at the later trial. She drove over to Westmoreland Street to pick up Ian and his dog, and she waited for him on the corner of the street as usual. She noted that the time was 11.00 am. When Ian saw the white vehicle he exploded with anger and told her that even the thickest policeman would be able to see exactly where they'd been. Myra asked him what she was expected to do and Ian calmed down. It wasn't ideal, but their plan could still go ahead.

Back in Smallshaw Lane, Ashton-under-Lyne, 12-year-old John Kilbride was at home annoying his five brothers and sisters. At 12, he was the oldest child of Irishman Pat and his wife Sheila Kilbride. He had already been to visit his grandmother Margaret Doran in nearby Rowley Street, and had helped her to tidy the garden and the house, which he did on an almost daily basis. He then went home for lunch with his siblings Danny, Pat, Terry, Sheila, Maria and Chris.

His mother Sheila recalled: 'John tormented his brothers and sisters and I said: 'Please go to the cinema John – stop tormenting your brothers and sisters, and don't forget when Pauline Reade was missing what I told you – whoever did it is only a train ride from here so always be on your guard', and he just grinned his cheeky grin and said 'bye' and off he went. 'In spite of the warnings he was too trusting, especially of a lady 'cause I'd never warned him about women. I didn't think there were any bad women about.'

John went to the local cinema with his friend John Ryan and they both went to the market at Ashton-under-Lyne to earn some money from helping the stallholders. He often did this, but without telling his parents. He would then spend any pennies he earned on broken biscuits. 'We went and fetched a trolley from the station for a man on the market. I got sixpence for this. John got about threepence or sixpence', recalled John Ryan at the trial.

Then we went to the man who sells carpets in the open market. There were two lads there, one from the same class as me. After I had some talk with them I decided to go home. When I set off to catch my bus John Kilbride was not with me. I last saw him beside one of the big salvage bins on the open market, near the carpet dealer's stall. There was no one with him. It was 17.25 when I last saw him.

John's father, Patrick, was actually in the market buying a new pair of shoes, he left at 4.45 pm. Had he been running late he may well have run into his son and dragged him home.

After Myra had picked Ian up, they set about establishing their alibis for the day. They drove, first of all, to Ramshaw Rocks in Leek, Staffordshire, and took some photographs of themselves. What happened from there until they wound up in Ashton Market we only have Myra's account for. She told both DCS Topping in 1987, and journalist Duncan Staff even later, that after leaving Ramshaw Rocks they drove north to Huddersfield where they stopped off for a coffee and a Danish pastry.

They then went to a hardware shop and picked up a roll of thin cord and a small kitchen knife with a serrated edge. She said she was wearing a black wig which she'd bought in Lewis's on Piccadilly Gardens, and a headscarf to hold it in place. Ian was waiting around the corner in the car when she did this.

Ian got out of the car as she approached and he opened the boot, which they had lined with black plastic. She then put the cord and knife inside, next to a torch and her rifle.

They then drove around looking for a cinema that was showing a film they had already seen and were in luck when they found one showing the James Bond film

Ian Brady at Ramshaw Rocks.

Above: Unseen photograph of Ian Brady at Ramshaw Rocks.

Left: Unseen photograph of Myra Hindley, taken on the day of John Kilbride's abduction.

From Russia With Love. They had seen it just the week before and would say they were watching that if they happened to be questioned by the police.

They drove to Ashton-under-Lyne and it was dark when they arrived, but the stalls in the market were well lit. There were many children around, which pleased them, and Myra recalled that there was no rush to pick one. She went to the toilet and noticed that her wig had started to slip, so she reset it and when she left, Ian

Right: Hindley in the clothes it's believed she used to abduct the children.

Below: Ashton Market.

immediately told her he had 'seen one', buying left-over food. He asked her if she was ready and had she remembered what to say, to which she replied that she did.

This time they walked side-by-side down the back of a line of stalls. John Kilbride was sitting on a wall eating a bag of broken biscuits. Ian walked off to make sure they hadn't been seen and to keep a look-out, and Myra spoke to John. She told him that she thought he was out late and that she had children herself. She looked around and saw Ian standing at one of the agreed viewing points and he gave her the signal that they were in the clear.

She told John that she would be worried if her kids were out in the dark so late and would he help her to carry some boxes back to her car. If he agreed, then she would give him a lift home. John agreed, put his remaining biscuits in his jacket pocket, jumped down off the wall and walked with Myra back to her car. Myra asked him his name and where he lived. Innocently, he told her.

Once Ian had seen them leave together, he darted off to their pre-arranged pick-up point, the tobacconist's. Myra drove by with John in the back and stopped outside to pick Ian up. Myra told Ian that John had helped her with the boxes and Ian acted as though he was impressed. He asked John if he would like a bottle of sherry as a reward, to which John seemed most keen. Ian told him that they would have to go to their home in Greenfield to collect it, was that alright with him? John said that it was.

As they pulled into Greenfield, Ian and Myra discussed going up to 'where we picnicked this afternoon and get the pair of gloves we left'. They told John that as they were nearly home, it wouldn't take long and that the gloves were given to them as a wedding anniversary present, so were important to them. Thinking that he was getting a bottle of sherry and a lift home, John said he didn't mind.

They soon pulled into the lay-by at Hollin Brown Knoll and the three then got out. Ian opened the boot of the car and quickly grabbed the torch, and he and John walked south onto the moor, on the opposite side of the road to where Pauline Reade had been raped, murdered and buried.

Myra specifically recalled a half-moon was helping to light the way as they walked down the shallow incline onto the moor. When Ian and John had walked a certain distance, Myra suddenly drove off south towards Greenfield. Ian had told her that she would be less conspicuous parked away from the lay-by, and that she was to go back to the lay-by after around half-an-hour and to flash her lights and wait for a response from his flashlight.

When Myra pulled away in the car, John panicked. He asked Ian some questions and Ian couldn't answer them, so John's senses were heightened. Ian quickly grabbed John by the throat from behind and John struggled to try to free himself. He was kicking Ian and trying to fight his way free, but he was no match for the 6ft tall Ian, who managed to drag him to the ground. John was still kicking wildly as Ian tried to pull his trousers and underpants down. He then tried to cut John's throat, but the serrated blade was too blunt and John was struggling too much, so he strangled John to death.

Myra had waited the thirty minutes and at 8.00 pm she drove back towards Hollin Brown Knoll. As she approached, she flashed her car lights twice and pulled into the lay-by. Ian responded with his torch almost immediately. She walked down towards Ian's torch flash, led by the moonlight, with the spade in her hand. When she got there she saw that John's trousers had been pulled down, along with his underpants, which were tied in a knot at the back. She could tell that Ian had raped him and it remains a distinct possibility that Ian had performed necrophilia.

Ian quickly dug a shallow grave and both he and Myra put his body in the hole, face down. Ian recalled that just before he shovelled the dirt back on top of John, he slapped John's naked backside, shook his fist at the sky and 'I shouted, "Take that you Bastard." This was my gesture in the face of whatever malignant force it is which underlies this universe, devoted only to chaos. I found a shoe nearby that I hadn't buried. I took it back to the car and we drove back to Myra's.' An argument quickly broke out as Ian blamed Myra for buying a knife that was too blunt to cut John's throat.

When they got back to Bannock Street, Myra helped Ian to cut up and burn their clothes and shoes. John's shoe was the first on the fire. Ian then threw the new knife on the fire and Myra wiped down the spade before putting it back in the cupboard. Learning from last time, they had covered almost every visible surface in a plastic sheeting, so this time all they had to do was to roll it up and wipe down the surfaces, which saved them a lot of time. He and Myra then threw some buckets of warm, soapy water over the car wheels and surfaces.

When that had finished, they each drank a bottle of wine, and then shared the third, before following them up with whisky chasers. They then almost undoubtedly had sex.

When John hadn't returned home by early evening, Sheila and Patrick Kilbride checked at the homes of relatives and friends of John's and then, when there was no sign of him, at 11.20 pm they called the police. Two officers went to the house to take a statement and John's brother, Danny, later recalled: 'All I saw my mother do for the next two years was cry.'

His gran, Margaret, said: 'I can almost see him sometimes, walking along the path at the side of the football ground across the road, in his usual cheerful way. I can't help wondering how he died; whether he suffered a lot….'

The following morning Myra dropped Ian at Westmoreland Street to see his mother while she returned the car to Warren's Auto's. It was 9.00 am and Myra was still drunk. The garage foreman, Peter Cantwell, later told at the trial that the car was particularly dirty and muddy, and looked as though it had been across a ploughed field. The mud was halfway up the sides, over the wheels and bonnet and on the windscreen.

Myra then returned home, where her gran chastised her for drinking so much, before she went up to bed to sleep off her hangover. She later recalled:

> Not only did I help procure the victims for him, I knew it was wrong, to put it mildly, that what we were doing was evil and depraved…. To him it had become a hobby, something one did to get absorbed into, interested and often fascinated with, and it had become literally a deadly obsession. And I knew that I was a part of his hobby and obsession.

DCI John Down took charge of the investigation and a huge search was launched:

> I took charge of the police search and enquiries to trace John Kilbride…. An intensive search was started on 24 November 1963. Market traders were interviewed and vehicles and skips were searched at Ashton-

under-Lyne market. A thorough search of the area was made and a house to house enquiry began in the area where John Kilbride lived. The press, radio and television gave extensive publicity to the missing boy. Posters were printed and distributed, about 500 posters…. There were over 700 statements taken from members of the public.

To help clear Myra's hangover, Ian took her to Sunny Brow Park on his motorbike. As they were sat on a bench they flicked through a copy of the *Gorton & Openshaw Reporter* and read about John Kilbride's disappearance. The newspaper printed John's home address in Smallshaw Lane and that was too much of an opportunity for Ian to pass up.

That evening they went out again on Ian's bike and ended up at the end of Smallshaw Lane. Myra later said that a small girl walked from the house to the end of the gate and looked up and down the road but didn't give them a second glance. She refuted all reports that she and Ian had gone to the house posing as police officers and taken away some items of clothing. It wasn't the last time they would sit and watch the house.

On 27 November Myra rented another car from Warren's Auto's. This time it was a red Morris Mini and was rented from 5.30 pm to 5.30 pm the following day. She drove herself and Ian up to Saddleworth Moor for what Ian called 'a reconnaissance', checking that the grave of John Kilbride hadn't been disturbed. Four days later, on 1 December, 2,000 volunteers searched every waste land, park and derelict building around Aston-under-Lyne market looking for any sign of John, while the police dragged all local canals, but nothing was found.

Ten days later, Myra again rented the same red Morris Mini from Warren's Auto's for another 24-hour period. They again went up to Saddleworth Moor to check that the graves of Pauline Reade and John Kilbride hadn't been disturbed, and they then went to do some target practice with the rifle.

That evening they drove to Strangeways Prison in the centre of Manchester, to heighten their sense of freedom.

> We watched prisoners in their windows swinging lines from cell to cell. This was their way of passing tobacco and newspapers to one another. They were too far away to make out the faces, of course, but you could hear the voices.
>
> We were just sat there, a nice sunny evening, in the car, smoking cigarettes, drinking wine. That wine tasted beautiful because we were watching people in prison.

Without the car, Myra was stuck at home most evenings. Ian was still disappearing at times to various homosexual pubs around Manchester, and she had no interest in what he got up to there. David Smith, who had been sacked again for poor time keeping, recalled many evenings when he was at Maureen's in Wiles Street when Myra would just turn up out of the blue. She'd tell Maureen: 'He's gone people-watching as per usual, at Central Station. Neddie likes to watch the maggots crawling about.'

Their final act of depravity for the year came on New Year's Eve when Ian drove Myra up to Hollin Brown Knoll on the back of his motorbike. They parked up in the lay-by and sat on the rocks. When midnight came around, Ian held his whisky bottle aloft to the moon and toasted, 'To John!'

Hollin Brown Knoll was becoming an obsession with Ian and Myra. On 3 January 1964 they again went up to Saddleworth Moor, but this time they took 'scenic' photographs which they later would say had no significance, but showed from where they were taken that the grave sites had not been disturbed.

Myra was still attending the gun club, but she wasn't very good and kept closing her eyes when she pulled the trigger. By the end of February she had decided that rifles weren't for her and she wanted to try pistols and revolvers instead. She asked George Clitheroe where she could buy a Luger; he told her she couldn't because she didn't have the correct certificate. She carried on at the gun club until the middle of April.

Myra had made other contacts at the club and illegally bought a Webley .45 and twenty rounds of ammunition from Mr John Boland from Barnsley; and from another member, Mr Alan Cottam (who did not enquire whether she had a firearms certificate) she bought a .38 Smith and Wesson without ammunition. Myra and Ian would go to various places, not just Saddleworth Moor, to practice with the guns and photograph themselves doing so.

Myra Hindley posing with a gun.

99

Above left: Ian Brady posing with a rifle.

Above right: Myra Hindley posing with a rifle.

Left: Ian Brady posing with a rifle.

Later in February Myra then bought an Austin A40 for about £40 and drove it to work at Millwards. Her boss, Tommy Craig, recalled: 'Everyone thought she'd gone ambitious', as only a relatively small percentage of households owned cars.

Despite the weather being cold and it having recently snowed, one of their first trips in the car was, unsurprisingly, up to Hollin Brown Knoll. They took a puppy with them called Puppet, who was the offspring that she had kept from the litter of her other dog, Lassie.

Myra Hindley on Hollin Brown Knoll with her puppy, Puppet, wrapped in her coat.

They parked in their usual spot, in a layby just below Hollin Brown Knoll, and walked up to the rocks above, with Myra holding Puppet close to her body, wrapped in her coat for warmth. When they got to one of their favourite spots, very close to where Pauline Reade had been buried, Ian took out his camera and photographed Myra.

They then returned to the road, crossed over and walked down towards where John Kilbride lay buried. Once they had located his grave, Myra crouched over it, half-smiling, as Ian took her photograph.

Years later, in prison therapy sessions, Myra told how her and Ian collected 'souvenirs' of their crimes, while at the same time trying to distance herself from the practice:

> [Ian] would have liked the victims to have suffered for the rest of their lives after he had abused them. He could only savour past experiences through the items that he kept under lock and key. Returning at a later date to rekindle the excitement…. Some of the photographs that we took on the moors were constructed with the location of the graves taken into consideration, [but] Ian did not need a camera's image, he could reproduce the image in his own head.

Brady took this photograph just a few weeks after killing John Kilbride. Myra is looking directly at John Kilbride's grave.

By March David Smith, who was by now living almost exclusively alone in Wiles Street, got Maureen Hindley pregnant. He admitted that he did this on purpose, as his father was away almost all of the time and he didn't want to be forced to move away to live with his uncle. His idea was to get Maureen pregnant so they would have to get a place together. He recalled: 'I tried for a long time to get her pregnant. I held her hands above her head, so that I could leave it in, so she didn't have any choice.'

He remembered that he was sitting in Sivori's when Maureen told him she was pregnant. 'I was delighted, absolutely over the moon … I felt on top of the world. She wasn't quite as thrilled because of having to tell her family. She didn't cry or get upset, but she was concerned.'

Above left: Myra on Hollin Brown Knoll. She recalled that 'My Guy' by Mary Wells was playing on the transistor radio.

Above right: Ian Brady on Hollin Brown Knoll. The grave site of Pauline Reade was less than 100 yards from where the photo was taken, with John Kilbride buried across the road.

Bob Hindley remained silent on the subject of his youngest daughter getting pregnant, but Nellie was furious and threw David out of the house. Somewhat surprisingly, Myra was accepting of the news. Maureen was forced to give up her job at Millwards in June 1964.

On the 6 May 1964, Myra changed her car again, this time part-exchanging her Austin A40 for a white Morris Mini pickup, registration number VDB 893. They took it up to Hollin Brown Knoll for another photographic session.

One night in the early summer of 1964, Ian told Myra that he was ready 'to do another one'. He said he needed to feel the power that committing such crimes gave him and that if he was in any way wronged or he wanted to take revenge against the world then he would satisfy himself in this way.

Chapter 8

Keith Bennett

On the 9 June 1964, David Smith got in trouble with the police again; he was given another year's probation on top of the two he was already serving for breaching the terms of his bail conditions.

Exactly one week later, on Tuesday 16 June, Ian gave Myra another record – Roy Orbison's 'It's Over'. They were on for another 'sacrifice'.

They followed their usual routine at work, with Ian and Myra making a working list from their 'Master List' before storing it back in the disused filing cabinet in the warehouse. After work, Myra drove Ian to his mother's house in Westmoreland Street before going home to Bannock Street for dinner. She arranged to pick him up afterwards, at around 7.40 pm, when they would go out looking for a child. They didn't have to look too far.

Keith Bennett had turned 12 years old just four days earlier. He lived with his mother, Winnie, stepfather Jimmy Johnson, and his five siblings – Alan, Margaret, Ian, Sylvia, and Susan – Jimmy's daughter from his previous relationship and the same age as Keith. Winnie recalled that Susan and Keith 'went everywhere together' due to their age.

> I can just see their little faces now, asking me if I'd give them the money for the pictures. And if they liked the film they'd stay in the cinema and see it twice…. And Margaret, she was only about 3 at the time, but she was devoted to Keith. She used to follow him around like a little dog.

The day before Keith was snatched, he had taken part in his school's swimming gala. He swam the length of the pool for the first time and was given a certificate for his achievement. Unfortunately, he dropped his glasses and broke them; due to his short-sightedness, his mother promised to get them fixed as soon as she could.

It had been pre-arranged that Keith, Alan, Ian and Margaret would spend the night at their grandmother's house, which wasn't out of the ordinary, while Winnie took Sylvia and Susan with her to bingo, which started at 8.00 pm at St Aloysius' School in Ardwick. The rest of the children had already gone ahead to their grandmother's, but Winnie was pregnant and running late with Keith, Sylvia and Susan. Winnie clearly remembered the day of his abduction: 'I gave him his tea and washed his face … I took him out – I was going to Bingo and the two girls were coming with me.' They walked up Eaton Street, on to Hathersage Road, crossed Plymouth Grove and then Keith bumped into two girls he knew from school and started messing around with them. Winnie, recalled: 'I shouted to him to be careful in case he hurt them girls. He just gave me one of them big grins of his, as much to say don't worry, Mam.

Winnie watched as she saw Keith across the main road (Stockport Road). He was wearing blue jeans, a T-shirt and new white jerkin. He had less than a 200-yard-walk to his gran's.

Myra was waiting around the corner for Ian to finish his dinner, thus establishing part of his alibi for the evening. When he emerged, he got into Myra's car. She looked around her to see if anyone had noticed her in the car and then put on her black wig, keeping it in place with a head scarf. Just as Keith had crossed Stockport Road, they drove away from Westmoreland Street, looking for someone to pick up. Their paths crossed just a few moments later.

Myra knew as soon as she saw Keith walking along Grey Street that he would meet with Ian's approval and so pulled over next to him. They asked him if he would help them to again find a glove up on Saddleworth Moor. As a reward, they offered him a bottle of drink. Fatefully, Keith accepted.

Myra, with Keith in the front next to her, drove towards the moor. Ian, who was in the back of the car, knocked on the glass panel behind Myra and got her to stop as they approached an off-licence just a few streets away. The roof on the back part of her car was detachable, and a glass sheet separated the front seat from the back. She pulled over and Ian quickly went into the shop to get what Keith believed would be his reward.

Ian and Myra both said that they drove up to Saddleworth Moor with Keith, but that Myra parked in a different lay-by, further into the moor. It is possible that the account they gave from here on in was a lie, and that Keith is actually buried close to the other victims, in order for them to increase the probability of nobody finding his remains and therefore keeping their 'perfect murder'.

Their accounts both state that Keith went willingly with both of them onto the moor, and as Myra said later: 'He went like a lamb to the slaughter.' They walked for quite a way (as far as 3 miles if you believe Brady's version of events, and just over 1 mile if you believe Myra's). They went past the confluence of Hoe Grain and Shiny

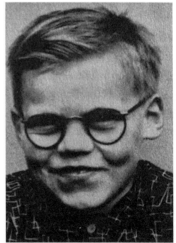

Keith Bennett.

105

Brook streams to Ian and Myra's 'special place', where they would go to practice with the guns and have sex.

Keith was beginning to get anxious, according to Ian, and said that his grandmother would start to worry if he didn't arrive there within the next hour as he was staying there for the night. Ian remained almost silent through the entire walk, and Myra offered Keith some words of comfort.

At this point their stories differ. Myra says Ian motioned to her to go and climb the plateau that rises above Hoe Grain and Shiny Brook to keep a lookout. She said that she sat down there with her back to the stream and listened to the wind and the fast-flowing water. Off to her right she could see the tall shape of Greystones.

She then stated that after about half an hour Ian whistled to her. She looked down and saw him waving at her to join him. Keith was not with him. They made their way back up Hoe Grain towards the car. On the way they buried the spade in the shale of the steep left-hand bank.

According to Ian, as the three of them reached the spot where Keith was to be murdered, Myra was carrying both a spade and a rifle, wrapped in a plastic mac. Ian then started to whistle, which was Myra's signal to overtake Keith. As they entered a gully, Ian grabbed Keith's throat from behind. He sank to the ground and screamed in panic. He tried to kick Ian, so Myra grabbed his legs. Ian said that Keith fought just as hard as John Kilbride had. Myra held Keith's legs while Ian pulled Keith's trousers and underpants down, before sexually assaulting him. He then strangled Keith to death with his bare hands. He recalled that it was all over in a matter of minutes. When he was later interviewed by Dr Alan Keightley, Ian said that Myra 'was a yard away from me. I couldn't keep her away – she enjoyed it.'

They both agreed that Ian took at least one photograph of Keith's body before they buried him. Ian said that he put a large rock on the grave as a marker, 'like a headstone'. When interviewed, he said that he was surprised that metal detectors hadn't located Keith's body from the metal zip on the jacket he was wearing.

It was dark on their way back to the car and they had to use the lights of passing cars to guide them. Myra lost one of her shoes in the peat and they had to go back and find it.

It was late when they got back to Gorton. Having work the next day meant that there wasn't much time to clean the car up. They burned their trousers and counted the buttons on their coats while ticking off their working list. Their shoes had the remnants of shale on them and so were also burned. Ian's also had spots of blood on them. They gave the car a quick clean and then drank wine. They probably had sex too, before Myra dropped Ian off at Westmoreland Street. He was desperate to develop the photograph(s) he had taken of Keith's body.

The following morning, Ian drove to Myra's early on his motorbike and they cleaned the car more thoroughly, before going off to work. Ian showed Myra the photograph. It showed Keith laying on his back, with his trousers down and blood on his body. Ian said that he was upset that it was out of focus and they both said that he destroyed it, but the probability is that it was put with the Master List and other items in the filing cabinet when they got to work.

Back at Keith's home, Winnie remembered that,

> My mam came to our house and I said, 'Where's Keith?' because she normally brought him up with her on her way to her job. She was a cleaner at Toc H in Victoria Park in them days, so she'd bring the kiddies back early.
>
> She said he hadn't come to her last night. She said she'd been expecting him, but then she thought I must have made some other arrangements. We both started to panic. I was more than seven months pregnant. I went up to the school and the clinic, where I thought he might have gone about his broken glasses. But there was no sign, so I went to the police. They took his description but said they couldn't do anything till he'd been missing forty-eight hours.

When there was still no sign of Keith, the police launched a huge search. They conducted house-to-house enquiries, looked through empty buildings, dragged reservoirs and canals, put up posters and posted thousands of leaflets. They tore up the floorboards in the family home and looked under the concrete in their backyard. Keith's stepfather, Jimmy Johnson was questioned four times:

> They accused me of killing him, because I was his stepfather. I don't blame them, I'm glad they explored every possibility, they had a job to do. But it was terrible at the time. I was very fond of the lad, and to be accused of doing away with him was too much, what with all the other upset. Every time I spent the day at the police station I'd come home and all the neighbours would be hanging over their gates, ever so friendly like, dying to know what was happening. They'd seen me being driven off in a cop car, and I'm sure that was enough to make half of them think I was guilty.

Winnie added:

> The worst time was one Sunday morning when we was all in bed, and the police came and hauled Jimmy away. He didn't come back all day. Apparently someone had told the police that Jimmy had been drinking in the town and talking about what he'd done to Keith. They released him, of course. But Jimmy was getting really sick of it. He started blaming me. It was beginning to affect our marriage. In the end I went

down to Bootle Street police station and said to the head of CID, 'Do you think I'd have stayed with my husband if I thought he had anything to do with Keith? You're splitting my family up. And if that happens you'll have my death and the death of four kiddies on your conscience, because I'll kill myself and take them with me.

Eventually the police laid off. But other people didn't. I was walking along Stockport Road one day with my mother and two of the kiddies when a woman stopped me. She said, 'You're Keith's mum, aren't you?' Do you want to know what's happened to him? He's been chopped up and fed to pigs.' I was upset for days after that.

The police released a short statement: 'We are investigating every possible explanation. Crime cannot be ruled out.... We are determined to find his body quickly.' They linked Keith's disappearance to that of John Kilbride, as they lived just eight miles apart, were of a similar age, and neither had reason to run away. They looked at Pauline Reade's file too, but still suspected that she may have run away with someone from a fairground. The possible links were made known to the parents of the missing children, and it wasn't long before Winnie Johnson went to visit Sheila Kilbride, as she was the only person who knew how she felt.

David Smith and Maureen Hindley on their wedding day.

Meanwhile, life for others moved on as normal; on 15 August 1964, David Smith, aged just 16, married Maureen Hindley, aged 18, at All Saints Registry Office.

Maureen's mother, Nellie, refused to attend the wedding as she hated David's history of violence and the way he spoke to, and treated, her daughter. Myra and Ian refused to attend the ceremony too. David recalled the day many years later and said that neither he nor Maureen were bothered about getting married, and that they were pressured into it by their parents as illegitimacy was still a social stigma back then. Maureen moved in with David and his father while the wedding arrangements were made – David's father bought their wedding rings.

Late in the evening following the wedding, out of the blue, Myra knocked on David's door in Wiles Street and told him, 'Ian would like a drink with you.' They immediately got dressed for going out and went over to Bannock Street, where her and Myra's grandmother was already in bed. The record player was on in the background and there was a bottle of red wine warming by the fire in the living room. There was also a lot of other drink in the room, including white wine, whisky and a jug of red wine on the table. Myra was already half drunk as she talked to Maureen and Ian was chatting to David.

> That was the first time I'd socialised with them as a couple. When we arrived, Ian was nothing like the person I'd seen on the street.... He chilled out that night.... A lot of drink flowed. Ian had a taste for Liebfraumilch, which I've never liked, and he'd brought whisky and jugged red wine from the offy [off-licence] near Westmoreland Street. We downed the whisky and warm red wine and the girls sipped the Liebfraumilch. Beer wasn't really Ian's thing – I think he thought it was a bit common.

David relaxed almost instantly in the house, playing with the two dogs – Lassie, and her puppy Puppet. 'It was the girls who really created the atmosphere. My friendship with Ian developed because of them. Myra stood near the record player, a drink in one hand and a cigarette in the other, bopping about and choosing the vinyl for us.'

> The girls danced and sang together, and I got up and had a jive as well. It felt like a small party, just the four of us, celebrating the wedding – a regular happy occasion. They made a fuss of us that night – Ian was *Mein Host*, hovering with his bottle so that no one's glass was empty. He'd squeeze past Myra with a fag hanging from the corner of his lip and give her an affectionate hug.... We went home in the early hours. I was three sheets to the wind and singing, and Maureen was laughing like a drain as we stumbled back to Wiles Street in the dark.

The following day Myra again went to Wiles Street and called for David and Maureen. They were still in bed sleeping off their hangover, but Myra told them to get dressed as she and Ian would be calling for them in about an hour's time. She told them that they had a surprise for them.

David and Maureen got dressed and were ready and waiting when Myra pulled up in her Morris Mini pickup. Maureen slid into the front next to Myra, while Ian and David sat behind the partition in the back. They told the newlyweds that they were taking them out for the day to the Lake District.

Myra Hindley at home.

Myra and her Mini.

Myra crouching at the side of her Mini.

Unseen photograph of Myra pouring something away in a ditch.

They left at 2.30 that afternoon and Ian made sure that there were sandwiches, cigarettes, beer and six bottles of red wine for them to enjoy during the journey. They headed for Windermere first, with Ian and David drinking heavily, but when they arrived it was too busy, so Myra drove them to Bowness where it was quieter. They parked the car up and Ian paid for all four of them to take a speedboat out on the lake. They then went for dinner in a restaurant which Ian again paid for. They set off for home at around 8.00 pm that night, and when they reached Preston, Ian knocked on the partition and Myra stopped off at a pub. Having drank all the alcohol that Ian had in the car they had a pint of bitter each in the pub before Ian bought half a bottle of whisky for them to drink on the journey home.

During the journey, Ian spoke to David about work and told him how much he hated it. He told him that there were easier ways of making a living if you were willing to break the law. They told each other about their past criminal records and exploits during the long journey home, which took even longer due to the traffic coming out of Blackpool. It was 1.00 am when they got back to Bannock Street, where all four of them had another meal and more to drink. David and Maureen then walked home and climbed into bed at 4.00 am.

On two other occasions shortly after, Ian and Myra called on the newlyweds unexpectedly at Wiles Street, taking ample supplies of wine with them and staying up talking until the early hours. David loved it as he never had to put his hand in his pocket for alcohol.

From then on, the two couples would meet up every fortnight or so, where they would get fish & chips, play cards, drink and listen to music. David recalled:

> It was a very ordinary time, no heavy conversations or hints of what was to come. The relationship between Ian and Myra was normal, as far as I could see, too. There was no question of one dominating the other. She could give as good as she got, anyway. They rowed occasionally, but only over daft stuff … if he got very drunk and started rambling or raising his voice about something, she'd give him a withering look like women do and he'd belt up.

David's relationship with Myra had thawed considerably by now too.

> We were OK with each other then. If I saw her in the street, she'd stop for a chat, arms crossed as always, asking what I was up to and how was Maureen. She'd accepted that I was married to her sister – what else could she do, with a baby on the way as well? But she was fine with it. She'd had her moment, reading me the ground rules, telling me not to lay a finger on Maureen or mess her about, but after that everything was OK. I felt very comfortable around her then.

David, however, did often beat Maureen.

Like Ian, David Smith was also attracted to men. He said that he wasn't bisexual, as Ian clearly was, but he enjoyed the company of other men. He even admitted that

Above left: Maureen Smith, Ian Brady and Myra Hindley.

Above right: Myra Hindley with a drink in her hand.

Above: Myra Hindley sat at home.

Right: Myra Hindley drinking at home.

Above left: Unseen photo of Ian Brady and Myra Hindley at home.

Above right: Ian Brady and Myra Hindley at home.

during his last year at school he had flirted secretly with two other boys. As far as it is known, Maureen knew nothing about this.

Ian introduced David to his and Myra's guns fairly early on, when they discussed crime. He said that his feelings for other men disappeared as his relationship with Ian and Myra grew.

Towards the end of the summer, Ian and Myra went up to Glasgow and on the way back they stopped off at the Lake District and took some more photographs.

Above left: Ian Brady in the Lake District.

Above right: Myra Hindley in the Lake District.

Left: Myra Hindley in the Lake District.

Chapter 9

Wardle Brook Avenue

On 17 September 1964, Ian, Myra and her gran, along with the two dogs, Lassie and Puppet, moved from Gorton as part of a slum clearance programme. They were moved by the council into a two-bedroom end of terrace house at 16 Wardle Brook Avenue, Hattersley, Cheshire – just a fifteen-minute car journey away – and closer to Saddleworth Moor. Myra's mother, Nellie, was also offered a house in the area but refused to move there as she had begun an affair with a man whom she would later marry, Bill Moulton.

Before they moved in, David Smith helped Ian to decorate, painting the walls in the living room pink, and putting imitation brick wallpaper around the fireplace. While they were busy decorating, Myra went out and bought the furnishings. She bought new fireside chairs, new curtains and a new red carpet with her friend May Hill, whose family had also moved to the estate and lived directly behind them at number 2.

In the house next to them was a Jamaican man named Phoenix Braithwaite, his wife Tessa and their three young children Mercedes, Carole and Barrington. Because

16 Wardle Brook
Avenue on the left.

they were black, Ian and Myra openly displayed their racist feelings towards them and ignored them whenever possible.

Myra's gran still disliked Ian and hadn't wanted him to move to the new house in Wardle Brook Avenue with her and Myra; after all, the house was in her sole name and Myra and Ian were technically just lodgers, but Myra persuaded her to let Ian move with them.

A friend of Mrs Maybury's recalled one day waiting around the corner until she saw Ian and Myra leave the house, as she had been warned that Ian would be angry if she had any visitors. She recalled that Mrs Maybury was very nervous when she told her, and that it was made very clear to her that she no longer wanted anyone else to visit her at home.

At this time Myra changed cars again, this time getting a Morris Mini van. She purchased the car but only took out a four-month licence on the vehicle, knowing full well that it would be used in another murder before long and so she would have to change vehicles again.

Despite now having to travel six miles to see her gran and sister, Maureen and David kept meeting them for drunken evenings at least once every fortnight. Some things did start to change, however. As usual, Myra and Ian would turn up out of the blue in Wiles Street with wine and whisky and the two couples would make a night of it, but when David and Maureen went to Wardle Brook Avenue, they had to make arrangements in advance.

On one occasion they turned up unannounced; they were greeted by Maureen's gran and shown into the living room. Ian and Myra both stood up and walked upstairs without saying a word. They waited upstairs in Myra's bedroom until the couple had gone, giving no explanation.

On another occasion, Maureen had been making cushion covers for the new house and took them over to Wardle Brook Avenue. It was about 9.00 pm when she knocked on the door, but there was no answer. Her gran was in bed, but she could see Myra's car parked outside and the lights were on. As she walked away, Ian suddenly opened the door. As she walked back towards the door, she could see that he was angry. He put his arm across the door to stop her from going in and told her that she couldn't go in because he and Myra had company. She told him she had brought the cushion covers for them, Ian grabbed them off her and slammed the door closed in her face.

When the visits were arranged, Ian always brought between four and eight bottles of Spanish or German wine and they nearly always drank into the early hours of the morning; Maureen also drank, despite being heavily pregnant at this stage. Myra and Maureen would go upstairs to sleep in Myra's single bed at around 1.30 am, and Ian and David would carry on drinking downstairs until they passed out.

In November 1967 Myra's former fiancé, Ronnie Sinclair, recalled sitting in a pub in Gorton, 'The Three Arrows', one weekend when Ian (whom he didn't know) came in and started to talk to him. Interestingly, the conversation turned to Myra, and then

Ian told him that he was in the area to collect his winnings from the bookies next door. Ian seemed to know (obviously from Myra) about Ronnie's past, as he had also been in Borstal for breaking and entering. Ian soon turned the conversation around to robbery and told Ronnie that he hated having to work for a living. He told Ronnie he'd been thinking about robbing the Co-Op in Mount Road as he'd been watching it and thought it would be an easy job. He asked Ronnie if he wanted in as a look-out, but Ronnie declined and told Ian that there was nothing there worth robbing.

Ian then told him about all the previous robberies he had carried out and how he was always well armed, as well as the various people he had beaten up, including one whom he attacked in a nightclub with a razor and hoped he had killed.

He was obviously trying to both impress Ronnie and maybe intimidate him too, showing him how

Pat Hodges.

Myra had upgraded in partners. Suddenly, Ian leaned forward and discreetly pulled a photograph out from the inside pocket of his coat. It was of a young girl, naked, with her hands behind her back. Ronnie thought that the girl looked about 13 or 14, and Ian told him that he had taken the photograph himself. Ian then asked him if he knew any girls who would be willing to pose for such photographs, to which Ronnie replied that he didn't and that he wasn't interested in that type of thing. Ian persisted and told him that he was primarily looking for girls aged 16–20 and that he could show him better quality photographs, but Ronnie again insisted that he wasn't into that sort of thing. Both men left the pub shortly after. Who this girl was we will never know for sure, but it is possible that she was one of Ian's new neighbours, Pat Hodges.

Both Ian and Myra had become friendly with 12-year-old Pat, who lived a couple of doors down at number 12. Pat was one of seven children but the only one who visited Ian and Myra, mostly alone, but sometimes with her mother, Elsie Masterson.

Pat called at the house one day to see if her mother was there and later recalled at the trial:

> Myra asked me into the house, I stayed for about twenty minutes. When I went to the house I think there were two dogs, they were called Puppet and Lassie. Puppet was a black and white dog. We had been living at number 12 about three or four weeks before we got to know Ian and Myra. Myra might have called occasionally at our house before I went to visit her at number 16, but I am not sure.

Ian was still going to his mum's in Westmoreland Street for dinner after work and Pat recalled:

> When I visited Myra she suggested I should go with her down Longsight, she said she was going to pick Ian up, I went with her in a little grey Mini van. Myra drove the van, and we went just off the Stockport Road, this was into a side street. We both stayed in the car after it had stopped, eventually Ian joined us in the car, Myra said she didn't go to his house because his mother kept her talking. After we had picked Ian up, I was driven straight home. I used to go with Myra every night to the same place, every night we picked up Ian Brady there.… We were waiting for Brady who was in his mother's house.
>
> About two or three weeks after I started going with Myra to collect Brady, Myra suggested, I think, I should go with them on the moors, she said it was just for a run out. I agreed to go with them on the moors on the first occasion, I was taken on the moors in the van with Myra driving, I know where we went to … it was through Greenfield. When we got there on the first occasion we just sat in the van, it was dark, we just sat there talking.
>
> We went up on the moors together about once or twice a week, they took wine up with them. They took wine with them nearly every time. We went to the same spot except for a couple of times when we went further down the road, that is, a place nearer Greenfield than the place we usually went to.
>
> There were occasions when both of them brought something back from the moor, this was soil. They carried it in sacks. They took empty sacks up with them in the van. They took a spade and sometimes they used to borrow ours. I used to hold the sacks for them when they did this. They got the soil from just off the road about a yard or two from the road edge. When they put the soil in the sacks they brought it back in the van with them. They put the soil on the back garden.
>
> Once Myra and I went to get soil without Brady – on the other occasions Brady came too. This happened about ten times. This happened sometimes in the day and sometimes at night.
>
> When they took wine with them they sometimes went up in the day and sometimes at night. Sometimes they took half a bottle of wine and sometimes a full bottle. I had some of the wine, it was given to me sometimes by Myra and sometimes by Brady – I had it from the bottle.
>
> I used to go to the house, 16 Wardle Brook Avenue, very regularly after I got to know them. I have had wine there. When I had it there

I had it in a glass. I just used to have my glass filled up. I would have about four glasses of wine on a visit to the house.

On two occasions I went for walks on the moor with Ian and Myra. On both these occasions we started off from the same place … where Myra used to stop the van. On one occasion we walked on one side of the road and on the other occasion we walked on the other side of the road … when we went for a walk we went beyond the rocks. When we went it was daylight. Nothing was said as to why we should go for a walk in this direction, we walked about ten yards past the rocks. We didn't stop there at all we just turned round and came back. We may have stopped for a minute. They never had the dogs with them when they went on the moors.

When we went for a walk at night we went on the opposite side of the road from the rocks and it was just going dark then. They did not say why we were going for a walk in this direction … it was on the opposite side from that which we had gone for a walk before … I was thirsty and I just had a drink from a stream down there. Ian said have a drink from there as it's clean.

We walked about six yards from the road, we didn't go beyond the stream. We only stopped while I had a drink. We stopped a couple of minutes after that. I can't remember anything that was said by Ian or Myra on this occasion. After we had been for a walk and had a drink from the stream we went back to the car and then drove home.

She knew that tape recorders were kept in the house and she knew that Ian was a keen photographer:

On occasions when I went to Wardle Brook Avenue, I have seen Brady using a camera. He took photographs of Myra and I with the dog. This happened once. He had a little camera. Myra said it was a German camera. He had another one which folded up.

The Medico-Legal Society is an organisation of lawyers and medical professional whose aim is to promote medico-legal knowledge. In November 1967, Mr W.L. Mars-Jones QC gave a talk on Brady and Hindley during one of the Society's regular monthly meetings, and there is a strange comment by a Mr Ingram in which he states: 'They had shown some affection towards this little girl [Pat Hodges]. They had also shown some of their sexual perversity towards her because she had been subject to assault in the presence of Myra.' This is the only known record of any suggestion that Pat Hodges may have been abused by the couple.

Pat Hodges, Myra and Puppet laying on Myra's bed.

Above left: Pat Hodges with Myra Hindley next to her.

Above right: Unseen photograph of Pat Hodges sat next to Myra Hindley.

During the reinvestigation in 1987, Myra told DCS Peter Topping that both she and Ian had an affectionate relationship with 'Patty', but there was nothing sexual about it. She also told him that when all three of them went out in her car, 'Patty' would sometimes sit on Ian's knee.

On the 9 October 1964, David Smith was again in court and was convicted of two cases of common assault at Manchester Juvenile Court. He was fined £3 for each offence and bound over to keep the peace for twelve months. There was no action regarding his probation as the Magistrates felt that David had suffered a certain amount of provocation and the fact that his wife was due to give birth soon certainly influenced their decision.

The charges had arisen as part of a private summons issued against him after a woman had reported him and alleged that he had assaulted a 21-year-old man and his mother. David's defence was that he was walking down the street with his father and Maureen when the 21-year-old deliberately obstructed him, so he simply 'moved him' out of the way.

Soon afterwards, Maureen went into labour and gave birth to a daughter – Angela Dawn Smith. David recalled:

> There was no longer any friction between Dad and Maureen, and straight after work I'd play with Angela before sitting down at the table with Dad to eat the dinner Maureen had cooked. At weekends and in the evenings, we'd take Angela out in her pram and walk the dogs … now the older people on the street smiled, chatted to Maureen and made baby-talk to Angela. I felt content and didn't even make a fuss over visiting the in-laws on a Sunday afternoon. Maureen laughed a lot and Dad was a changed man – he would babysit while the two of us had a night out … Nellie had mellowed as well, and was just as you'd expect a grandma to be … Bob was too wrapped up in his own misery to care.

Ian and Myra were still regular visitors to Wiles Street, but neither were interested in the baby: 'There was no doting Auntie Myra and Uncle Ian. Myra's only concern was for Maureen … She wasn't a touchy-feely auntie and *never* held Angela.'

Ian's relationship with David's father was fraught; when Ian and Myra went to his house one particular Friday evening, things became explosive. It was payday and so David's father spent the evening in the pub. As usual, the girls were drinking and having a dance in the living room while David and Ian sat and talked. Later that evening David went outside for some fresh air and Ian joined him. David was enjoying a cigarette and Ian a glass of whisky when Amos and Joan Reade walked past them. They acknowledged David before going into their house.

Ian asked David if they were the parents of the missing girl and what he thought had happened to her. David said it was rumoured that Pauline had met a lad from the fairground and run off with him. He then told Ian about the police questioning him and his father; Ian was interested to know what kind of questions the police had asked, and he replied just the usual, such as what sort of girl was she, and was she the sort to just disappear. David told him that she wasn't that sort of girl.

They went back inside, and Ian took over the record player. He had brought some records with him and played 'The Goons', which he and Myra thought were hysterical. When that had finished Ian put on one of his German marching records. Maureen went into the kitchen, leaving David, paralysed by drink, sitting in the chair;

he recalled Ian and Myra talking to each other in German, and Ian telling David exactly what Hitler was saying.

David's father arrived home drunk from the pub. He was outraged to find Ian sitting in his chair and playing German marching songs. He yelled at Ian to get out of his chair, to take the record off and get out of the house. Ian enraged him further by calmly refusing and then smirking at him. To avoid the situation getting out of hand, David bundled his father off to bed, leaving Ian and Myra laughing to themselves.

In November 1964 the new CID chief at Ashton-under-Lyne reopened the investigation into John Kilbride's disappearance. DCI Joe Mounsey was determined to solve the case of all missing children on his patch and as such, his colleagues referred to John as 'Mounsey's Lad'.

John's younger brother, Danny, recalled: 'None of us had any hope then that John would come back, but what Mounsey did was to get things moving towards finding out who was responsible. He decided to reconstruct John's last known movements in Ashton market to try and jog people's memories. He needed someone to play John's part and I said straightaway, 'I'll do it.' I was 12 at the time and I looked a lot like him. We did the reconstruction around the time of the first anniversary of John going missing.'

Chapter 10

Lesley Ann Downey

As Christmas approached, Pat Hodge's mother told Myra that her kids had been invited to a Christmas party at the Braithwaite's house. She recalled:

> Myra hated the Jamaican next door. She said to me, 'Dirt is better than him…. You're not letting them go, are you? I wouldn't let my children go nowhere near a black's party. Tell them I'm taking them to see Santa Claus.' But my little girls went and Mr Braithwaite was very kind. He kept playing records and jiving about like a teenager.

During their lunch break a couple of days before Christmas 1964 Ian and Myra went to a branch of Tesco's in Newton Heath because the store had been advertising cut-price wine and spirits and they wanted to get some in for Christmas and the New Year. On the way they saw posters advertising a funfair running over Christmas and decided it would be an excellent opportunity for them to make another 'sacrifice'. They debated the location of the fairground, as neither knew that area of Manchester very well, and decided that whoever they picked up should be taken back to their home in Wardle Brook Avenue for photographs to be taken. They knew that they would have the house to themselves on Boxing Day as Myra's grandmother would be out visiting her son Jim (Myra's uncle) for his birthday.

They went back to work and Ian spent the rest of the day consulting the Master List and trying to make a working list from it. That evening they got the map out and checked the area that the fairground was in, before driving to Manchester Central station and depositing two suitcases full of possibly incriminating evidence concerned with their crimes committed so far in the 'left luggage'. On the way home they checked the area out in the car and thought it was a great prospect.

On Christmas Eve, Pat Hodges called at 16 Wardle Brook Avenue to see Ian and Myra, and the couple saw this as an excellent opportunity for a dry run. Pat recalled that she was alone with the couple and they gave her some wine, whisky and gin to drink. Her mother then came to the house and spoke with Ian and Myra for a while; it was nearly 11.30 pm before she left with her daughter. Pat was not given any alcohol while her mother was there. A few minutes after getting home, Myra knocked on their door and told Pat's mother that she and Ian were going for a drive up to the moors and did Pat want to go with them? Pat's mother, Elsie, recalled: 'I thought they were a nice couple. They seemed to like Pat a lot and she often took her dolls and toys there. Pat was very insistent about going that night.'

Pat recalled:

> I went off with them to the moors that night. We went in the white Mini van. Myra was driving. I never saw anyone but Myra driving that white Mini van.
>
> We went to the usual place on the moors, nearer to Greenfield, just before where we used to go for soil on the opposite side. We sat in the van mostly looking out of the window when we got there. It was dark. Myra took some sandwiches. I might have had a little bit of wine. I think they were drinking wine. We stayed there until about 00:30. Myra said: 'Shall we go home and get some blankets and come back for the night?' Ian said: 'Alright'. Myra then drove me back home.
>
> It was about 01:30 when I got in. Shortly after I got in the house I heard the van drive off. I don't think I saw either Myra or Ian on Christmas Day. I did not see either Ian or Myra on Boxing Day.

Her mother, Elsie later said:

> Looking back now I know I should have been worried. I still have nightmares of what could have happened to Pat with those devil people. I lie awake at night thinking what might have happened if they had kept her. They must have had second thoughts or something like that.

There is no doubt that when Ian and Myra went back up to the Moors on their own on what was effectively Christmas Day morning they used the time to plan the final stages of their next murder, and possibly even dig the grave in advance for their next victim.

It was Boxing Day 1964 when Ian and Myra put their sordid plan into operation. Ian gave Myra a copy of 'Girl Don't Come' by Sandie Shaw as a memento to remember the day by. They spent the early morning going over the final details of their planned abduction in snatched conversations when Myra's grandmother was out of earshot. Ian told Myra that he wanted a girl this time as it would be easier to sell the photographs, and they decided to pack boxes around the girl when she was in the car so that she would be mostly hidden from any prying eyes.

Myra then drove her grandmother to spend the afternoon with Jim at his home in Combermere Street, Dukinfield, where. Myra did this every other Saturday, when she wasn't working, and this day was also Jim's birthday. He recalled that they arrived

Above left: Pat Hodges.

Above right: Lesley Ann Downey and her brother, Tommy.

around 2.00 pm but Myra didn't stay for long, and said she'd be back at around 9.30 pm as usual to take her grandmother home.

Meanwhile, back at Wardle Brook Avenue, Ian was busy setting up his camera and photographic lighting equipment in Myra's bedroom. He also set up his reel-to-reel tape recorder, with attached microphone, and left it next to the front door.

When Myra returned, he showed her what he had been up to and then the couple got into Myra's car and drove to the shops where they deliberately bought slightly more items than they could carry, before heading to Silcock's Wonder Fair in Hulme Hall Lane where they would take their next victim, 10-year-old Lesley Ann Downey.

Lesley Ann's mother, Ann, recalled:

> I think everybody loved Lesley. She never gave cheek. I never had to smack her. She always did as she was told. She came in from school of a night and she would go up, change out of uniform, make her bed, come down and do her homework. She was perfect.

It was 3.30 pm when Lesley Ann asked her mother if she could go to the fair. She told her mother that the next-door neighbour's children were going and that their mother, Mrs Clarke, would supervise them all. The fairground was so close that the music could be heard from Lesley Ann's kitchen window.

Alan West, Lesley Ann's stepfather, told her 'Mrs Clarke will see you don't get up to any pranks.' He then told her and her brother Tommy: 'When you've spent your money we want you both back here sharpish. Your mum's laying tea for five o'clock and you'll need to get cleaned up after the fair.'

It was 3.45 pm when Lesley Ann left for the fair with her younger brothers Tommy and Brett. They went straight to their neighbour's and met up with Mrs Clarke's children Linda, her brother Roy, and their sister Ann. Lesley Ann's older brother Terry had wanted to go along too, but he was ill with the flu. He had been to the fair a couple of days before, however, and had won a string of white beads and a matching bracelet, which he gave to his sister.

Mary Clarke, who was supposed to go and supervise the children, decided at the last minute not to go, leaving them to go by themselves. Unfortunately for all concerned, she never informed Lesley Ann's mother.

Mary's daughter, Linda, recalled that she and Lesley Ann went on a roundabout-like ride and then to the machines. Once they had spent all their money they decided to go home. Linda went home with her sister, Ann, at 5.15 pm, leaving her brother, Roy, and Lesley Ann's brothers, Brett and Tommy, at the fair. Lesley Ann said she would go and find them and go home with them as she wanted another look around the funfair. Linda and her sister got home at around 5.30 pm.

Lesley Ann never met up with her brothers but was seen by her 10-year-old schoolfriend Bernard King, who was in the year below her, at around 5.45 pm standing by the dodgems. Bernard recalled:

> I used to play with her brother Terry, I did know her quite well …
> I went to the fair by myself. I walked there; it is about five minutes'
> walk from our house. I saw Lesley Ann Downey at the fair, she was
> standing by the Dodgems when I was standing by the Waltzer. She
> was more than fifteen yards away from me. I saw Lesley Ann about
> two or three minutes after I got to the fair. I didn't speak to Lesley Ann
> Downey at all. There was no one with her when I saw her. I walked past
> her to the Cyclone and then I didn't see her. There was no one with her
> when I passed her on my way to the Cyclone, she was still standing by
> the Dodgems…. After I passed her … I did not see her again.

What actually happened between Lesley Ann being alone at the funfair and her arriving at Wardle Brook Avenue is up for some debate. Myra found this the most difficult murder to talk about, probably because there was more evidence of her involvement in this case than any of the others, and so could not offer an alternative explanation for some of the established facts.

She told DCS Peter Topping in the mid-1980s that both her and Ian went into the fairground carrying some bags and boxes of shopping; once they had seen that Lesley Ann was alone (after they had been watching her for five to ten minutes) they walked next to her and purposely dropped one of the bags. Lesley Ann helped them to pick up the contents and they offered her some money if she would carry that bag back to the car for them. She was then offered more money if she would help them unpack the shopping at their home. When she got into the car she was put into the back and had the bags and boxes of shopping piled up around her for the almost thirty-minute trip.

Ian denied that he went into the fair with Myra and insisted that he was waiting on a road nearby when Myra pulled up with Lesley Ann already in the vehicle.

As Lesley Ann was being driven to Wardle Brook Avenue, her brothers Tommy and Brett had arrived home; they asked where Lesley Ann was, assuming she had left earlier with Linda Clarke. Tommy told their mother that he had last seen his sister on the Wall of Death. Ann sent him to Mrs Clarke's, assuming that Lesley Ann had gone there with Linda and her mother. He didn't return for another fifteen minutes, but when he did, he had worrying news. He told his mother that when he discovered that Lesley Ann wasn't there, he had run back to the fairground for another look for her but couldn't find her. He then told her: 'She didn't go with Mrs Clarke ... she went with Mrs Clarke's daughter. I've been down to the Rec again but she's nowhere to be seen.'

Lesley Ann's stepfather, Alan, became concerned and asked Tommy to go into more detail. Tommy said: 'Mrs Clarke didn't go to the fair. She was tired and didn't feel like going. Their Linda went with Lesley. I've just been over to the fair again, but I can't see her. I've looked everywhere – honest.'

With that, Alan and Ann went out looking for her. They searched the entire fairground twice and knocked on the doors of everyone who knew Lesley Ann, in case she had gone there. Ann went to see Mrs Clarke, and in her book *For the Love of Lesley* she recounts how:

> All my fear burst out in hysterical accusations and angry threats when we got to the Clarkes. I raved at Mary for not going to the wretched fair. Almost out of control, I accused them of negligence, cursed them for being so irresponsible as to allow a 9-year-old like Linda to go on her own with Lesley. Her guilt and my fury were a potent and explosive mixture.

Mary Clarke's husband, Roy, offered to help in the search and the three of them, along with Tommy, went back for a third look around the fairground. With no luck, Alan tried to send Ann home while he and some others went to look along the bank of a stream, but she insisted on going with them. Ann recalled: 'I was hysterical. The boys were crying. They'd all be round with her friends looking for her. She wasn't there.'

They reported her missing to the police at Mill Street station just after 6.00 pm, but the policeman they spoke to wasn't particularly interested. He told them:

> Apart from the fact it's Christmas and we have a number of officers on leave, there is no way we can mount a search for a kiddy that's an hour late home. If we did that every time a child gets reported missing we'd never have time to do anything else.

He told them to go home and come back at around 11.00 pm if she wasn't home by then. They thought of places she might have gone, including an old cotton mill on Butler Street, to see if she was there, but there was no sign of her anywhere.

As this was going on, back at Wardle Brook Avenue, Myra, Ian and Lesley Ann arrived at number 16. The time was roughly 6.30 pm. Ian went in first and immediately switched on the tape recorder he had left by the front door.

A transcript of the tape was played at the trial and is reproduced here in full:

> **Brady:** Get out of the fucking road. Get in the fucking basket. [Presumably talking to the dogs].
>
> *Then there are various noises, a door banging, crackling. Footsteps, heavy, steps across the room, recording noises, blowing sounds in the microphone, more footsteps.* [Brady putting the tape recorder in Myra's bedroom].
>
> *Hindley's voice, quiet and indecipherable. Footsteps, light, walking across the room. Whispered conversation, at the same time footsteps. Speech, distant, containing word 'Upstairs'. Then two footsteps, two sets.* [The conversation between Brady and Hindley was probably just to check that the machine was working. Hindley then went to bring Lesley Ann in].
>
> **Lesley Ann:** (*Screaming*) Don't. Mum. Ah. [It has never been established why Lesley Ann called Ian and Myra 'Mum' and 'Dad']
>
> **Hindley:** Shut up!
>
> **Lesley Ann:** Please, God, help me, ah, please, oh.
>
> **Hindley:** Come on*! (Whispering, footsteps).* Shut up! (*More whispering*).
>
> **Lesley Ann:** Oh, please, please. Oh. (*then faintly*) Help, oh. I can't go on, you've got hold of my neck. Oh. (*Scream*). Help! (*There then follows a gurgling noise. Heavy breathing, sounds of distress, laboured breathing*).
>
> **Hindley:** Shh. Shh. Shut up, shut up.
>
> *Screams and gurgles. Lesley Ann crying.*
>
> **Hindley:** (*Whispering*). Keep (*unintelligible*). You will be right. Sit down and be quiet. (*Whispers*).
>
> **Brady:** Come on. (*Whispers. Footsteps on stairs, then entering room.*) *Lesley Ann, crying, muffled.*

Brady: Here (*whispered*)

Hindley: Hush, hush, go on. Sit. (*Indecipherable.*) *Lesley Ann crying.*

Hindley: You are all right. Hush, hush. Put it in your mouth. *Lesley Ann crying.*

Hindley: Put it in your mouth and keep it in and you will be all right. Put it in. Stop it. If you don't … .Shh. (*Lesley Ann crying*)

Hindley: In your mouth. Hush, hush. Shut up or I'll forget myself and hit you one! I'll hit you one! Keep it in! (*Lesley Ann whimpering*)

Brady: Put it in!

Hindley: Put it in! (*Spoken quickly*)

Brady then speaks but words indecipherable except for 'in'. Then footsteps.

Brady: Put it in. Keep it in. Stop it now, stop it now.

Hindley: I am only doing this and you will be all right. Put it in your mouth. Put it in now. *Further words are spoken by Hindley but are indecipherable except for 'put it in'. Will you stop it. Stop it! Hindley's voice again but indecipherable.*

Lesley Ann: (*Whimpering*). Can I tell you summat? I must tell you summat…. Please take your hands off me a minute. Please, mummy, daddy, please…. I can't tell you. I can't tell you. I can't breathe. Oh…. I can't bear it….Please, God!

Brady: I want to take some photos, that's all.

Lesley Ann: Don't undress me, will you?

Brady: No.

Indecipherable talk.

Lesley Ann: I want to see mummy, honest to God … I will swear on the Bible.

Brady: The quicker you do this the quicker you get home.

Lesley Ann: I will have to go because I am going out with mam. Leave me, please. Please help me, will you?… What are you going to do with me?

Brady: I am going to take some photographs. Put it in your mouth.

Lesley Ann: What for?

Brady: Put it in your mouth…. Right in.

Lesley Ann: I am not going to do 'owt.

Brady: Put it in. If you don't keep that hand down I'll slit your neck…. Put it in!

Lesley Ann: Won't you let me go, please?

Brady: No, no, put it in. Stop talking…. What is your name?

Lesley Ann: Lesley. Lesley Ann.

Brady: What is your second name?

Lesley Ann: Westford.

Brady: Westford?

Lesley Ann: I have to go home for eight o'clock. I have to get or I'll get killed if I don't…. Honest to God.

Brady: Yes!

There are then quick footsteps of Hindley leaving the room and going downstairs. Then there is a click, then the sound of a door closing, then Hindley's footsteps coming upstairs, followed by eight longer steps.

Brady: What is it?

Hindley: I have left the light on.

Brady: You have?

Hindley: So that…. *The next part of the tape is unrecognisable, then Lesley Ann is heard crying.*

Lesley Ann: It hurts me neck.

Brady: Put it in your mouth and you'll be all right.

Hindley: Shut up crying!

Lesley Ann: (*Crying*) It hurts me

Hindley: (*Interrupting*) Hush. Shut up now. Put it in and don't dally. Just keep your mouth shut please…. Wait a bit. I'll put this on again. Do you get me?

Lesley Ann: (*Whining*) No, I…*Sentence indecipherable*

Hindley: Shh. Shush! Put it in your mouth again, packed more solid.

There is then a whispered sentence which is indecipherable.

Lesley Ann: I want to go home. Honest to God I'll … before eight o'clock.

Hindley: No, it's all right.

Brady: Eh?

Music begins to play with a country-style tune, followed by the tune of Jolly Old St Nicholas and The Little Drummer Boy. Three loud cracks are then heard on the tape (believed to be Brady's tripod extending) and there are various non-vocal noises. The music of The Little Drummer Boy grows fainter, then there is a sound of footsteps. The tape ends.

Ian and Myra then took photographs of Lesley Ann in various pornographic poses, with a gag in her mouth, kept in place by a scarf wrapped around her head and neck.

Lesley Ann was then subjected to a horrific sexual attack by both Ian and Myra before being strangled to death. Myra's claim that she was sent by Ian to the bathroom to run a bath of warm water while she assumed Ian was raping and killing Lesley Ann is quite frankly unbelievable.

Ian later claimed that Myra took part in the sexual acts committed against Lesley Ann and that they were both partially clothed too. At the trial, Ian slipped up when giving his evidence, and said: 'After completion, we all got dressed and went downstairs.'

Lesley Ann begged Ian and Myra to let her go, she pleaded for her life, but they weren't finished with her. After being raped, she was then possibly photographed some more before being strangled to death. Ian claimed that Myra had strangled Lesley Ann with a silk cord and had then openly played with it in local pubs in the weeks following the murder, but at the trial, Dr David Gee gave evidence regarding his post-mortem examination and he ruled out strangulation by ligature as the cause of death. Whoever killed Lesley Ann, it was likely that they did so with their bare hands.

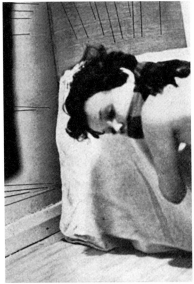

The edited photograph taken by Ian Brady as he tortured Lesley Ann Downey before raping and murdering her.

It was then that Myra ran a bath and Ian carried Lesley Ann's bleeding body into the bathroom. They washed the blood off, as well as the fibres and dog hairs that may have been on the body from Myra's bed. They then lifted Lesley Ann's body onto a bed sheet and wrapped her up. They placed her clothing on top of the bundle. Myra was due to collect her grandmother, but they still had the body to get rid of and they had run out of time. It was also beginning to snow.

Back at Lesley Ann's home, her mother remembered that her sister Elsie and her husband John were due to visit that evening. Grasping at straws as to where her daughter could be, she thought that maybe Lesley Ann had got on a bus and gone to visit her aunt and uncle. Ann and Alan jumped onto a bus and took the seven mile trip to their house; when they arrived, of course, there was no sign of Lesley Ann. They all returned to Ann and Alan's house by bus to help look for Lesley Ann. By now it was 8.30 pm.

As the evening wore on and there was still no sign of Lesley Ann, they went back to Mill Street police station. The same desk sergeant was on duty and this time took them far more seriously.

Myra left Wardle Brook Avenue and drove to Dukinfield; she took the same route over Saddleworth Moor as she would have if she and Ian had been going to bury Lesley Ann's body. She left Ian at home, alone, with the body.

Myra arrived to collect her grandmother at 11.00 pm – 90 minutes later than she had originally intended – telling her uncle Jim that she was late because the roads were 'really bad' with the snow. She said the roads were so bad, in fact, that she couldn't drive her gran home, yet she had been able to drive there – and fully intended on driving herself home again. Her uncle began to argue with her, saying that there was nowhere for the 'old lady' to sleep, and that if she was making the journey home herself then why couldn't she take her grandmother? He could see traffic moving at the end of the road and could see that there was no more than a dusting of snow on the roads and told Myra that she was being silly. They argued for over fifteen minutes before Myra stormed out, telling her grandmother: 'I can't take you, Gran, and that's that!' She drove off, leaving her 77-year-old grandmother to spend the night sleeping on the floor in a bed made up of cushions and blankets.

Police Inspector John Chaddock told the court at the subsequent trial that on Boxing Day 1964, he spent the day in the Saddleworth Moor area. He said it was a cold and frosty day and that there had been snow the day before,

> not a heavy fall but some of this remained and in the late afternoon and early evening of Boxing Day a further fall took place – this was only a moderate fall. Neither the frost nor the snow affected the A635 road. Traffic was moving along the road all day. Rock salt was applied from the early evening.

When Myra got home she and Ian knew there was now no rush to dispose of Lesley Ann's body. They had a lot of wine and whisky to celebrate their 'sacrifice' and probably had sex too, before falling asleep downstairs on the sofa bed.

Early the following morning Ian and Myra were awoken by a gritting lorry. They went upstairs and found Lesley Ann's body was cold and lying face down on the bed. Ian picked her up, wrapped in a sheet, and put her into the boot of the car. Myra then drove them up to Hollin Brown Knoll. When the coast was clear, Myra pulled over into their usual layby and Ian got out and ran up the incline with a spade, towards the burial place of Pauline Reade and out of sight of the road. He then began to dig a shallow grave through a thin layer of snow, about 90 yards from the road.

Myra waited in the car with the body, as this was the first time a victim had not walked willingly onto the moor. Just then, a police car pulled up beside her and the officer asked her if there was something wrong. Myra managed not to panic and told the officer that she was just drying out her spark plugs, hoping that he didn't go up and look over the rocks and that Ian didn't come back down, as she knew there would be a dead policeman to bury too.

The policeman accepted the explanation and drove off. Ian then returned and ran up the incline with Lesley Ann's body over his shoulder, as he had practiced with Myra. He put her into the grave with her legs doubled up to her abdomen and lying on her right side. Her clothes were buried at her feet.

Myra then drove the couple home and they ticked off everything on the 'Working List', made sure that everything was clean, and Myra drove off alone to collect her grandmother, arriving there about 10.30 am. In the meantime, Ian was burning any possible evidence, such as their clothing, from the night before.

Myra and Ian didn't see David or Maureen on Boxing Day, despite saying otherwise at the subsequent trial. Maureen and David spent most of the day at home with their baby and David's father. David's father went to the pub at around 7.00 pm, and David and Maureen went for a drink at 9.30 pm in the Three Arrows pub on Hyde Road, leaving the baby with Nellie Hindley in Eaton Street. They left about an hour later and were home by 11.10 pm

At 5.00 pm on 27 December, two CID officers called at Lesley Ann Downey's home and asked Ann and Alan to accompany them to the station. A few minutes after arriving at the station they were led into separate interview rooms where they were asked some very probing questions. Ann was asked if Alan had ever smacked Lesley Ann, and whether Lesley Ann had ever flirted with her stepfather. They asked further questions in trying to establish whether Alan could be a paedophile, and when Ann insisted that he wasn't, they questioned her on whether either of them had smacked or beaten Lesley Ann which had made her run away. Alan had a similarly tough interview, with questions being asked along the same lines. He later said that if the interview had gone on much longer he would have confessed, just to get the officers to stop.

It was almost 10.00 pm when Ann was let out of the interview room. As she walked into the waiting area she saw her 8-year-old son, Tommy, walking out of an interview room wearing just his pyjamas with a coat wrapped around his shoulders. Ann found out that after her and Alan had been taken to the police station, another police car had arrived and the detectives made the babysitter, Margaret Glennen, get Tommy out of bed so they could question him at the station. Ann was apoplectic, and the detectives eventually explained to her that as he was the last known person to see Lesley Ann, he was an important witness who was needed to eradicate 'certain possibilities'.

Two CID officers drove the three of them home, where they insisted on being allowed into the house. Ann collapsed, exhausted, onto the sofa with a sleeping Tommy in her arms, and Alan was made to lead the detectives on a tour of the home. They examined Lesley Ann's bedroom first, before going through the rest of the rooms, searching any space that could be big enough to hide a dead body. The two detectives left, empty-handed and none the wiser, over an hour later.

Manchester Regional Crime Squad took over the investigation and over the next few days the funfair was torn apart, the caravans were searched and hundreds of people were interviewed. Every member of the fairground staff was questioned but no leads emerged. Extra police and dogs were drafted in to go through factories and warehouses in the district, and neighbouring canals were dragged. Shopkeepers and householders were asked to check their premises and an appeal was launched a few days later to catch people who had been away for the holiday period. Police and Fire Brigade cadets searched wasteland around the fairground; 6,000 posters and 5,000 handbills with Lesley Ann's picture on were handed out around the local cafés, pubs, factories, shops and public notice boards. Lesley Ann's father joined in the search as soon as he found out, and her uncle Patrick had 2,000 posters printed and distributed them himself. Six thousand interviews were recorded by the police and, with press and TV coverage, Lesley Ann's disappearance became national news in just a few days.

On 29 December, Lesley Ann's disappearance was first linked in the newspapers with those of Pauline Reade, John Kilbride and Keith Bennett.

On New Year's Eve, Ian and Myra went to David and Maureen's in Wiles Street for a party. Also there were Nellie and Bob Hindley, David's father and David's friend Keith Blinston and his partner, Pauline. At the subsequent trial, Keith gave the following account of the night:

> We got to the house at Gorton where the Smiths were living, I don't know the address but it is in Gorton.
>
> We sat talking and had a cup of tea, having called and collected the baby which was at Maureen's mother's house.
>
> While at Smith's house, about 01:00-01:30 on New Year's Day, Myra Hindley and Ian Brady called. They came in a Mini van. They brought drink with them, whisky, gin, and rum. A bottle of each.

Soon after they arrived, either Maureen or Myra went out, and brought their mother back. David Smith and I went out then and brought Mr Hindley back to the house as well. We had to help him, as he had just had a heart attack, and could not walk, or use his limbs very well.

Later in the morning, about an hour later, Myra took her mother and father home in the van. One of the others went with Myra, but I can't recollect who. It definitely was not Pauline or me. Myra and whoever went with her, apart from her mother and father, returned to Smith's house and rejoined us.

We all stayed there, just talking about general things. About 04:00 Maureen Smith and Pauline went to bed in Smith's house.

Brady and Smith were talking about books, the Bible was mentioned. I was bored. I have no interest in books. About 05:00 I went upstairs and went to bed, leaving David Smith, Myra Hindley and Brady downstairs.

Pauline and I got up about 08:00, Myra Hindley and Ian Brady had gone. Smith was in bed with his wife. Pauline and I left Smith's house, after Pauline had said goodbye to Maureen. This would be about 08:30.

While the drink was flowing, Myra told Maureen that she and Ian had been up to the moors on Christmas Eve and had taken some blankets with them as they had intended on staying the night, but that they ended up going home because it was too cold. Myra then told her sister that she and Ian hadn't done anything on Christmas Day and Boxing Day.

The subject of Lesley Ann Downey was brought up at the party as it was the hot topic of conversation in the area, but Myra and Ian remained poker faced throughout.

The following morning, New Year's Day, Ian and Myra were visited by Pat Hodges. The three of them sat in the living room drinking wine and Pat was reading from the local newspaper, the *Gorton & Openshaw Reporter*. Unbeknown to her, Ian and Myra were recording the conversation on Ian's tape recorder.

After their arrest, the police were able to play back the tape to Pat Hodges, and she was able to recall the conversation and confirm that the other voices on the tape were Myra and Ian.

On one occasion I think Myra operated the tape recorder while I was there. It was played back to me what had been recorded. I did not know that the conversation was being recorded at the time. I did not see any microphone around the place, they never showed me where the microphone was kept.

As Pat read the newspaper about the disappearance of Lesley Ann Downey, she commented that 'that girl from Ancoats' lived near a friend of hers, but told Myra she

135

didn't know her. She is also heard reading out the words, 'Last seen on Fairground on Boxing Day.'

The conversation then turned to something that Ian was playing with. Pat thought that it was a shaver and wouldn't believe that it was a camera when Ian told her so. He explained to her that it was a special German one.

The search for Lesley Ann intensified and the police began treating her disappearance as a murder inquiry. Female officers were sent to schools to lecture children not to talk to strangers and asked them if anyone had been approached by a stranger. Linda Clarke, who went to the fairground with Lesley Ann, appeared on the children's news TV programme, 'Headliners', and made an appeal for all children to help find Lesley Ann. Not long after, Mary Clarke, the neighbour who should have accompanied Lesley Ann and her children to the fair, suddenly moved out of the area.

Two weeks into the New Year, Lesley Ann's mother appealed in the very same newspaper that Ian and Myra read: The *Gorton & Openshaw Reporter*. She said:

> To whoever is holding my Lesley, if only they knew the agony that myself and my family are going through. Her little brothers keep asking when is she coming home … to be parted from a child like Lesley is heart-breaking enough without the agony of not knowing whether she is safe. I plead with all mothers never to let their children out of their sight because they do not know the heartbreak of losing them until it happens.

Her brother, Terry, added: 'Whoever is holding our Lesley, please look after her because she will be very sad and ill being away from Mum.' This, no doubt, gave Myra and Ian a kick to read, knowing that her family were holding on to false hope that their Lesley Ann might be returned to them.

One afternoon in January 1965, Ann and Alan received a message that Mary Waugh, who ran a small grocer's shop on Bradford Road, wanted to see them. When they got there Mary took them into a back room and explained that, together with some of the neighbours in the district, she had organised a collection and in just a few days they had managed to raise £100 – a considerable sum in those days. She also explained that they were having posters printed with Lesley Ann's photo on them and would be distributing them all over Manchester.

In early 1965, Ian and Myra began planning a holiday, and were hoping 12-year-old Pat Hodges would accompany them. Myra asked Pat's mum Elsie if the girl could go with them to Scotland, explaining that while Ian stayed in Glasgow visiting family, she and Pat would camp in the van at Loch Lomond. Although the two households were close (Myra spent hours training Pat's dog, Duke, not to bark constantly), Elsie declined the offer.

By February, the relationship between Ian, Myra and Pat had come to an end. Pat recalled:

> I used to go to 16 Wardle Brook Avenue to take the dogs for a walk. This was about 19:00 every night. These were the only occasions I went to the house without being asked. When I went other times Myra would say, when I took the dogs back, 'Would you like to come down and collect Ian', and she would say, 'I'll call for you at such and such a time.' I kept on going out with Ian and Myra after Boxing Day – both to the moors and to Manchester to collect Ian … I stopped going out with them because two girls came to live near us, just up the road from us, and I started going around with them. They were twins.
>
> Shortly after I had started going around with them, I remember meeting Ian Brady. It was about three weeks after I had stopped going around with Ian and Myra. I had climbed over a wall at the side of the house. A lot of people do that. Ian said that Myra's gran had said that me and my friend Margaret had been in the garden. I said: 'We weren't in the garden.' He said: 'You were.' I said: 'I only came over the wall.' He said: 'Don't let me cop you in the garden again.' He was telling me off. He said: 'I'll break your back if I cop you in here again.' I never spoke to Myra or Ian again after that.

According to Ian, this was the end of the 'Moors Murders'. Years later he commented:

> Contrary to popular perception, the so-called Moors Murders were merely an existential exercise of just over a year, which was concluded in December 1964…. The final ten months of our freedom in 1965 were entirely preoccupied with return to mercenary priorities, reorganising logistics and eradicating liabilities.

He offered the acquisition of the pistols, the sale of the Tiger Cub and Myra's purchase of a new car as supporting evidence:

> All these facts testify that the Moors Murders ended in December 1964, and that throughout 1965 we were hurrying to make up for wasted time, cutting reliance

Pat Hodges.

on others down to the bone, with Myra doubling as driver and sole armed back-up. All we required was a 'mule' to pick up and carry during robberies.

That 'mule' would be David Smith.

At the end of March, Ian and Myra went to Wiles Street to visit David and Maureen, as they sometimes did on a Saturday night. As usual, Ian took plenty of wine with him and it wasn't long before all four of them were drunk. At around 1.00 am Myra was tired and asked Maureen if it was OK if her and Ian stayed the night, as they had done many times before. Myra and Maureen went off to share Maureen's bed, leaving Ian and David to finish off the wine and sleep on the chairs.

As the sisters were getting ready for bed, Maureen mentioned Lesley Ann Downey, and having read in one of the local newspapers that Lesley Ann's mother was now offering a £100 reward for information leading to the whereabouts of her daughter. She said Lesley Ann's mother must think a lot about her to offer so much money. At the subsequent trial, Maureen told the court that Myra had burst out laughing at this.

In July 1965, just over six months since their last visit, Silcock's Wonder Fair returned to Manchester, and Lesley Ann Downey's mother went there searching for her daughter and asking questions.

Chapter 11

Drunken Evenings & Missed Opportunities

By April 1965, Ian and Myra had found a replacement for Pat Hodges in 10-year-old Carol Waterhouse and her 14-year-old brother David, who lived at 11 Wardle Brook Avenue.

Carol remembered that,

> they used to go out of their way to be friendly. I first met Myra when she came round to borrow an onion. My brother David and I used to wash the car out for money and sweets. They seemed so sophisticated. They drank wine. Well, for a working-class person like my mam to be invited in and offered wine was quite something. It just didn't happen.

She recalled: 'They were adults, but not like parents. That's what made them so attractive. She was quiet, he was chatty. He kept his sunglasses on all the time.'

David Waterhouse, in his police statement, said:

> About March or April of this year I got to know a girl called Myra who lived with her grandmother and her boyfriend Ian…. My sister Carol and I used to help Myra wash her car every other week and she gave us a few shillings for this. I saw very little of her boyfriend Ian and he never spoke to me.

Carol Waterhouse added in her statement: 'When we started cleaning the car for her, afterwards she used to go for some petrol and she used to take me to Hyde for some sweets. Ian never came with us then.'

They didn't spend many a fortnight washing Myra's car, however, as on the 5 April Myra sold her Morris Mini van to

Unseen photograph of Carol Waterhouse.

'Kings of Oxford'. Ian also sold his motorbike, and it is believed that they were trying to save enough money to buy guns for a bank robbery, but disaster was about to hit the family.

On 25 April, Maureen and David's baby, Angela Dawn, passed away from Bronchitis. David tore the hospital room to pieces in anger, and Maureen was a hysterical mess. She later explained that she had put the baby down in her cot for an afternoon nap and when she went to wake her later, she couldn't.

On the way home from the hospital, David, Maureen and her mother Nellie called round to Wardle Brook Avenue to tell Myra what had happened. She and Ian were sat watching a BBC programme about the Shakespeare's *Richard III*; Ian was nonplussed about the news and secretly told Myra that he was angry they had interrupted his viewing. Myra took David, Maureen, Nellie and her grandmother over to her uncle's in Dukinfield to try to digest the news.

When they got back home from Maureen's uncle's, David ironed and packed all of Angela Dawn's clothing and belongings into an old suitcase, walked down to the railway embankment and threw it over the fence. He said that he felt 'a pain so acute' that it made him vomit.

When he got home, his actions caused a huge row with his wife Maureen, who felt that he was being heartless, and she went to stay with her mother and father in Eaton Street. David didn't want to be in the house where his daughter had just died, so he went to stay with his grandfather in Aked Street. Two days later the baby, in her coffin, was taken to Aked Street, where David and Maureen put her in the parlour. They would never recover from such a big blow at such a young age.

Various relations went to the house to pay their respects and to say goodbye to the baby. David struggled to cope with the emotions of the day and ended up going out to the pub and getting more drunk than he ever had before. While this was going on, Myra picked up her new car, a surf blue Austin Mini Countryman.

The following day, that of the funeral, Myra and Ian called round. Myra went into the house and took some flowers and a card, which read: 'Another flower in God's garden.' Myra had tears in her eyes and her mascara had just started to run as she looked down at the baby and said: 'Oh God, look at her.' David later recalled how this was the only time he ever saw Myra show any emotion. She borrowed some make up from Maureen and asked her not to say anything to Ian about her crying. Ian stayed sat in the car outside, refusing to go into the house or even acknowledge David as he stood at the door smoking a cigarette. Just as David took the last drag, Myra emerged and hugged Maureen, while nodding at David. She got into the car, without even looking at Ian, and David recalled: 'They drove away facing the windscreen like a pair of crash-test dummies.'

The following weekend, with Myra's grandmother again in Dukinfield visiting her son, Myra and Ian invited David and Maureen over for some drinks. They thought they could take advantage of the situation and they needed David in order to help with their planned future robbery activities.

The two couples had been out on the moors (according to Maureen they had been to Woodhead) early in the afternoon and they returned home around 9.00 pm, where they drank more wine and sat down to play cards. As usual with Ian and cards, he soon lost his temper and blamed the crass stupidity of everyone else. The four of them just sat there in silence for a while.

Later on, around 10 30 pm, Ian jumped up out of his chair and insisted everyone go back up to Saddleworth Moor. They got in the car, girls in the front and men in the back as usual, and they stopped off on the way to buy more wine, before continuing on their journey. Maureen remembered Ian suggesting that he and David should go for a walk. He said he wanted to show David the reservoir and how nice it looked at night with the moon shining on it. They walked off in the direction of John Kilbride's grave.

David recalled that Ian was very drunk, but that he could walk straight and knew exactly where he was going. Ian suddenly stopped, grabbed David's hand, and said: 'There it is. There is the reservoir, doesn't it look beautiful?' David recalled that it was cloudy and he could only just make out where the stretch of water was. They went back up to the car and drove off. The foursome had been to the moor for less than twenty minutes. It was only months later, when he was taken up to the spot by police, he realised he had been practically standing on John Kilbride's grave.

Roughly three weeks later, David and Maureen were fully reconciled and he moved in with her, Nellie and Bob for the next two months. To get back to some sense of normality, Maureen also returned to her former job as a part-time machinist with her mother at a factory in Gorton.

It was from here on in that Maureen and David played an even more common role in the lives of Ian and Myra. During the drunken evenings, after Myra and Maureen had gone to bed, Ian spoke more and more about robberies and crime to David. He told David that he was sick and tired of working and David agreed with him, saying that he hated working too and was fed up of being between jobs all the time. Ian asked David what he considered to be a 'big job' and David replied: 'Robbing a supermarket with a van.' Ian laughed at his suggestion and told him that he wasn't thinking big enough. 'There's only one big job and that's a bank!'

Ian confessed to David that he and Myra had two guns and that if he wanted him to, he could arrange for David to see them and even try them out. The following Saturday morning, Ian and Myra picked David up and drove out to Saddleworth Moor. Myra stayed in the van while the two men started to walk over the moor. Ian knew exactly where he was going and after about ten minutes they came to a valley, well hidden from the road. They stopped about 20 yards from where an old railway sleeper lay on the ground. On top of it was an old oil drum and Ian drew out the Webley .45 from his holster and fired twice at the drum, hitting it once.

He then gave the gun to David, who missed with his two shots. Ian took it back and swapped it for the Smith & Wesson .38. David shot twice with it and hit the drum once before Ian reloaded the Webley .45 and emptied half of the bullets into the drum with his right hand, swapped the gun into his left hand and hit it three more times. He'd clearly been practicing.

He then went and picked up all of the empty shells before the two men walked back to the car. On the way Ian asked David if he was impressed, and David said he was. They drove to 'The Wagon and Horses' pub in Gorton, where the three of them had a few drinks, and Ian told David that they were going to use the guns on the bank job that he was planning. At one point, Myra joked: 'I wonder what would happen if we had Mo as a watch.' All three burst out laughing. There was never any proof, or even suggestion, that Maureen knew anything about either the planned bank jobs or the disappearance of the children.

Ian and Myra took David back to the moors on two further occasions, and both times to different areas. David later recalled that one of the locations was where the body of Lesley Ann Downey was later discovered. David got better each time he practiced with the guns and Ian talked about the bank robberies more and more, while Myra and Maureen waited in the car.

Ian told David that guns would be carried on the bank job and that he mustn't be afraid to use them if the need arose. He also told David that he was going to nick the ends of the bullets, which meant that they would make a small entry hole but a large exit hole. David told him that he didn't mind carrying a gun, but he didn't want to use live ammunition. Ian just laughed at him.

Ian showed David maps and drawings he had made of the streets surrounding the bank that he had been watching 'for years'. He told David that he knew how the money left the bank and how many men were employed to guard it. Sometimes the money was carried on foot and sometimes a car was used. He told him that Myra's job was to be the getaway driver. At the trial, David recalled:

> We were talking about the robbery, and what sort of robbery it would be, and the way we were going about it, and what risks we would have to take and he mentioned that guns would be carried, one by Myra and one by himself, and that they would be loaded with live ammunition. He called it a safeguard, an insurance, in case there was any obstruction, and then they would be used with the live ammunition in them.

He said that when they next spoke of the robbery: 'I had a small starter pistol that made a big bang. I showed it to Ian and he was impressed by the noise. He still insisted that the two guns should have live ammunition.'

Ian and Myra set about taking advantage of the young couple. Maureen and David were happy to be given free drinks as it helped them to numb the pain of their daughter's death. In the words of the prosecutor at the later trial of Ian and Myra: 'Brady's interest in Smith went far beyond ordinary friendship. The association was one of steady corruption of a youth by a man … Brady was interested in murder and wanted to make Smith a student of murder.'

Shooting practice wasn't the only place that Myra and Ian took David and Maureen. They often went out on evening and weekend excursions to various places including Derbyshire's Snake Pass, Whaley Bridge, Woodhead and Saddleworth Moor – always stopping at places they seemed to know well.

In early spring, 9-year-old Anne Ashmore was walking along Armdale Road, Dukinfield, with her 11-year-old sister, Susan, when a Mini Countryman, identical to Myra's at the time, glided up alongside them and, as the window slid open, a man's voice from the passenger seat called: 'Come here…' As the girls turned, the voice continued: 'Can you tell me…' There was something in the tone that made the girls immediately uncomfortable and the girls, remembering their mother's advice not to talk to strangers, ran away as fast as they could. Anne later recalled: 'My mother is convinced to this day that it was them. To think I might have been one of the victims….'

As a major coincidence of the case, Anne Ashmore later married Danny Kilbride – the brother of murdered John Kilbride.

It seems that Ian and Myra were still looking for more 'sacrifices', despite what Ian later said. In addition to what Anne Ashmore claimed, during the school summer holidays, 10-year-old David Gray would earn some money for his mother by delivering coal from a barrow around the streets near to his home. He recalled an encounter with Ian and Myra that left him chilled to the bone. 'I'd counted up my tips and it was 14s 6d. 14s was for my mother and I had 6d I could spend all on me.' He decided to go straight to the local sweet shop. 'I stepped into the shop thinking

Rare image of Myra Hindley and her dog. Photograph from the 'Tartan album'.

I could spend anything with that sixpence. I was just lost in thought. The shopkeeper was talking to an elderly lady and she just mentioned that there was a guy looking at the barrow outside the shop.' He stepped outside to check on his barrow when he encountered a man he later identified as Ian Brady.

> He wore a suit, white shirt, open collar, dark hair. He looked almost like a typical pop singer of the day. I had no idea who he was and there was a car parked at the curb and there was someone in the car. He turns and says, 'We're police officers. We're investigating meter robberies – and he'd heard the money in my pocket jangle – and he said, 'We have reason to believe that you could help us with our inquiries. We want you to come to the police station with us.'
>
> I asked him to show me a warrant card. He told me, 'You watch too much telly, sonny.' I must've stepped back, because I nudged the door and the shop door's bell jangled, and the driver of the car said, 'Come on Ian, we've gotta go.' [The interview doesn't record whether the driver was female or male] The guy just casually stepped towards the car, got in the car and they drove off. I'm stood there for a long time, afraid to move. I just remember, for the next few days, being really afraid.'

As the summer wore on, the longer days meant that the drinking sessions on the moors and at other places could go on for longer. At the trial, Maureen described the four of them going up to the moor:

> We went round the area where the bodies were found. We just got out of the car and had a walk around. We went down a slope and right across the moors, Brady and my husband went in the direction of the reservoir and Myra and I went in the opposite direction. We were out of sight of each other. Myra and I eventually came back to the car after about quarter of an hour. My husband and Brady had not returned when we got back. They eventually returned to the car after about 20 minutes. Nothing was said by either of them or Myra as to what they had been doing. When we had all got back into the car we went back to Hattersley. I mean to the accused's home. We stayed there all night. I am not sure but I think we went out again that evening. I think it was the same night that we went to Blackpool.

David Smith recalled one of these occasions when the four of them went up to the moors. He said that he was lying on his back on a blanket when Myra suddenly straddled him, pinned him down and held his arms above his head, while Maureen was laughing her head off at his predicament.

Above left: Myra, Ian and Maureen.

Above right: Maureen, Myra and Ian outside Wardle Brook Avenue.

Right: Unseen photograph of Ian Brady found in his 'Tartan album'.

Below: Myra Hindley at Ladybower Tor, near the Snake Pass.

Above left: Unseen photograph of Myra Hindley and her sister, Maureen.

Above right: Rare photograph of Myra and Maureen.

Left: Myra on Hollin Brown Knoll.

In this photo, Myra is wearing the same clothes as she is seen wearing as she squats looking at John Kilbride's grave. Here she is obscuring a sign behind Hollin Brown Knoll that was a marker for the recently laid trans-Pennine methane gas pipeline. The trench for the gas pipe was open at the time Keith Bennett disappeared and it is possible that his body was thrown in as it was left open and unattended at night. When the detectives inquired about uncovering the pipeline, they were quoted a cost of £10,000,000.

David Smith later recalled that he and Maureen had also been taken to a pine forest by Ian and Myra in the Peak District of Derbyshire. He thought it a completely random place to be taken, as to get there Myra had parked in a layby and they'd had to climb over a low, crumbling, stone wall, down a steep, rocky hillside and through some pine trees to a clearing with a tree that had fallen due to a lightning strike. It was 200 yards from the road.

Ian & Myra in the Peak District.

Above left: Ian Brady in a forest in the Peak District.

Above right: Ian brady holding a rifle and posing for a photograph.

Right: Unseen photograph of Ian Brady and his dog.

Above left: Unseen photograph of Ian Brady and his dog.

Above right: Ian Brady.

Left: Unseen photograph of Myra Hindley with dogs in the forest.

Below: Myra Hindley with her dog in the forest.

DRUNKEN EVENINGS & MISSED OPPORTUNITIES

On Myra's 23rd birthday, Maureen, David, David's father and their dog Bobbie moved into a third-floor flat in a new tower block that had been built less than 300 yards from Wardle Brook Avenue, called Underwood Court. Due to the close proximity, the all-weekend and all-night drinking sessions increased.

They had been rehoused on compassionate grounds, as Maureen had written to the council asking for different accommodation as they did not want to return to Wiles Street, where their daughter had died. David's father was working away a lot, and he eventually moved in permanently towards the end of the year.

Myra and Ian were not always happy to see the married couple though. Around this time there was a polio scare and mass inoculation was handed out to the population on sugar cubes. David recalled an occasion one weekend when Ian greeted them in a good mood, relaxed and friendly. Myra, however, was in a bad mood and went through to the kitchen to make a cup of tea. When she returned, she began to rant about the Polio scare and asked David if he'd had his vaccination, to which he replied that he hadn't. At this, Myra had gone crazy and shouted, 'You fucking moron! You stupid bastard! You could be carrying it, killing us all, and what happens then, eh? *Eh?* Go on, get out, get the fuck out of my house right now, you fucking moron!'

Above: David and Maureen.

Right: Underwood Court.

Below: David Smith.

David shouted back at her, telling her that it was up to him whether or not he had the vaccination, and Maureen began to cry. Myra screamed at him again to 'get the fuck out of my house', and threw a scalding teapot at him. David managed to duck as the teapot smashed against the wall behind him. Maureen bolted for the front door and David rose to his feet ready to fight Myra. At that point, Ian told Myra to 'cut it out', but she stood her ground, ready for a fight. Ian sternly told her to 'fucking stop it now'. At this, Myra backed down and David left to find Maureen, who was waiting for him outside at the end of the short path. They walked home, with Maureen still crying and David still raging.

That night, just as David and Maureen were getting ready for bed, the entry phone rang. Maureen answered it and buzzed the caller up. It was Myra. She was now dressed smartly and had her hair perfectly done so it was clear to him that she and Ian Brady had been out for the evening. She said that 'Ian's told me to come and say that I'm sorry.' David grudgingly accepted the apology and Myra and Maureen embraced each other. Myra told them that Ian had got some drinks in and invited them back to Wardle Brook Avenue.

The threesome then made their way over to Wardle Brook Avenue, where Ian smiled at them as he opened the door. On the table were three bottles of red wine, white wine and whisky, along with two plates of biscuits. Brady put his arm around David and guided him to a chair while telling him to help himself to the food. The drink quickly flowed and Myra and Maureen spoke of their childhood while Ian put the record player on and they listened to Glenn Miller. Mr Braithwaite from next door was on David's mind as the music was played louder and he spoke of this to Ian, who said: 'Fuck them niggers and monkeys next door and fuck the Jews as well.' David joined in: 'Yeah, dead right, fuck them, robbing Jew bastards.' Ian then put on one of his Hitler speeches and they joked in agreement to what he was saying, even though David couldn't speak German. Myra and Ian then rolled around on the carpet in hysterics as the Goons were played on the record player. This was one of their favourites, but David didn't find them funny. He was drunk and that was all he was interested in that night.

During these drunken evenings, Ian asked David if there was anyone in particular that he really hated and would prefer dead, just as he had to Myra years before. David had quite a long list, but top of it were his former best friend Sammy Jepson, and another called Tony Latham, as both had been mouthing around the local pubs that they'd been sexually involved with Maureen.

Ian asked him questions about both, such as the size of their families and where they lived and deduced that out of the two, it would be safer to kill Tony Latham, as Sammy Jepson lived too close. Ian then told David that if he was to kill Tony Latham for David, then he would need a photograph as Tony was a large man and Ian wanted the element of surprise. They agreed that David could use Ian's Polaroid camera and that the best place to photograph him was when he was in his local pub, where David could engage him in conversation and try to get a photograph as friends might do.

A couple of days later Myra drove Ian and David along Hyde Road and pulled up at the back of 'the Flea Pit', a local cinema. David got out and went into The Dolphin pub, where he saw Tony sitting with a group of friends. David joined them and the camera quickly became the topic of conversation. David found it easy to get a photograph of Tony, but the only problem was the shutter, which made an odd noise when he took the photograph.

He went into the toilets and locked himself in the cubicle and opened the back of the camera to check the film and immediately spotted his mistake – there was no film in the camera. David later recalled: 'I wanted him dead, and I went out to buy new flash bulbs especially for that night. I just didn't check to make sure that I had film in the camera.'

He made his excuses and left the pub, getting the bus home and worrying that Ian would think he was incompetent; when he went over to Wardle Brook Avenue the following day Ian wasn't upset but did ask if Tony had been at all suspicious. Nothing else was mentioned about killing Tony Latham after that. This may have been because Ian and Myra were distracted with Carol and David Waterhouse. They were taken up to Saddleworth Moor by the murderous couple, to the area known as Shiny Brook, where Myra later insisted that Ian had killed and buried Keith Bennett.

When the investigation into Keith Bennett was reopened in 1986, Carol said that the police failed to contact her in relation to the enquiry. She recalled 'broad yellow stones you can walk up the middle of the stream on'. When she later went back with author Duncan Staff, Professor John Hunter and his assistant Barrie Simpson – the former head of the West Midlands Police murder squad – she took them down Hoe Grain to the confluence with Shiny Brook and turned right, towards Wessenden Head Reservoir. Not being able to find where her and her brother had been taken, the foursome went back the way they came when Carol said: 'This is it! You can walk up the centre of the stream on the rocks. David and I stood in the middle and Ian took photographs. We all had a picnic together on the bank.' She was unable to remember the exact spot where they had picnicked but it was as they were heading towards the waterfall where Myra had posed for two pictures.

David Waterhouse recalled in his police statement:

> On August Bank Holiday my sister Carol told me that Myra had asked her to go for a run on the moors and I could go as well. My mother agreed to this and Myra, Ian, Carol and myself set off in Myra's car about 13:30.
>
> We drove through Stalybridge, Mossley, Greenfield and along the A635 up on to the moors.
>
> We stopped on the roadside and all four of us went for a walk along Shiny Brook Clough. We had a picnic at a large rock called Greystones.

Left: Myra Hindley
near the spot where
Keith Bennett is
believed to be
buried.

Below: Myra
Hindley near the
spot where Keith
Bennett is believed
to be buried.

We then walked further along the Clough to near Wessenden Reservoir. Ian took some photographs and after a while we went back to the car.

We then drove over the hills to Glossop and on to Mottram where we took some more photographs at a farm. Then we came home. Nothing unusual took place that day. This was the first time I had met Ian.

About a fortnight later I went with Carol and my mother to Myra's house to see the slides of the photographs we had taken on the moors and some others.

His sister Carol's statement said:

I've only been to the moors once with Myra and Ian and that was on August Bank Holiday this year, 1965.

Myra asked me if me and David would go to the moors with them and told me to ask me mum.

Me mum said we could go, so we all left Hattersley about 13:30. Me and David sat in the back of the car and Ian and Myra sat in the front. Myra drove there and back. We drove through Stalybridge, Mossley, Greenfield and along the A635 up on the moors.

We stopped on the roadside and went for a walk along Shiny Brook Clough. We had a picnic of egg and tomato sandwiches and tea and sat by a big rock called Greystones. Ian took some photographs of our David and me and Myra. We walked along for a bit, near to Wessenden Reservoir. The place we went to is the one I've already shown the police.

Then we drove over the hills to Glossop and on to Mottram. We stopped near a farm and Ian took some more photographs of us three with a horse.

We didn't see anyone at the farm and I don't think they knew them really.

From there we went on to Werneth Low to have a look at the monument. We just drove past it.

While we were on Werneth Low, Ian took photographs of the Hattersley Estate. Then we went back home. It was about 17:00–17:30 when we got home.

That was the only time I ever went on the moors with Ian and Myra. Myra didn't ask about it again.

Myra didn't do anything wrong that day to me or David or any other time.

I've only been in their house twice. Once was when they invited Mum in to have a look at some photographs. I went in with her and our

David. We all sat in the living room and Ian showed us the photographs of us that he took on the moors on August Monday. He put them on a screen. This was one evening. That evening they gave me mum a glass of wine, but they didn't give me or David any.

Another time, Myra called me in and gave me a blouse. That's the one I've given to the police.

Those are the only times I've been in Myra's house. I've only been in the living room. We never went in when we used to clean the car or anything. Myra used to bring the stuff out to us. She never asked us in.

I've never talked to Ian very much at all and didn't know him very well. I was more friendly with Myra.

When we went on the moors, I walked with Myra and our David walked with Ian.

Myra nor Ian never gave me anything to drink at any time.

Also, they never did anything wrong to me.

By September 1965, David Smith was out of a job again and running low on money. The bank job was looking better and better to him, so Ian instructed him to keep a watch on a particular bank, Williams and Glynn, on Ashton Old Road. He later recalled that Ian and Myra drove him down to the bank, which was opposite Grey Mare Lane market, before driving off. He had his notepad and pen with him and noted down any movement that could be useful in regards to the robbery. He was there from 8.30 am until closing time before catching a bus back to Hattersley and going straight to see Ian. He thought they were getting close to the robbery taking place, but when he got to Wardle Brook Avenue and showed Ian his work and answered a couple of questions, Ian simply tossed the notebook onto the coffee table and walked off to the kitchen.

David then told how that night all four of them took part in their heaviest drinking session to date. Myra and Maureen went up to sleep in Myra's bed, leaving Ian and David alone downstairs. David heard a noise and looked up, only to find Ian holding the Webley .45 and pointing it straight at him. Ian didn't think that David believed him when he said he could kill and told David, in no uncertain terms, to look down the barrel of the gun and then slowly look into Ian's eyes, before telling him 'You're about to die.'

Ian pulled the trigger, but nothing happened. David then watched him disengage the chamber and one bullet fell out. David had been that close to being murdered. Ian then said to him: 'That's how easy it is, Dave. You just have to press the fucking trigger.'

Ian then loaned David books to read, along the lines of the ones he had given to Myra during the early days of their relationship, such as Geoffrey Gorer's *Life and Ideas of the Marquis de Sade*, and de Sade's pornographic novel *Justine*.

Ian (whose IQ was 170) knew David wouldn't fully understand what he was reading and asked him to write notes about anything he found interesting. When they were found in Ian and Myra's suitcases during the later investigation, they showed that David agreed with many of Ian's views. One of the notes David had written said:

Three authors, three books, three different dates, all writing about sexual pleasure in perversion, De Sade's 'Justine' is by far the superior book, as he deals solely with perversion, not only sexual but also logically. De Sade's works are about pleasure and life, the pleasures obtained from life. Every man and woman is one of two things, a masochist or a sadist, only a few practice what they feel, the remainder because some organisation says it is wrong, and they fear some mighty indestructible force, rather sit back and rot away, until the end. These people enjoy what they are told to enjoy, they feel the way they are taught to feel, they live the way they are taught is the proper way of living; they breed the way one man tells them to breed. They live by laws that were made thousands of years ago, and they fear the God they are taught is kind and loving. Perversion is the way a man thinks, the way he feels, the way he lives. People are like maggots small, blind worthless fish bait. Rape, is not a crime, it's a state of mind, murder is a hobby and a supreme pleasure, God is a disease, a plague a weight around a man's neck, a disease which eats away his instincts, God is a superstition, a cancer, a man made cancer, which is injected into the brain in the form of religion, an infant is taken from its parents and for the first time in its life it is forcibly introduced to the cancer; from the age of 5 to 16 its mind is forcibly fed with trash. A parent is faced with two forms of education C of E and R.C., both feed their subject's religion, at least twice a day for eleven years, this form of mass brainwashing must, in the long run, do considerable damage to the subject. Many are captured in the pit of life, few escape as clean as they entered, these unquestionably are the sane, the perverts against mass brainwashing. Take your place in this hole as quietly as possible, you are the pervert, people disagree with you so you must be wrong! But remember they are merely machines repeating and listening to what the masters feed them. You are your own master. You live for one thing, supreme pleasure in everything you do. Sadism is the supreme pleasure!!! Look around, watch the fools doing exactly what their fathers did before them. The book, they live by the book!!!

On 18 September, Ian and Myra went up to Scotland for a week's holiday, returning on 26 September. Ian decided that the time was right and finally introduced Myra to his foster family, the Sloans, but rather than stay with them, they opted to stay in a hotel instead.

On the first night, Ian went out and told Myra she couldn't go with him, so she spent the evening alone in the hotel. When he returned, he told Myra that he had been to see his foster-sisters, May and Jean. 'I told them I have a girlfriend, and that I would probably stay with her for the rest of my life', he later recalled.

The following day Ian introduced Myra to the family, before the couple went and toured Scotland.

They then travelled on to St Monans, leaving the car near the cemetery and walking to Newark Castle.

Above left: Ian Brady in Scotland.

Above right: Myra Hindley in Scotland.

Myra Hindley at St Monans.

Above: Myra Hindley in the remains of Newark Castle, Fife, Scotland.

Right: Ian Brady in the remains of Newark Castle, Fife, Scotland.

In his first letter to Myra after their trial, Ian recalled the trip:

> Firstly we reached the round, stone structure on top of the cliff, the daisy-strewn valley diving down and up to the castle.
>
> We progressed at a leisurely rate, your photo and mine taken on a resting place of my childhood 17 years in the past.
>
> Off towards our fated night's resting spot, the Y-sign street, the meal, the manoeuvring about till situated in an ideal spot, the couple with their children.
>
> The final setting down, the warmth as we lay together, the radio playing and wine sipped lazily as the summer dusk darkened around our glade, the solitary bird calls dwindling to peaceful silence, the soft beat of our hearts leading us to blissful slumber.

They then went to Dunning, but Ian was frustrated by their inability to find the cottage he had stayed in with the Sloans as a boy. As they left the village, they spotted Maggie Wall's cross at the roadside and they stopped to have a look. It was a monument to where Maggie Wall was burned to death in 1657, because locals suspected she was a witch. Ian took the last photos he was to ever take of his homeland and he and Myra took it in turns to sit on the witch's monument.

It was almost midnight on 26 September when Ian and Myra got back from Scotland. They went straight over to Underwood Court to see David and Maureen and took bottles of wine with them. When they arrived, David was in bed having spent the evening drinking heavily and then vomiting. He had learned that his father, who still partly lived in Wiles Street and kept the dogs there, had arranged to have his dog, Peggy, put to sleep because it was going days without being fed while he was away working. David recalled:

> Ian walked into the bedroom and he asked me if I was all right. Then he turned round and he said, 'It's that bleeder who should have got the needle and not the dog'… Myra went out of her way to try and save the dog. She drove all the way down to the dogs' home…. She was just too late. The dog was in the house on its own because my father was working in London.

It was around an hour-and-a-half later that Maureen and Myra went to bed, leaving Ian and David talking about the race riots in Los Angeles. When the women were

Above left: Unseen photograph of Myra Hindley at Maggie Walls' monument.

Above right: Ian Brady at Maggie Walls' monument.

asleep, Ian switched the conversation to robbery again and David thought that he was obsessed with carrying out the bank robbery, as he had spoken of not much else to him for the past few months.

It was on this occasion that Ian first mentioned to David that he had killed before, and asked David: 'Are you capable of murder? I've done it … I've done two or three. You and Maureen have been sat near one.' David didn't answer, so Ian continued to probe.

> You think I'm lying, don't you? You think I'm a lying cunt, but it's been done, I've killed, more than once. Ach, but you don't believe me. Maggots, they're all fucking maggots…
>
> I've got photographic proof, and you've sat on one of the graves. Get the bastards over 16, that's the easiest way, they're nothing to the police then, just some sad kid missing, runaways who've fucked off to London and the bright lights, file and forget. Jews, winos, queers – who gives a shit about them? They're fucking germs and worth fuck all, even the police see them as numbers and know the world's well rid. Who's gonna give a fuck about some dirty little shirt-lifter? Hitler had the right idea, that's just my point, he had the right fucking idea…

Still, he didn't believe that David believed him, so he carried on: 'Well, I have. There are two ways I do it. I pick a street and sit in the car waiting until it is quiet and nobody about, then, when someone comes along, I just get out and kill them.' He told David that if he chose this way then he had to wash his shoes, brush down his clothes, wipe all his buttons and make sure there were no dog hairs in the car. He then told David that the other way was 'to pick someone up in town and take them home and then do it. Then I bury them on the moors – I've got photographs to prove it. The ones that are sixteen to twenty are the best because the police don't bother much. They just list them as missing persons.'

In one of his later police interviews, David talked about this conversation and added: 'I didn't know whether to believe him because he didn't give any reason for wanting to kill people apart from the bank job, although he sounded quite serious about it.'

When he had sobered up the following day, Ian could tell that he had made a mistake in telling David that he had killed as he didn't get the response that he had hoped for. That evening he and Myra went out in the car to the Derbyshire hills near Buxton and had a frank discussion on whether or not to kill David Smith. Ian was unhappy that David had failed in his mission regarding Tony Latham which, in turn, had denied him the opportunity to show David that he could kill. He was also fully aware that David could get drunk and say the wrong thing to the wrong person and implicate both himself, but more importantly to him, Myra. Ian recalled:

Myra outside her home.

'I offered to just kill him, you know, like in a film. We were just sitting, discussing it as if we were discussing some triviality. But it was real.'

Myra was concerned about the effect it would have on Maureen and that concealing their responsibility would be a big problem, but Ian told her that in time an opportunity would present itself. Myra vetoed the idea and so David's life was spared. This angered Ian, who years later blamed Myra. 'It was always Mo this, and Mo that. She didn't want to hurt Mo.'

Ian later gave an account of the perfect opportunity which arose a few days later in which he could have killed David. He told how Maureen and David had had a huge argument because Maureen had discovered she was pregnant again; Maureen went to Wardle Brook Avenue and asked Myra to drive her to their mum's. After they had gone, David came over and asked to see Maureen – and this is when Ian said he would have killed him.

He said that he would've waited until Myra came back, then offered to take him out in the car. Once on the move, 'Head out of Manchester. Take the .38 Smith and Wesson. Blow his head off. Mo some days or weeks later would have enquired if we had heard anything from him. Nothing.'

He was certain that the trail would never have led to him and Myra. David would have just gone on record as a missing person, and because of his age, the police wouldn't be too interested. They would've just put it down to a matrimonial row and not a police matter. Myra told DCS Topping, in the mid-1980s, that they had discussed killing David Smith, but it was because he and Maureen were always arguing and Ian had told her that he had grown tired of David's constant domestic difficulties.

On Saturday 2 October 1965, Ian and Myra were working at Millwards until lunchtime. As Myra left work on her break, she bumped into Anne Murdoch, her former Ryder Brow rounders teammate. Anne recalled:

I hadn't seen Myra for a long time. Then I heard from a lad she used to hang about with at school that she was working at Millwards. It was a rotten, scruffy-looking place near the big launderette. On this particular Saturday, I put my 2-year-old daughter Sharon in her pram and went shopping at Gorton Cross. I met up with two other lasses I knew from school, Mary and Marge. They had tots as well. When we were walking home, I spotted Myra coming out of Millwards, on the other side of the road. She saw the three of us with our toddlers and

shouted sarcastically, 'By God, you've all ended up with good jobs.'
I shouted back, 'You've got an even better one there.' She snorted at
me, 'You do my job then and I'll take the babies for a walk.' I didn't
answer. She went off, clicking down the street in her high heels.

After work, Myra called at Mottram police station and informed PC Reeves that she
had sold her .22 rifle to a woman in Stockport and wished her Firearms Certificate to
be modified. The officer asked Myra if she'd completed the Firearms Certificate of
the person to whom she had sold the rifle; Myra said she wasn't sure of the address,
but would find out.

The officer retained Myra's Firearm Certificate but she didn't return to the
station as promised. The police made their own enquiries and Mrs Freda Harvey,
a 48-year-old headmistress, was traced as being the person who had bought the
rifle. The purchase had been negotiated through George Clitheroe – Freda Harvey's
brother-in-law and a co-worker of Myra. Harvey had applied for a variation of her
own Firearm Certificate issued by Stockport County Borough Police to acquire the
rifle, but the Chief Constable refused the application a week later on the grounds
that authorisation should have been obtained before the rifle was bought. The police
took possession of the rifle and destroyed it after the trial. Freda Harvey said in her
statement:

> My brother-in-law came home from work and said that a woman named
> Myra, who worked in his office, had a .22 rifle for sale … I do quite a
> bit of shooting with .22 rifles and I wanted one of my own…
>
> On Saturday 2 October 1965 I gave my nephew £5 and he went
> down to my brother-in-law's place of work, picked up the rifle from
> Myra, paid her and brought the weapon home. It remained in the house
> until Wednesday 6 October when my brother-in-law tested it. The next
> day, Thursday 7 October, he took it to work to return to Myra until my
> certificate was varied.

Chapter 12

Edward Evans

On Saturday 2 October, Ian and Myra went to Underwood Court at around midnight, taking six bottles of wine with them. By 2.00 am Myra and Maureen were asleep in Maureen's bed, leaving Ian and David to finish off the drink and once again the talk soon turned to murder. Ian said: 'You don't believe I'm capable of it, do you? I tell you I've done two or three.' David was more interested in the free wine than what Ian was saying, but he persisted: 'You don't believe I have killed people but I have, and another will be done... It won't count – I'm not due for another one for three months.'

He then told David how he took Pro-Plus to stimulate him and then again outlined his two preferred methods – waiting in a car and jumping out on someone or taking someone back to his home and killing them there. He then explained how he eradicated any sign of possible evidence, and said it was easier if the murder was committed in the house as he could take his time cleaning up afterwards. He also told David about making a working list which would be ticked off and covered everything that he had been wearing. Then he told David about his golden rule, which was to remove everything – 'writing materials, books, photographs, tape recordings' – beforehand.

Clearly, Ian and Myra had been discussing their next move, and Ian felt that until David believed that he could kill, he couldn't fully indoctrinate him nor trust him to not squeal if they pulled off a bank job and Ian or Myra had to kill someone in the process. They formulated a plan over the coming days at work and on Tuesday 5 October, at around 7.30 pm, Ian went alone to Underwood Court. He told David to get all of his books on sadomasochism (and notes on those books) together, as well as anything else that could possibly be illegal, and take them over as soon as possible to Wardle Brook Avenue, telling him that he would hide them. David did as Ian instructed, thinking that plans were afoot for the bank robbery. Ian then left and David told him that he wouldn't be long. He wrapped up the books, such as *Mein Kampf*, *Tropic of Cancer*, *Kiss of The Whip*, *Justine* and *The Life and Ideas of Marquis de Sade*, along with his notebook and written notes on these books, into a bundle and walked them over to Wardle Brook Avenue, along with another nine books, a cosh, his starter pistol and the blank shells that went with it.

It was 8.00 pm when David arrived at Wardle Brook Avenue. Myra opened the door and welcomed him in, and David put the bundle onto the table in the living room. Ian carried it straight upstairs, leaving David downstairs talking to Myra and her grandmother. He emerged again after 5-10 minutes and was carrying two suitcases, one blue and one brown. David's police statement then takes up the story:

> Ian, Myra and I went out of the front door of 16 Wardle Brook Avenue. Ian was carrying the two suitcases while Myra climbed over the front fence which runs alongside the front garden. She went down the bank to her Mini Traveller [David identifies the car incorrectly here. It was the Mini van purchased in Autumn 1964] which was parked on the roadway and opened the back door. Ian passed one of the suitcases over to her and then I passed the other one over to her. As I was passing mine over Ian said: 'Don't drop it, else it will blow us all up.' When the suitcases had both been passed over Myra put them in the back of the Mini.
>
> Ian and Myra got in the Mini and drove off. Neither of them said where they were going or what they were going to do with the suitcases. I walked home then.
>
> Although Ian didn't tell me what was in the suitcases I was fairly certain that it was the tape recordings he had of German and the books and writings I had taken round. I knew he had a lot of tape recordings of German and music but I did not know of any others.

Maureen confirmed that David was only gone for about fifteen minutes. Myra and Ian drove to Manchester Central Station and deposited the suitcases in the 'left luggage' area. When they got home, Ian picked Myra's prayer book out from the bottom drawer of the dresser and tucked the tickets for the suitcases down the spine of the book, before placing it back on the shelf.

Before the couple went off to work the following morning, Wednesday 6 October, Ian gave Myra another record as a gift, this time 'It's All Over Now Baby Blue' by Joan Baez, who was one of Myra's favourite singers. While at work at Millwards, Ian and Myra spent the day finalising their plan for the evening, where they planned to pick up another 'sacrifice', only this time they decided to involve David Smith, to see if he had what it took to join them as a force.

When Ian and Myra got home from work that day, they took the dogs out for a quick walk and bumped into Carol Waterhouse. Ian had his camera on him and wanted to use up the last of the film and so he took the last photograph he would ever take.

David Smith had spent the whole day worrying. He was sat at home in his flat wondering what he was going to do about a note that had been posted through his

Rare colour photograph of Carol Waterhouse with Myra. This was the last photo Brady took.

letterbox that morning warning him that he was in arrears with his rent and that having a dog at the property was against his tenancy agreement. The note read:

> I want £14 12s.6d. at the town hall, Saturday, or I shall take legal proceedings. Mr Paige is doing his job and if that dog is not out of the building tonight I shall have you evicted. If there are any more complaints of Teddy Boys and noise I shall take further action.

The part about 'Teddy Boys' was explained by Maureen at the trial. She said that the night before the note arrived, David had seen two people that he knew. It was raining and they had nowhere to go so he let them stay the night in the flat. When they left the following morning the caretaker of the flats, Mr Paige, had seen them.

As Ian was taking the photograph of Carol Waterhouse and David was at home having dinner and planning to visit Ian and Myra for advice on his situation, Edward Evans, a 17-year-old apprentice engineer at Associated Electrical Industries Ltd, was leaving home at 55 Addison Street, Ardwick, where he lived with his parents Edith and John and siblings Edith and Allan. He was heading for the centre of Manchester where he hoped to meet a friend in the pub before going to watch a football match.

He went into one of his usual pubs, 'Auntie's Bar' on Oxford Road, where he got talking to the landlord, George Smith. George remembered that it was unusual to see

EDWARD EVANS

Evans on his own, as he had always been with friends on previous occasions. After a short while Evans left and headed in the direction of Oxford Street and on to Old Trafford to watch the match. That was the last time he was seen alive in public.

Edward had thought he was going to Old Trafford to watch Manchester United v Helsinki with his friend Michael Mahone, but in the end he went alone. Michael later recalled: 'On the previous Sunday he was at our house for tea. His last words were:

> I'll see you on Monday or Tuesday'. As he never came and, therefore, we had made no proper arrangements to go to the game, I never turned up to meet him. I wasn't feeling too well at the time – I had my leg in plaster – and wasn't sure that he would turn up anyway.

Michael spent a long time blaming himself for what happened next to Edward and made himself so ill that he had to spend three weeks in hospital with a perforated ulcer.

It was 8.00 pm when David called at Wardle Brook Avenue to speak to Ian and Myra. Myra answered the door and he explained what the situation was regarding the note through his door that morning. As she was telling him in no uncertain terms that neither she nor Ian could help him out financially, Ian appeared over her shoulder and told David to come in. He had heard David's predicament and a plan was formulating in his mind.

As David went into the house, Myra's grandmother was also there. David recalled that Ian wasn't really listening to what he was saying as he was busy putting his cufflinks in a fresh clean shirt. Myra was also busy putting the finishing touches to her make-up and sorting her hair out. It was clear to him that they were going out for the evening and Myra soon packed her grandmother off to bed.

With both Myra and Ian knowing full well that a 'sacrifice' was to be made that night, Ian changed the plan slightly and told David not to worry as he would get him the money. They came up with a plan to 'roll a queer'. This was a common term at the time, and as homosexuality was illegal, it involved a straight man going somewhere quiet with a homosexual man and then robbing him. The homosexual man wouldn't go to the police, as he would then have to admit that he had intended for homosexual acts to take place and would likely be arrested. David was led to believe that Ian would carry this out with the help of Myra and they would then give him the money he needed for the rent. Little did he know what Ian and Myra really had in store for him.

Edward Evans.

At 8.30pm Ian, Myra and David left the house; Ian and Myra drove off and David walked home. When he got home a few minutes later, he lied to Maureen that he would get the money for the rent tomorrow and that Ian and Myra had gone out for the night. He didn't give her any information about where the money was actually going to come from. Pleased at this news, Maureen wrote a reply to that morning's note. It stated:

> Dear Sir,
> My husband and I are at work, and because we are not on the best of terms with Mr Page, [*sic*] I shall personally deliver the rent to the Town Hall this Saturday morning without fail.
>
> Mrs M Smith
Flat 18

As Ian and Myra drove towards central Manchester, the car in front of them hit a dog which had run out across the road. Myra pulled over and both she and Ian got out to try to find the dog which had run off. They found it cowering and whimpering down an alleyway and were checking it for injuries when the owners caught up with them. Myra offered to take the dog to the vets, but the owners said that it wasn't necessary. They got back in their car and Myra drove on, parking outside Manchester Central station. Ian got out and went off on the hunt by himself, telling her that he shouldn't be too long. Myra was annoyed that Ian had partly changed their plan to suit David and she sat in the car stewing by herself.

Just a couple of minutes after Ian had left her, Myra was scared by a knock at her window. There stood a policeman, asking her to wind her window down. When she did, he told her that she was parked illegally on a double yellow line and that she needed to move on. Myra kept her cool, apologised to the officer, and explained that she was waiting for her boyfriend who should be there in a couple of minutes. The officer told her that he would go and have a walk around the block, but if she was still there when he came back then he would have to give her a ticket.

A minute or two later, Ian appeared with Edward Evans in tow and, according to Myra, he introduced her to him as his sister. Myra also told the police that Edward introduced himself to her as 'Eddie' and told her and Ian that he was an apprentice and had just been to see Manchester United play. He was meant to go with his mate, Jeff, but he had to stay home to look after his sick mother. (Edward had meant to go with his friend Michael, so note the contradiction in Myra's account).

Ian later told how he had met Edward standing at a milk-vending machine nearby. Edward had gone to the station after the match hoping to get something to drink but had arrived just a minute or two too late and the buffet bar was shut. Ian and Edward got talking and Ian said that he offered Edward a drink back at his house and a lift home afterwards, which Edward accepted.

When the three of them drove back to Wardle Brook Avenue Ian opened a bottle of wine and he and Edward sat in the living room while Myra let the dogs out. They tried to create a relaxing atmosphere, so Myra went upstairs and put more comfortable clothes on. Ian then motioned for Myra to go and get David Smith. As she left, Ian made it clear to her that there was going to be some sexual activity between him and Edward. It has never been established whether Edward was a homosexual, as Ian always claimed.

Maureen and David were in bed when Myra rang the buzzer at 11.30 pm. They had been in bed for about half an hour when Maureen got up and answered the call. When she realised it was her sister, she told David who put on some trousers and went into the living room. He recalled what happened when Myra made it to their front door:

> Earlier that evening, at Wardle Brook Avenue, she was ultra-dressed up. Full war paint, tight dress, hair sprayed into a stiff beehive – far beyond the smart secretary look she normally wore. But when she turned up at our flat, she had on an old skirt with the hem hanging down, a cardigan and scruffy pumps. The lacquer had gone from her hair and her make-up was smudged. Something had happened before she came to us. She looked a proper mess. It wasn't even that she'd got changed out of her evening gear into something more comfy – she looked a right state … the expression on her face was … well, she wasn't smiling, put it like that. She was edgy, very edgy.

What happened next was told by Maureen:

> Myra asked if I would give a message to my mother. She said to tell her she'd see her tomorrow. I asked her why she'd come round so late. She said she'd forgotten to come round earlier on. She asked David if he would walk her home because all the lights were out. David said he would walk her home and would only be a couple of minutes.

Myra was lying about the streetlights being out; the police later consulted Mr Leslie Wright, the Assistant Lighting Superintendent for Hyde, who confirmed they were lit.

While David finished getting dressed, Myra asked her sister how she was going to find the money to pay the rent. David overheard and told her that they were going to borrow the money from his father. When David was dressed, he picked up his dog's stick to take out with him. The stick had string wrapped around the top of it and a loop for David to put his wrist through. He always took the stick with him when he went out by himself, mostly to use as a deterrent to anyone who may be wondering the streets looking to pick a fight.

Above: David and Maureen Smith.

Left: Unseen photograph of the kitchen of 16 Wardle Brook Avenue.

According to David:

> We got almost to Myra's house. I intended to leave her there, then she said, 'Ian has some miniature wine bottles, come and collect them now.'
>
> As we got to the front door Myra stopped walking and said, 'Wait over the road, watch for the landing light to flick twice.' I didn't think

168

this was unusual because I've had to do this before, while she went in to see if Ian would have me in. He's a very temperamental sort of fellow.

I waited across the road as Myra had told me to, and then the light flicked twice so I walked up and knocked on the front door. Ian opened the front door and he said in a very loud voice for him, he normally speaks soft: 'Do you want those miniatures?' I nodded my head to say yes and he led me into the kitchen which is directly opposite the front door, and he gave me three miniature bottles of spirits and said, 'Do you want the rest?'

When I first walked into the house the door to the living room, on my right, was closed. After he'd put the bottles down Ian went into the living room and I waited in the kitchen.

The following account of what happened next is taken from Myra's, David's and Ian's accounts of Edward Evans's murder. It was clear that Ian and Myra could have killed Edward by themselves, but Ian felt he needed to show David that he was not a liar and that he could kill. If David went along with what was to happen next, then Ian felt that they would be as entwined as he was with Myra, and therefore would be unable to back out of any crime that Ian then suggested.

Edward was sat on the sofa in the living room talking to Myra when Ian went in on the pretence of getting the miniatures for David. He went behind Edward, and in his own words:

> I picked up an axe that had been placed out of sight and I brought it down with great force on to Evans's head. I was aiming for the back of his head to kill him instantly, but he turned round at the last split second and the blade of the axe bounced off the crown of his head. It should have taken only one hit.

David heard a 'really high-pitched' scream, followed by a couple more and then Myra shouted 'Dave, help him', very loudly.

Ian recalled: 'Evans screamed out as I rained down blows to his head. He was writhing on the floor to protect himself. Myra was in the room watching. The two dogs were excited and barking in the kitchen.'

David's account:

> When I ran in, I just stood inside the living room and saw a young lad. He was lying with his head and shoulders on the couch and his legs were on the floor. He was facing upwards. Ian was standing over him, facing him, with his legs on either side of the young lad's legs. The lad was still screaming. He didn't look injured then, but there was only a

small television light on, the big light was off. Ian had a hatchet in his hand, his right hand, he was holding it above his head and then he hit the lad on the left side of his head with the hatchet. I heard the blow, it was a terrible hard blow, it sounded horrible. They were heavy blows, they were not blows aimed in a frenzy. They were almost positioned.

The young lad was still screaming and he half fell and half wriggled off the couch on to the floor, on to his stomach. He was still screaming. Ian went after him and stood over him and kept hacking away at the young lad with the hatchet. I don't know how many times he hit the lad, but it was a lot, about the head, the neck, and the shoulders and that. Brady had hold of him and was hitting him. He was holding him by the jacket.

David then moved from the door to the fireplace, and the attack was going on no more than two feet in front of him.

Brady was stood astride the lad and the lad groaned. Brady had his left hand on his knee. He was half bent and he lifted the axe up and hit him on the back of the head with it. He waited while the lad groaned again and then hit him with the axe. He hit him on the back of the head. The lad stopped groaning. He was making a gurgling sound.

One of the blows had grazed Myra's head and another had cut David's leg, but both were only superficial wounds. David recalled that 'there was blood all over the place, on the walls, fireplace, everywhere.'

Ian recalled: 'Myra's grandmother had been woken up by the noise and shouted down to ask what was happening, Myra shouted something in reply but I was too occupied to know what it was.' Myra had in fact told her grandmother that she had just dropped something on her foot, but that she was ok and that she should go back to bed.

Remarkably, Edward Evans was still alive after fourteen blows from the axe. Ian then recalled: 'I went into the kitchen to fetch a length of electrical flex. I put a cushion over his head and strangled him by wrapping the wire round his neck.' David recalled that Ian was pulling the cord as tight as he could and calling Edward a 'fucking dirty bastard.'

As Edward drew his last breath, the room fell silent. Myra then stepped over the body of Edward Evans and could see that Ian had hurt his ankle. She was only concerned with Ian's condition. He then told her: 'It's done. It's the messiest yet. It normally only takes one blow.'

This was the point of no return. David had two choices: to run and hope that Ian and Myra didn't catch him before he had the chance to get to safety, or to stay and see it through – whatever 'it' may entail. He weighed up his options and decided that he wouldn't get out of the front door before Ian would catch him and he was under no illusions that Ian would have beaten him to death with the axe too, so he decided to wait where he was.

Ian then told Myra to go and fetch some warm, soapy water and some old cloths or clothes, before lighting himself a cigarette and pouring a glass of wine for David and himself. 'I handed the axe to Smith so that his fingerprints were on the handle', Ian later recalled. He then said to David: 'Feel the weight of this. How did he take it?' He then looked down and told David that his stick had got a bit wet, and David realised that he must have dropped it when he first entered the room. It now had blood from Edward on it.

With the body still lying on the floor, David and Ian sat on the sofa, shoulders almost touching, each drinking wine and smoking a cigarette. David could see, through the serving hatch, Myra in the kitchen 'organising bowls and cloths for the clean-up'. Ian asked her how the dogs were, and Myra replied that they were OK, just a bit quiet. Ian then said: 'The fuckers could smell the blood, couldn't they, eh? I was worried they would get too excited.' He then turned to David and said: 'We'll finish up in here and then get a cup of tea down us. How does that sound?' David agreed.

Myra then called through the hatch to say that she was going to pop upstairs to check on her gran. A minute or two later Myra appeared in the room and told them that her gran was OK and that she told her that the noise was because she had dropped a record player on her toe.

She went out into the kitchen and then went straight back into the living room with a mop, bucket, a bowl of warm, soapy water and some old cloth. She stepped over Edward Evans's body and put it all down by the fireplace. Ian then pointed out to David: 'There's a hole in the wall next to the fireplace, put your finger in that. I felt the fucking thing bounce of his fucking head, that's when it swung back into the wall…'

The three of them then set about cleaning up the room as best they could, David doing so for fear of what would happen if he didn't. Ian recalled:

> I opened Evans's wallet and found a green National Insurance card giving his personal particulars. His occupation was given as 'engineer'. There was also a pay packet and an old letter from a girl named Wendy in North Wales. I put the wallet, the axe and Evans's shoes in a carrier bag with other rubbish. I had sprained my left ankle and realised that this would delay the disposal of Evans's body. We would have to put the corpse in the empty bedroom upstairs until tomorrow.

At this point Myra came back into the room, carrying bed sheets, sheets of polythene and an old blanket that she had got from her bedroom. She and Ian then spread them out on the floor.

Ian told David to grab the body by the ankles, while he lifted the shoulders, and they put it on the polythene sheet. Ian then untied string that was on the end of David's stick and used it to tie Edward's hands together across his chest. Myra was cleaning the floor where Edward had lain at this point. David recalled this moment years later:

> I put my hands on Edward. His blood is very thick and slippy, and it's everywhere. Ian holds his feet and dumps him on the sheets on his back, head covered, trousers undone. Ian uses my string to tie him roughly, using a lot of force, pressing down on him with his knee and pulling the string as taut as possible. 'Get the bastard's legs and push them back.' I grab one leg and the other drops sideways out of my hands. Ian stands above me: 'Use your weight, I need them right back.' I hold Edward's knees together and bend his legs, pushing them against his chest. 'Fucking hell!' I turn my head away; the smell is full in my face and putrid. [As often happens at death, Edward's bowels had relaxed and David got a lung full.] I keep the pressure on Edward's legs and Ian uses the string to truss him up until he's in the shape of a ball, head forward to meet his knees. We wrap him in the blanket and then it's time for a break.

Ian asked David if he knew Edward, as they were both the same age and from the Ardwick area of Manchester, but David replied that he didn't.

Unseen. Edward's National Insurance card.

They then got back to it and wrapped a grey blanket around the bundle that was now Edward Evans, carrying him in a cradle fashion up the stairs. As they struggled to carry him, Ian joked: 'Eddie's a dead weight.' David recalled: 'Both he and Myra thought it was bloody hilarious. I didn't see anything to laugh about.'

While Ian and David were carrying the body up the stairs, Myra was just in front of them and held her gran's bedroom door closed. When the body was in Myra's bedroom, they pushed it under the window while Myra ran back downstairs and grabbed the carrier bag containing the hatchet and other items that Ian had put in there. She then put the bag next to the body. Ian recalled:

> I was wearing a shoulder holster and a gun that was hindering my movements. I took them off and put them into Myra's empty bedroom. This was a fatal mistake. I should have asked Smith to carry Evans single-handedly. I would then have no reason to put the gun upstairs. It would have been under the divan bed downstairs and I could have used it at the arrest.

The bedroom door was then locked and all three of them went downstairs to finish clearing up. Ian recalled: 'It took the three of us almost three hours to clean up the blood in the living room, using buckets of soapy water and rags. The carpets were the most troublesome.'

However, it wasn't just blood that they were clearing up. The attack had been so ferocious that they also picked up pieces of hair, skin, skull and brain. The three of them sat and drank cups of tea in the same room in which Edward had just been murdered. While Ian told David how he had hit Edward with the axe, Myra was tending to his injured ankle and put a cold compress on it. He then said to Myra: 'How the fuck did he take that?' She replied: 'I don't know, love, but you could see the blow register in his eyes, he didn't know what hit him, I was looking right at him and he didn't know a thing. You should have seen the look on his face. His eyes registered astonishment.'

The discussion then turned to how to get rid of the body. Myra spoke to Ian, mainly for David's benefit, in reference to the burial of Lesley Ann Downey, and said:

> Do you remember that time we were burying a body on the moors and a policeman came up? I was in the Mini with a body in the back. It was partitioned off with a plastic sheet. Ian was digging a hole when a policeman came and asked me what the trouble was. I told him I was drying my sparking plugs and he drove off. I was praying that Ian wouldn't come back over the hill while I was there.

Ian quickly wrote out a hasty 'Working List'. There was absolutely nothing to connect Edward Evans with Wardle Brook Avenue, so they decided that there was no need to dispose of the body immediately. They considered burying Edward Evans in Penistone or waiting a couple of weeks and disposing of him on a fire during bonfire night, and even considered burying him in the small back garden, but there were too many windows overlooking.

Oddly, the best plan they could come up with was for David to meet Myra the following evening outside Millwards, where they would drive to his grandfather's house and collect the pram that was Angela Dawn's and had been stored there since she passed away. Ian would stay off work for the day with his ankle, and make sure that Myra's grandmother didn't try to access Myra's bedroom. They then planned to take the pram to Wardle Brook Avenue and put the bundle that was Evans's body in it and wheel it out to the car, where they would then drive up to the moors and bury it.

It was now 3.00 am and the conversation had started to wane. David thought that now was his chance to get out of the house alive. When he suggested that he had better be off, otherwise Maureen would be worried, Ian agreed and saw him to the front door. David feared for his life still and was afraid that Ian and Myra would come after him, so as soon as he was out of sight of the front door, he ran as fast as he could back to Underwood Court.

As Ian went back inside, he and Myra began chain-smoking. Both were concerned that David would tell Maureen what had happened. Myra suddenly remembered that the chain needed to be locked on the steering wheel of her car. She said she couldn't face the darkness, so Ian went out and limped down the grass slope to secure the car. As he stooped down to put the chain on the steering wheel his wallet fell out of his pocket and he picked it up and put it on the dashboard. He then forgot to put it back in his pocket once he had finished. The disposal plan was in his wallet.

Ian then climbed back up the slope, and he and Myra fell asleep for a couple of hours on the sofa where Edward had first been struck with the axe. It was to be the last night they would spend together.

Chapter 13

Arrest

As Ian and Myra began to settle down for a couple of hours sleep, David arrived home. He undressed and got into bed with Maureen, but after a few moments got up and rushed to the bathroom where he was violently sick. This woke Maureen up and she went to see if he was OK. It was then that she spotted David's bloodstained clothing on the floor; she was concerned it was his and that he might be hurt. He assured her that the blood wasn't his and that he was OK, but then told her he had seen Ian and Myra kill a man. Thinking that David must be drunk, she made him a cup of tea to help sober him up and talk sense, but he just kept repeating himself. He had seen Ian kill a man with an axe and Myra was involved right up to her neck.

Drinking the tea made David vomit even more, and once he had nothing left to bring up, he told her exactly what had gone on that night when he had arrived. They discussed what was best to do and decided that they had no choice other than to go to the police. David was scared for his life and didn't want to go out again in the dark, so they waited until daybreak.

It was at 6.00 am when David and Maureen Smith left their flat, barely three hours since David had escaped from Wardle Brook Avenue. Afraid that Ian and Myra might be watching them, David armed himself with a large kitchen knife and a screwdriver in case he needed to defend himself and his wife and they made their way to the nearest telephone box, which was 300 yards away on Hattersley Road West.

At 6.10 am David telephoned Stalybridge police and asked for a car to be sent to them, but didn't explain why. He told the officer that he would explain everything once he was safely at the station. Scared for their lives, he rang back a couple of minutes later to make sure a car was being sent. When they told him one should be with them shortly, David and Maureen hid behind a privet hedge in case Myra or Ian were out looking for them.

Five minutes later, a police car pulled up outside the phone box and David and Maureen jumped in, telling the policeman just to drive to the station. PC John Antrobus remembered that David was very agitated and very upset as he tried to get into the locked police car the moment it pulled up. Once safely inside, David immediately handed over the knife and screwdriver, which were put in the glove box, and the policeman then drove them to Hyde police station. Neither David nor Maureen said a word during the journey.

Once they were safely inside Hyde police station, David told the police everything, and Superintendent Bob Talbot was called in. He asked David to repeat what he had told the other officers, so he told him about the events of the previous evening and also that there were guns in the house at Wardle Brook Avenue.

DC Ian Fairley was one of the first officers to be involved in the case: 'I was called out about half past seven in the morning to be told that there had been a murder committed at 16 Wardle Brook Avenue, Hattersley the night before. The body was still believed to be in the house and also the occupants were in possession of firearms.'

At 8.20 that morning, Superintendent Bob Talbot, DC Fairley, DS Alex 'Jock' Carr and other officers took up posts around Wardle Brook Avenue, just as Myra was making her gran a cup of tea in bed and Ian was writing a note to his boss, Tommy Craig, to explain that he wouldn't be in work.

A traffic car was put at Godley, near the railway arches, and another car was set up near Mottram, in case Ian and Myra made a break for it. At 8.40, Superintendent Talbot knocked on the back door of 16 Wardle Brook Avenue and because there was a threat of firearms on the premises, he had borrowed the uniform of a driver who was delivering bread to some of the properties. Myra opened the door and saw the word 'Sunblest' on his white coat. She told him: 'You've got the wrong house, we have Mother's Pride.' Superintendent Talbot asked her if her husband was in, and Myra replied that she didn't have a husband. The policeman then told her: 'I am a police superintendent and I have reason to believe there is a man in the house.' She retorted: 'There is no man here', but Superintendent Talbot and DS Carr pushed past her and went into the kitchen. They told her that they were not satisfied with her answer and wouldn't leave the house, so Myra had no other option than to tell them that 'He's in the other room in bed.'

The officers walked into the living room and found Ian Brady wearing nothing other than a vest. He had just finished writing the note to his employer. The note read:

Tom,
Sorry I could not phone yesterday, my family are at Glasgow this week. I was crossing [the] road in town last night when someone on a bike came around the corner and knocked me down, except for a few bruises. I was alright until I got up this morning, my ankle would not take my weight. I must have weak ankles or something. If it's no better tomorrow, I'll have to see [a] doctor.

Ian

DS Carr could see that Ian had a cloth wrapped around his ankle as he swung his legs over to sit on the edge of the sofa but that he also removed it when he got dressed. Myra later recalled: 'I'll never forget his face when I took the police into the living room … it was expressionless, as it often was, but I saw him almost shrink before my eyes, helpless and powerless … it was all over.'

The officers took a look around the room and noted that everything looked clean and there didn't appear to be any sign of the struggle that David had told them had occurred less than ten hours earlier. Ian asked Superintendent Talbot what this was all about and was told, 'I have received a report that an act of violence took place here last night and we are investigating it.' At that moment Ian and Myra both knew that David had reported them.

Ian didn't say anything, perhaps angry with himself that his disciple had turned on him, but Myra, who was standing behind the detectives, said: 'There was nothing wrong here.' She told them that Ian, herself and her grandmother were the only people who lived in the house. Superintendent Talbot told her that they wanted to search the whole house, and Myra didn't object, so he asked a couple of other officers in to the house to help.

Myra was probably still hoping that Ian had his gun under the sofa, not realising that he had left it in her bedroom upstairs, and that he would use it to shoot the officers so the pair of them could make a run for it, as he had always told her he would do if they were ever cornered. If it came to it, he would shoot her and then himself, rather than let them be caught.

DC Fairley was one of those called in to the house: 'When we got into the living room there was a man in his underclothes in the bed in the lounge and that turned out to be Ian Brady. He was told why we were there and Bob Talbot and Alex Carr went to search the upstairs.' They went into the bedroom that was directly above the living room first, where Myra's grandmother was still in bed, before then going into the bathroom. When Myra's grandmother asked her what the police wanted, Myra told her that they were there because she had committed a traffic violation and that she was to stay in bed.

Superintendent Talbot then tried to get in to Myra's bedroom but it was locked and Myra told him that it was locked because that's where her guns were kept and that the key was at work. Superintendent Talbot then told her to get her coat and the police would take her to her work to collect it, but Myra insisted that it was not convenient for her to go then, despite her being about to leave for work when the police had knocked on her back door.

DC Fairley suggested they should get into the bedroom by forcing the door. Superintendent Talbot again asked Myra to get her coat so they could get the keys, but she just stared at Ian. He didn't react so Myra said to him: 'Well, you had better tell him.' Ian stood up and told the officers: 'There was a row last night, it's in the back bedroom.' He then told Myra to give the detectives the keys.

Superintendent Talbot and DS Alex Carr went upstairs, unlocked the door to Myra's bedroom and found the body of Edward Evans. Upon closer inspection, the detectives noticed some blood-stained books on top of a blanket and then saw a human foot poking out from underneath. DS Alex Carr recalled: 'When we went upstairs at Wardle Brook Avenue we saw in the corner of the bedroom was this body all wrapped up like you wrap up a chicken or a turkey and it turned out to be the body of Edward Evans.'

Beside the body was a carrier bag with a hatchet inside. On the floor was a stick which was also covered in blood. The two revolvers were discovered in a cardboard box, both fully loaded.

Ian told the detectives that 'Eddie and I had a row and the situation got out of hand.' Unbeknown to the police, he had just given Myra the story she was to stick to. Superintendent Talbot told Ian he was taking him to the station and cautioned him. Ian nodded and replied: 'Yes, I know.' It was at this moment, as he was putting on his shoes that he reached under the sofa for his revolver. He had already decided to shoot his way out of trouble but, as he felt some more, he remembered that he had moved the gun upstairs after the murder the previous night.

Myra was not arrested but she demanded to go to the police station with Brady. Superintendent Talbot agreed that it was a good idea as he had a few questions for her anyway. Then she suddenly remembered her gran. She said that she was going to have to get one of the neighbours to look after her and asked her grandmother

Above left: Myra Hindley's bedroom. The body of Edward Evans is under the blanket with books on top by the curtains. That is also the bed where Lesley Ann Downey was assaulted.

Above right: Unseen. The axe used by Ian Brady on Edward Evans.

Left: Unseen. The blood splatter on the cushion found next to Edward Evans' body.

to tell anyone who asked that she'd 'run someone over'. The detectives agreed and Myra took her grandmother over to the Hills around the corner. No one at the Hills believed Myra's story as her car was parked, undamaged, outside her house and there were far too many policemen around for that.

Granny Maybury never spoke about what happened the previous night. We will never know what she heard or even may have seen as Edward Evans was murdered and his body carried up the stairs. She certainly heard something, as Myra said she shouted down the stairs asking what the noise was and Myra had told her that she had dropped her typewriter on her foot (note the contradiction to her earlier account where she claimed to have dropped a record player on her toe). Did she take some more sleeping pills and go back to sleep and not hear another noise that night? Did she try to get out of her room as her granddaughter held the door shut? We may never know.

David was taken back to Wardle Brook Avenue by two detectives. They parked their car just below the house and he was asked to identify Ian and Myra as they passed. Ian passed first and their eyes met – confirmation for Ian as to who had shopped him to the police. Myra then followed a few yards behind and stared David straight in the face as she passed.

Myra was driven to the police station in the back of a panda car and she remembered Ian's words to her: 'Say nothing!' She had to take her dog Puppet with her as the police needed the house cleared so they could search it; it's not clear what happened to Lassie at this point. They were taken to Hyde police station where, at 9.33 am, Ian dictated a statement to DS Carr and DC Fairley – and the blackening of David Smith's name began. It read:

> I, Ian Brady, wish to make a statement. I want someone to write down what I say. I have been told that I need not say anything unless I wish to do so and whatever I say may be given in evidence.
>
> Last night I met Eddie in Manchester. We were drinking, then we went home to Hattersley. We had an argument and we came to blows. After the first few blows the situation was out of control. When the argument started David was at the front door, and Myra called him in. Eddie was on the floor by the living room door, and David hit him with a stick, and kicked him about three times. Eddie kicked me at the beginning on my ankle, and there was a hatchet at the fireplace which I hit Eddie with. After that the only noise Eddie made was gurgling, then Dave and I began cleaning up the blood. The gurgling stopped, then we tied up the body, that is Dave and I and nobody else, and Dave and I carried it upstairs. We sat in the house till three or four in the morning, then we decided to get rid of the body in the morning or the next night.

As can be read from the above statement, as well as implicating David in the murder, he was also insistent that Myra was not involved. He knew that he would go to prison now, but he didn't want Myra to be sent down too, so in all subsequent interviews, he tried to make it seem that Myra was either not involved, or knew very little about his crimes. As David was taken back to Hyde police station, he was taken in through a side door and had to walk directly past Myra, who was standing in a corridor with two officers. He was shown into a side room where his wife Maureen was waiting with their dog and some officers.

The neighbours at 14 Wardle Brook Avenue, Pheonix and Tessa Braithwaite, were questioned as to whether or not they heard anything the previous evening. They told the police that they had heard banging, shouting and one or two screams but thought it was just a lovers quarrel and had gone back to sleep.

At 10.40 am DC Derek Leighton, an official photographer for the Cheshire Constabulary, arrived at 16 Wardle Brook Avenue where he photographed the interior and exterior of the house.

He was still there at 1.15 pm when the Home Office Pathologist, Dr Charles St Hill, removed the coverings from the body of Edward Evans and took photographs of the position of the body and other objects in the immediate vicinity. He found the body of Edward Evans trussed up and the head severely damaged, with a piece of electric flex around the neck. There was a blood-stained letter, addressed to Edward Evans that identified him.

Myra was not allowed back to her house or into her car, so she went to stay with her aunt and uncle. DS Alex Carr recalled: 'To our mind Brady was the main culprit … we arrested him and took him out of circulation straight away. It was five days later that I arrested Myra Hindley in Hyde police station.'

Unseen police photograph of the living room at Wardle Brook Avenue.

ARREST

Unseen police photograph of the Living Room where Edward Evans was murdered at 16 Wardle Brook Avenue.

Between 11.45 am and 1.10 pm, David Smith was interviewed and made his first full statement to the police:

At 11.30 pm last night I was at home with my wife Maureen Smith. That's Wednesday night, October 6, 1965. Me and my wife live alone, and we were in bed, but we were awake. It's the flats we live in, and the internal telephone rang from the main door to our flat and my wife Maureen answered the telephone. Maureen said 'It's Myra'. That's her sister, who lives at 16, Wardle Brook Avenue, Hattersley, and then she said that Myra sounded worried. Maureen pressed the button which unlocks the main entry door, where Myra would be standing using the 'phone, and two or three minutes after, Myra knocked on our flat door and I let her in.

She seemed normal at the time. She gave a reason for coming to our flat, but to tell the truth, I can't remember what she said, but it was unusual in itself for her to be round our place at that time of night, but I can't remember what reason she gave for coming, the wife will probably know, because Myra did say something to her which I didn't quite catch. She, Myra that is, was only there for about 10 minutes at the most, and then she asked me to walk home with her to 16 Wardle Brook Avenue, as she was a bit scared of walking about on the estate in the dark. I'd got dressed after I got out of bed just after she'd phoned from the main entrance of the flats, and I left our flat with her about quarter to twelve midnight, or about that time.

181

My wife Maureen stayed in our flat. I told my wife Maureen that I wouldn't be long. I left our flat with Myra, and we walked across, I think it's Pudding Lane and then into Wardle Brook Avenue. It's not far, it only took us about 3 or 4 minutes to walk it. We got almost to Myra's home at 16, Wardle Brook Avenue, I intended to leave her there, because she was almost home and in sight of her house, and then she said 'Ian has a few miniature wine bottles for you, come and collect them now.' Ian is Myra's boyfriend, but he lives at 16 Wardle Brook Avenue with Myra and her grandmother.

He then told how Myra asked him wait across the road and to look out for the light to flick twice. He did this and when he saw the signal he knocked on the door and Ian opened up. Ian then asked him loudly if he wanted the miniature drinks bottles and was shown into the kitchen, directly opposite the front door. His statement continued:

When I first walked in to the house, the door to the living room, which was on my right standing at the front door was closed. After he'd put the three bottles down in the kitchen, Ian went into the living room and I waited in the kitchen. I waited in the kitchen about a minute or two, and then suddenly I heard a hell of a scream, it sounded like a woman, really high pitched. Then the screams carried on, one after another, really loud. Then I heard Myra shout 'Dave, help him', very loud. It sounded as though she was shouting from the living room, I rushed into the living room, as I didn't know what was happening, the living room door was wide open.

He then told how he ran into the living room and saw Ian standing over the youth, who was on the floor, but couldn't tell if he was injured because the only light was coming from the TV. As recounted earlier, he saw Ian hit the youth multiple times with a hatchet. His statement continues:

I didn't do anything once I first entered the room, and saw all this, I couldn't. I felt my stomach turn when I saw what Ian did, and some sick came up and then it went down again. I couldn't move. When he, Ian that is, was hacking at the lad, they got close to me, and one of the blows Ian did at the lad, nearly hit me and grazed my right leg. I remember, Ian was swinging about with the hatchet, and one blow grazed the top of Myra's head. I never heard any conversation between the lad and Ian, and I never heard the young lad say anything.

After Ian stopped hitting the lad, he was lying on his face, with his feet near the living room door leading into the hall. I could hear like a gurgling noise in the lad's throat. When I saw Ian first that night, when he gave me the miniatures in the kitchen, he seemed normal enough, and there was nothing unusual about him that I could see. I didn't even know the lad was in the living room. I remember now, when Ian was hacking at the lad with the hatchet towards the end, he was kneeling down over the lad, and when he stopped hitting the lad, he dropped the hatchet and I remember he got a cover off one of the chairs, and wrapped it around the lad's head. I was shaking, I was frightened to death of moving, and my stomach was twisting, I couldn't move, there was blood all over the place, on the walls, fireplace, everywhere.

Ian never spoke a word, all this time, and he got a cord, I think it was electric wire, I don't know where he got it from, and he wrapped it round the lad's neck, one end of the cord in one hand, one end in the other, and he then crossed the cord and pulled and kept pulling until the gurgling stopped in the lad's throat. All the time Ian was doing this, he was strangling the lad, Ian was swearing, he was saying 'You dirty bastard'. He kept saying that over and over again, Myra was still there all this time, just looking. I moved away from the lad and Ian to the other side of the room. Then Ian looked up at Myra, and said something like 'It's done, it's the messiest yet. It normally only takes one blow.'

Myra just looked at him, she didn't say anything at all. Ian got up then, the little light was still the only one on, and he lit himself a cigarette up, after he'd wiped his hands on a piece of some material, I don't know what it was. Then Ian turned the big lights on and he told Myra to go into the kitchen and get a mop and bucket of warm water, and a bowl with soapy water in it and some rags. Myra did that and Ian turned to me then and said 'Your stick's a bit wet' and he grinned at me. The stick he meant, was a stick I'd taken with me when I went with Myra from our place. It's like a walking stick, and the only thing I can think is that when I rushed into the living room at first, I'd dropped it because it was lying on the floor near the young lad, who had finished up lying near the living room door. Then Myra came in then with the bowls of water and that, she didn't appear upset and she just stepped over they young lad's body, and placed the bowls of water and that on the carpet in front of the fireplace.

Then Ian looked at me like, and said 'Give us a lift with this mess.' I was frightened and I did what he said and I helped to clean the mess up. I was wiping the blood off the walls and floor and Myra and Ian were doing the same. No one spoke while this was going on, then after we'd cleaned up most of it, Ian, he was speaking to Myra said, 'Do you think anybody heard the screams?' Myra said 'Yes, me gran did.' The old grandmother was 78, she meant the old grandmother who lives with them, and Myra said 'I told her I'd dropped something on my toe.' Then Myra left the living room, I think she went either in the kitchen or upstairs, and while she was out, Ian offered me a bottle of wine. I drank it because he handed it to me, and my stomach began to settle a bit then. The young lad was still lying on the floor. Myra came in with a white bed sheet. I think Ian had told her to get one, and a lot of pieces of Polythene, fairly big they were, and a large blanket. Then Myra and Ian laid the blanket, sheet and pieces of polythene out on the floor and then Ian told me to get hold of the lad's legs, which I did and Ian got hold of the lad's shoulders and we lifted him into the sheets and blankets. The only reason I did this was out of sheer bloody fear. We placed the lad in the middle and then Ian came out with a joke, he said 'Eddie's a dead weight', and both Ian and Myra thought it was bloody hilarious. I didn't see anything to laugh about. I was too interested trying not to look at the lad. When Ian said Eddie, I understood that was his name. On the stick I had, the one I mentioned to you, there is some bound string, and Ian took the stick and unwound the string, and cut it into lengths, about 2-3 foot in length and he gave me one end, and he tied the lad's legs up in a funny way, so that the lad's legs were together, and bent up into his stomach. Then Ian carried on tying the lad up, it was like a maze of bloody knots.

He didn't speak while he was tying the lad up. Then he told me to get hold of the ends of the white sheet, and I had to help him while he folded the corners together, with the lad in the middle, and then he tied the corners together. Then he made me do the same with him with the polythene sheets, and he tied them and last of all came the blanket. He didn't tie that, it was like a kind of cradle. Myra was mopping up all this time. Then Ian told Myra 'Go upstairs and hold your gran's door to', and then he said to me, 'Lift your end up' and between us we carried the young lad upstairs, into Myra's bedroom and we put him down near the window. Then we came downstairs and I saw a wallet lying on the floor. Ian picked it up and pulled out a green sort of card and said, 'That's his name, do you know him.' I looked at the card and saw the name Edward Evans. I didn't know him. I saw a pair of shoes lying on the living room floor as well as the wallet and Ian picked them up and a couple of letters that were lying there, and put the shoes, wallet and the letter in a shopping bag. He was looking round and picked the hatchet up, gave it to me and said something like 'Feel the weight of that, how did he take it.' I said nothing and gave it him back. I was frightened of him using it on me. He put the hatchet in with the rest of the things

I think, that's the wallet and that, and he took them upstairs. I don't
know where he put them. Myra was still clearing up and by this time
the house was looking something like normal. I didn't turn my back
on Ian at no time, I watched him. Then Ian went on to describe how
he'd done it. How he said he'd stood behind the settee looking for some
miniatures for me, and the lad Eddie was sat on the settee. He said 'I
held the axe with my two hands and brought it down on his head.' Myra
said, 'His eyes registered astonishment when you hit him,' those are
the exact words she said, and they were to Ian while I was there. Ian
was complaining because he'd hurt his ankle and they'd have to keep
the lad's body upstairs all night, and he wouldn't be able to carry the
lad down to the car because of his ankle. Myra suggested that they
use my wife's and my baby trolley to carry the lad's body to their car.
Well it's Myra's car. I agreed straight away. I'd have agreed to anything
they said. We agreed to meet where Myra works in Manchester tonight,
that's Thursday, October 7, 1965, at 5 o'clock to pick up the trolley
from my granddad's at Ardwick and bring it to Hattersley and use it.

Later he remembered other details and he added:

After we had cleaned up Evans's blood, Myra made a cup of tea and
she and Brady sat talking. She said: 'Do you remember that time we
were burying a body on the moors and a policeman came up?' I can't
remember if Brady made any comment but then she drew me into the
conversation and said: 'I was in the Mini with a body in the back, it
was portioned off with a plastic sheet. Ian was digging a hole when a
policeman came and asked me what the trouble was. I told him I was
drying my sparking plugs and he drove off. I was praying that Ian
wouldn't come back over the hill while he was there.'

His original statement continued:

I said I'd better be off, I wanted to go and they let me go, and I ran
all the way home, they were both unconcerned. I let myself into the
flat right away, woke Maureen up and had a wash, there was a bit of
blood just round my nails off the cloths that had been used for wiping
up. After I had a wash, I had a cup of tea, I didn't tell her what had
happened and I got in bed. It was about 3 to half past in the morning
then. I couldn't get to sleep, I kept thinking about the lad, about the
screams and the gurgling he was making. I got up after a bit, put the
light on, woke Maureen up and I told her I had something terrible to

tell her. I told her all about it then. Then she got up, she was crying and upset, and we sat down and tried to decide what to do. I expected Ian and Myra to be outside my flat in their car waiting for me to do something. I was frightened of leaving the place, waiting till people on the estate started moving about. It got to about 6 o'clock. We decided it was the best time to go about, so I armed myself with a carving knife and a screwdriver, in case I met Ian and Myra. Maureen came with me and we walked to the telephone kiosk in Hattersley Road West and telephoned the police. That's it. I didn't take any part in the killing of the lad, I only helped them because I was frightened that I'd get the same, or my wife would, if I didn't do as they told me. Neither Myra or Ian was drunk, when she came to our place she was normal as far as I could see. I've known Ian for about fourteen months and I've known Myra for about four years.

Mr Mars-Jones, QC, told the Medico-Legal Journal in 1967 that,

the Pathologist who did the post mortem … found that at least fourteen blows had been struck on the man's head by an instrument, undoubtedly the axe. The greater part of the right side of the skull was smashed in. He had a depressed fracture of the right frontal region, but he still had lived, and in the end Brady had to strangle him with a piece of flex before he could extinguish his life. One of the astonishing things about the case is how that young man suffered a terrible assault and still was alive. He survived everything that Brady did. Until he extinguished his life with that piece of flex.

His body was later removed by police and taken to Hyde Mortuary.
Dr Charles St Hill recalled at the subsequent trial of Brady and Hindley:

I found that the body was that of a fairly slim youth, 5ft 6in tall and of about 9-10 stone. It was fully dressed but there were no shoes on the feet.
There were fourteen irregular lacerations distributed over the scalp, right cheek and ear, with surrounding bruising. These lacerations measured from 1-5in in length. Around the neck was a slightly depressed white band in the flesh, corresponding in position and width to the electric light flex. There was a little reddening of the skin in one or two places along the edge of this band. There was widespread bruising of the back of the neck and over the back of the tops of the shoulders and upper back. There was a 1 inch bruise in the small of

the back. There was extensive lacerating and bruising of the backs of both hands, the left forearm and the right upper arm; these wounds are accurately described as 'defence wounds'. I found the greater part of the right side of the skull was fragmented and a somewhat rounded depressed fracture was present on the right frontal region.

I came to the conclusion that the injuries to the skull could have been produced by the axe found in the house; I think probably by both the blade side and the back of the axe.

There was much blood on the surface of the brain with extensive bruising on both sides. The mouth and pharynx were normal. The trachea contained a little frothy fluid. The lungs were congested with a few small haemorrhages on their surfaces. The right side of the heart was dilated and there were numerous haemorrhages on this surface. The coronary arteries and great vessels were normal. In the abdomen the stomach contained a little turbid fluid only. I came to the conclusion that the cause of death was cerebral contusion and haemorrhage due to fractures of the skull due to blows to the head, accelerated by strangulation by ligature.

I removed hair from the head, eyebrows, pubis and around the anus. I found two loose fibres around the anus; also numerous fibres on both hands. I also took a swab from the mouth and the anus of the deceased; two swabs were taken from the skin of the penis.

Spots of blood found on Hindley's shoes were consistent with blood falling on them; spots of blood on David Smith's shoes could have been obtained in the same way. Smith's shoes are soft-toed, and I do not think they could have caused the lacerations.

Ian and Myra hadn't done as good a job at clearing up as they thought. A thorough inspection by forensic officers found bloodstains on the settee covers, mattress and floor in Myra's bedroom, two blood spots under the window in Myra's bedroom, a bloodstained sock from behind a cushion in her bedroom, a bloodstained silk cushion cover from the easy chair behind the door in the living room, blood on the legs of the easy chair, scrapings of blood from under the lino in the living room, blood splashes on the wall opposite the fireplace, blood spots from the pouffe, blood on a cigarette butt found by the fireplace and a piece of bone from the living room carpet.

Back at Hyde police station Hindley was questioned at 2.00 pm by Detective Policewoman Margaret Campion.

Hindley was sitting in the police station canteen with her dog Puppet at her feet when the detective asked her if she could answer some questions. Hindley replied that she wanted some food for her dog, which Campion agreed to – provided she answer some questions first.

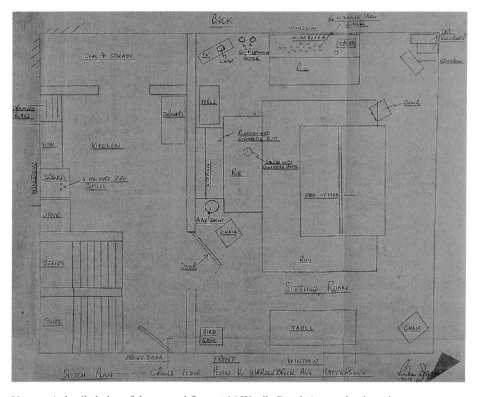

Unseen. A detailed plan of the ground floor at 16 Wardle Brook Avenue by detectives.

Campion: A man's body was found in your house this morning. Who was he?

Hindley: I don't know and I'm not saying anything. Ask Ian, my story's the same as Ian's.

Campion: Come on, what was the story of last night?

Hindley: We came home from work about six o'clock and went out about eight o'clock. We went to the outdoor [off-licence shop] in Stockport Road for some wine; we often go there. Then we went up Glossop way near the moors and sat talking for ages. It was just a normal evening out before all this happened. It was the same as hundreds of other evenings out. Now, can I have some food for my dog?

Campion: Would you care to tell me what happened at your house?

Hindley: All I'm saying is that I didn't do it and Ian didn't do it. We are involved in something we didn't do. We never left each other, we never do. What happened last night was an accident. It should never have happened.

Campion: An accident? If what you say is true, it is in your interests to tell the truth of what did happen.

Hindley: No. Ask Ian. His story is the same as mine. We never left each other. Ian can't drive and that's that. What are they going to do with Ian? Because whatever he's done, I've done.

Campion: Do you realise how serious this matter is?

Hindley: Yes, I also know David Smith told you all this and he's a liar.

Campion: David Smith says you cleaned up the mess in the living room after the murder of this man. Is this true?

Hindley: Yes, and I suppose he told you he sat on the chair benevolently looking on while I cleaned up.

Campion: Did you go to David Smith's house last night and did he walk you home? What time was that?

Hindley: Yes and I'm not saying what time it was. All this happened because there was an argument. Ian will tell you and I agree with what he says.

Campion: How did this man get to your house? Who brought him there?

Hindley: I'm not saying how he got there or when. I have told you before, I'm not saying anything.

Campion: Do I understand by this that you're refusing to say how the youth came to your house, when he came, or what happened to him?

Hindley: I told you before. My story is the same as Ian's…. What he has told you my story is the same as his. We didn't do it and I'm not talking any more about it. Please get me some food for my dog…

She was interviewed again at 4.00 that afternoon, this time by Detective Chief Superintendent Benfield, with Detective Policewoman Campion present:

Benfield: I have been to No. 16 Wardle Brook Avenue, Hattersley and I have seen the body of a young man trussed up and wrapped in a bundle in the bedroom there.

He cautioned her then and she replied:

> **Hindley:** I didn't do it. Ian didn't do it, David Smith is a liar. I am saying nothing else until I have seen Ian.
>
> **Benfield:** From information I have received you were present when a youth was attacked in your house in the living room, surely in your own interest you would wish to give some explanation?
>
> **Hindley:** We should never have been involved. I am saying nothing else until I have seen Ian; let me see Ian and I will make a statement.
>
> **Benfield:** I cannot allow that. Would you care to tell me where you and Ian went last night?
>
> **Hindley:** To Glossop. I bought some wine from an off-licence in Grey Street. We went to Glossop, stopped the car and had a drink.
>
> **Benfield:** According to Ian he went to Manchester where he met Eddie and brought him back to Hattersley. Were you with Ian?
>
> **Hindley:** I was with Ian all night. I should like to see Ian before I say anything else. Ian didn't do it, I didn't do it and that's all I'm saying.

By 4.00 pm Mrs Edith Evans had identified her son Edward at Hyde Public Mortuary which was across the road from the police station.

David and Maureen Smith were allowed to leave the station but were told to come back again the following day. Maureen caught sight of her mother, Nellie, and her Uncle Bert and Aunt Ann, but as she called to them her mother just ignored her, thinking that whatever had gone on, it was probably David's fault. They left the police station and went to stay with David's grandfather in Ardwick for the night.

Myra's mother Nellie and her Uncle Bert were shown into the police canteen so they could sit with her. This was the last thing that Nellie Hindley needed, as her husband Bob had suffered another stroke, adding to the already bad atmosphere in the house. They begged her to tell the police the truth about what had happened the previous night; to them, her version made it sound as though she was innocent, but Myra was insistent. Nellie had brought her Myra a set of her own clothes as the police wanted the ones she was wearing for forensic testing. After a couple of minutes DCS Benfield interrupted them and asked Myra for the keys to her pale blue Mini Countryman.

A search by Chief Superintendent Benfield of her car found Ian's brown leather wallet on the dashboard and inside it were three sheets of paper containing a list of abbreviated words such as HAT, ALI, GN, OB, DET, CARR, STN, REC, PRO and END. This was Ian's 'Working List'.

Unseen photograph of Myra's Mini.

The papers also contained notes about changing car seat covers; burning the shaft and burying the head of the hatchet; cleaning clothing and the car; and ten 'BUTS' for buttons.

Although police found loaded guns at the house, there was nothing to connect Brady or Hindley with any other crimes. DS Roy Dean then discovered an old exercise book with Ian's handwriting in. One of the pages in the notebook had some odd sketches and a list of names, mainly of film stars but there was a name that made them realise there may be some truth to David Smith's claims that Brady had told him he'd killed more people: John Kilbride.

As he was from Ashton-under-Lyne, Lancashire Police became involved in the case. Officers from Manchester Police soon arrived at Hyde police station wanting to talk to Brady about the other missing children from across the city – Pauline Reade, Keith Bennett and Lesley Ann Downey. Brady admitted nothing other than his involvement in the death of Edward Evans.

At 8.00 pm Brady was interviewed by DCS Benfield and asked about the note found in the wallet:

Benfield: I wish to put some questions to you about a letter found in the house, 16 Wardle Brook Avenue, addressed to Mr Craig.

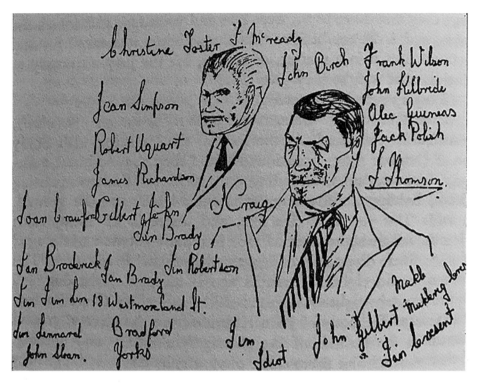

John Kilbride's name, written by Brady, is second from the top in the right-hand list.

He then cautioned Brady.

> **Benfield:** [showing the letter to Brady] This letter is signed 'Ian', did you write it?
>
> **Brady:** Yes, I had to tell him some tale to cover up.
>
> **Benfield:** I have also found a wallet in Myra's car which has some notes written in it. Do you recognise this?
>
> **Brady:** Yes, it's mine.
>
> **Benfield:** Inside the wallet are several pieces of paper on which are written certain words and abbreviations, would you care to tell me what they mean?
>
> **Brady:** Yes, that was the plan for the disposal of Eddie. We planned that after it happened. We sat up doing it.

DCS Benfield then asked him what the abbreviations stood for:

ARREST

Benfield: GN – What does this mean?

Brady: Gun. If anybody had seen us burying the body. For self-protection.

The rest of the codes were worked out, partly with Brady's help. OB stood for object; DET for detail; HAT for hatchet; CARR for car; REC for reconnaissance; PRO P for the stimulant Pro-Plus; PTS for prints [fingerprints]; END stood for finish.

According to the list, the object (the hatchet), should, under the heading 'detail', be cleaned before, wiped for prints and at the 'End' have the head buried and the shaft burnt. Then: 'Object: Car; Detail: Remove all removable objects, clean covers, floor and seat poly (polythene); End: Count all moveables. Destroy poly. Inspect car for spots. Object: Reconnaissance; Detail: check periodically to see if unmoved; End: W/H.'

DCS Benfield was confused as to what W/H meant and was also confused as to what 'check periodically to see if unmoved' meant, but he carried on with his questioning. 'Object: Pro-Plus; Detail: Stimulate. Object: TIC; Detail: Place P/B.' DCS Benfield asked Brady what P/B stood for and he instantly told him that it stood for 'Penistone Burn'. But it did not mean that at all. He was later to discover that TIC meant 'ticket', but Penistone Burn didn't make any sense to him.

Brady insisted that the plan was prepared after Edwards Evans's death, but the tense of some of the wording proved it to be a previously prepared plan and showed that the murder had been premeditated. One item in the programme read 'Drop me off. Pass agreed point every 5 minutes.' Brady explained that this meant he would

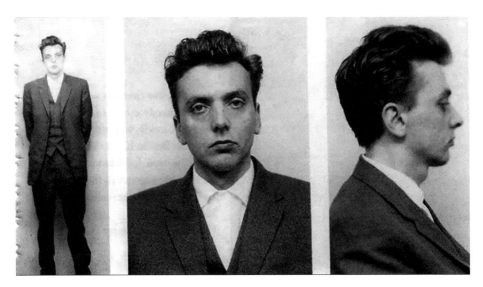

Ian Brady's mugshots.

193

be dropped off from the car in which Evans's body was being carried in order to find the spot selected for the burial place. The car (to be driven by Myra) was then to go to and fro every five minutes to avoid the risk of being noticed while stationary, and indicated conclusively that both Brady and Hindley were to be actively involved in the operation.

At 8.20 pm Brady was charged with the murder of Edward Evans by DS Carr, in the presence of Superintendent Bob Talbot. Brady replied: 'I stand on the statement made this morning.' He then had his mugshots taken:

Hindley was again questioned at 9.00 pm, this time with her mother and uncle present, by DCS Benfield and Detective Policewoman Campion.

> **Benfield:** Do you wish to say anything to me about what happened last night?

> **Hindley:** No, not until you let me see Ian first.

DCS Benfield told her that Brady had been charged with the murder of Edward Evans and that he would be appearing in court in the morning. Her only reply was: 'I'll be at court and I'll see you after I've seen Ian.'

After just a couple of minutes Myra was allowed to leave the station, but as her home was now a crime scene, she was told she could not stay there. She went to stay with her mother in Clayton, a suburb of Manchester, and had to leave the station in her mother's spare clothes as hers were taken away for evidence. She later told Duncan Staff that she was questioned heavily by her family that evening and they were not happy with her answers. They tried to persuade her to 'come clean', to look after her own interests, but she wouldn't listen. DC Fairley recalled:

> A decision was made not to charge Smith, the argument being if you're going to charge Hindley, you're going to charge Smith, because what you had at that time was Hindley helping clear up, no more than that. Who else helped to clear up? Smith. We took Smith's shoes off; there was blood on his shoes and Brady said Smith had kicked Evans. He had this stick, too, and the stick wasn't as thick as your finger, bit of string tied on it, that had blood on it…. The dilemma is: Brady admits the murder, the other two are both accusing the other. In those days, you didn't lock people up easily, so Smith and Hindley left, and Brady was kept in custody.

The following morning, 8 October, Brady appeared in court, charged with the murder of Edward Evans. Myra was in court to watch the proceedings and when Brady saw her he thought that she had been charged too. He asked the policeman at his side if they could share the same solicitor. This slip up was passed on to the detectives. When the court proceedings had concluded, Myra attended Hyde police station again and at 11.45 am and was interviewed by DCS Benfield and Detective Policewoman Campion.

> **Benfield:** Ian Brady has been before the court now. You said you would see me again after he had been to court. Do you wish to say anything to me?
>
> **Hindley:** No. All I am saying is that Ian didn't do it and I didn't do it.
>
> **Benfield:** Well who did?
>
> **Hindley:** I am saying nothing else until I've seen Ian's solicitor.

She was again interviewed at 3.00 pm by DCS Benfield and Detective Policewoman Campion:

> **Benfield:** You have now seen Ian's solicitor. Do you wish to tell me anything?
>
> **Hindley:** No, I want to see Ian first. I am saying nothing until then. I will see him at court at Stalybridge on Monday and then I might tell you.

At the house, police had discovered a large collection of photographs, mostly of scenic views, but also some of Hindley, her dog and Brady. Many of them had been taken against the backdrop of Saddleworth Moor. In total, police took away 149 negatives, 170 prints and a tartan-backed photograph album. Policewoman Pat Clayton remembered:

> Joe [Mounsey] said 'There's more to this than a straight up and down Brady/Evans murder'. From then on he got his teeth into it and he wouldn't let go. He was wanting to get to the bottom of where these children had gone, and then of course when the photographs were found of various strange places, strange photographs of places on the moor, he spent hours and hours on the moors with Ray Gilder, Mike Massheder and various other officers, trying to trace the exact location of these photographs.

Dr John Bennett was called to Hyde police station at 2.30 pm where he examined Brady.

> He was making a complaint about pain sited in the back of his left foot. I examined this foot and found a small superficial abrasion on the foot just in front of the lateral malleolus. This abrasion took the form

of being in the shape of a circle with three small lines running into a segment.

There was no bruising or swelling on the foot when I examined him … I would describe the injury as a trivial injury.

A report in the *Manchester Evening News* was read by Brady's boss at Millwards, Tommy Craig. When he read that there had been a murder at 16 Wardle Brook Avenue, he assumed that it was Ian who had been killed – and wasn't particularly bothered as he didn't like him.

He was so bad tempered about anything that upset him. If you ticked him off about something he would fly into a rage. He had a shocking temper and his language was dreadful, but I used to pass it over just to keep the pace. He was reasonable at his job but he would have been sacked long before if it hadn't been that it was difficult to get staff. In the six years he worked here, I can't say I ever got to know him at all. In an office, the lads usually chat a bit about football or something like that, but Brady wasn't interested in anything like that. Sometimes in the morning he might join in a conversation about what was on the TV the night before, but I noticed he only talked about the crime films or

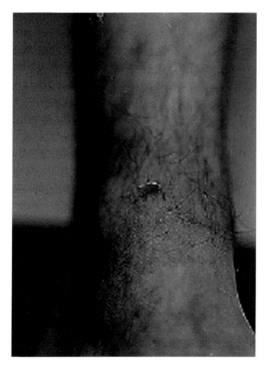

Unseen. Ian Brady's ankle 'injury'.

the 'Hitchcock Hour', things with a bit of horror or brutality in them. He often had a book with him – I don't remember any of them, but they were always those paperbacks with a bit of filth in them. I think it was his first clerical job and he was just adequate and no more. He wasn't the sort of fellow I liked to have around.

Of Myra, he said:

She was a good shorthand typist, I'll say that for her, and she was always smartly dressed. She wore these short skirts and boots and fancy stockings. But she would have been fired too if it wasn't that it would have been difficult to get a replacement. With most of the girls in an office you have a bit of a lark around, you pull their legs and everyone tries to get a bit of fun out of their work. But Myra was heavy going. You got no response out of her at all. She was surly at the best of times and aggressive if you spoke to her the wrong way. She didn't come in contact much with the other girls, but still she managed to have a bad effect on everybody. The pair of them were just plain surly and unsociable.

DC Ian Fairley recalled:

I was at Millwards on the Friday. I spoke to staff and searched the place, then went on to Brady's mother's house in Heywood. She lived in a block of flats and was a well-mannered woman, quite timid, refined. I told her Ian had been arrested for murder and she couldn't believe it.

The following day, Saturday 9 October, Myra helped her mother to carry a large bag of washing to the launderette opposite Millwards. As always with Myra though, she had an ulterior motive. While her mother loaded the machine up, Myra told her that she was just popping across the road to see her colleagues. When she got in, she saw that the office fire was burning which meant that the cleaners had been in, but she knew that she was in well before her boss Tommy would turn up. She walked quickly through the main building and into the store at the back of the warehouse, where she found exactly what she was looking for – the file containing the 'Master List'. According to Ian, the file also contained envelopes in which were lists of contacts, maps of projects and photographs, address books, tapes and other incriminating material.

Unfortunately for all concerned Myra burnt the items, one by one, in the office fire. It is highly probable that the files contained photographs of their victims, as well as possibly others that we do not yet know about. It is also highly likely that the evidence in them proved Myra's participation in such crimes beyond question. It may also have contained the mementoes of their killings, such as Pauline Reade's underwear, John Kilbride's shoe and further photographs of Lesley Ann Downey and Keith Bennett. They hadn't the time to get a memento from Edward Evans.

After they had all been burned, Myra's boss, Tommy Craig, arrived and Myra asked him to sack her so she could go on the dole, but he refused. He told her that whatever had happened he was sure she had nothing to do with it and that he'd keep her job open for her until everything had been 'sorted out'... But Ian would have to be sacked.

At 9.00 am David Smith went back to the police station for more questioning, but as the police were still not 100 per cent sure of his involvement in Edward Evans's murder, the questioning was probing and difficult. The detectives focused a lot on the hatchet and asked him questions such as had he seen it before? And where was it normally kept? But David was adamant that he had never seen the hatchet before that night and had no idea why it was in the sitting room.

The detectives then took David back to Underwood Court so that he could show them the route he took that night with Myra. While at the house on Wardle Brook Avenue, with David running through events again, the detectives re-enacted what had happened. It was then that David mentioned a tape recorder that was normally kept in the living room that didn't appear to be there. This was news to the detectives.

The following day, Sunday 10 October 1965, detectives took both Maureen and David Smith up to the moors to locate the place where Ian had taken David to practice with the guns. They arrived near Woodhead, which Ian had told the detectives was what the W/H had stood for in his 'Working List'. Ian had chosen the small valley because there was a shooting range nearby and that would mask the noises of their revolvers if anyone were to hear gun fire from the road.

Meanwhile, Myra visited her gran, who still didn't know the truth behind Ian's arrest. Her Uncle Bert and his wife Kath were there, and Jim Masterson and his wife Anita arrived shortly afterwards. Arrangements were made for Myra's gran to move in with her daughter Annie, in Gorton's Railway View. Eventually she ended up living with Myra's mother Nellie and her partner Bill Moulton in Clayton, after Nellie split from Bob.

Following the weekend, the investigation went up another gear and the police returned to the spot near Woodhead, where David had taken them two days previously. They had an idea that Brady was linked with the disappearances of children in the Manchester area after finding John Kilbride's name in his exercise book and finding it odd to take photographs of what most people would call 'next to nothing' on the moors. They marked the area out with yellow dye while senior officers met at Ashton police station to discuss the organisation of a search and the best way to proceed in the investigation.

ARREST

Inspector John Chaddock from Uppermill, whose police station covered the area to be searched, was consulted and his experience and knowledge of the moors proved invaluable to the investigation. Plans for the search then went ahead and Cheshire Police started to integrate the services of the neighbouring police forces.

Back at Hyde Town Hall, the East Cheshire Coroner, Mr Herbert Sidebotham, opened the inquest on Edward Evans. It was adjourned for three months shortly after hearing from Edward's mother, to allow the investigation to progress.

Brady then appeared on remand before magistrates at Stalybridge and his solicitor, Mr Charles Fitzpatrick, complained that he was unable to get a copy of the original statement his client had made to the police.

> I understand a written statement has been taken and I have made verbal and written applications for a copy. I have been told that it is subject to the Director of Public Prosecutions. I must say the police have been most helpful and courteous to me in all things except this one, but I cannot hope to begin preparing a defence until I have an opportunity of seeing this statement. Surely the accused himself is entitled to have a look at his own statement, and I am entitled to be present when he does so and make a copy. Why it must depend on the Director of Public Prosecutions I fail to see, but even he is not on another planet and some communication could be made to him almost immediately as to whether he will or will not release this statement. If he does not, I want to know why and on what grounds.

Superintendent Bob Talbot said that Mr Fitzpatrick's application was in the hands of the Chief Constable and he had to await further instructions. The magistrates directed the prosecution to hand over the statement as soon as possible.

After hearing how Evans's body was found and Brady had been arrested, the magistrates remanded him for another week. Myra was in the court again as a member of the public. She was later interviewed by DCS Benfield with Detective Policewoman Campion present:

> **Benfield:** When I saw you last Friday you said you might tell me something when you had been to Stalybridge Court and seen Ian Brady.

> **Hindley:** I want to see Ian's solicitor first.

DCS Benfield told her that she and Brady had not been as clever as they had thought and that the police had all the evidence they needed. They had Evans's body, David Smith's confession, and she and Brady had not been as clever with the clean-up as they thought. There was a blood-stained cigarette butt in front of the fireplace and blood splatter on her shoes.

At 2.05 pm Hindley was told she was going to be charged as an accessory after the fact to the murder of Edward Evans. She replied: 'I am saying nothing.' At 3.05 pm she was arrested and charged by DS Carr with being an accessory to the murder of Edward Evans in the presence of her mother and uncle. The words of the charge were that she 'did receive, comfort, harbour, assist and maintain' Ian Brady. She refused to say anything incriminating in any of her interviews. DS Alex Carr recalled:

> Why she wasn't arrested at the time was because she could've been under the duress of Brady for all we knew. As it turned out, she wasn't. I came to think of her as being worse than Brady for the opposite reason because she was a female and had participated in these awful crimes which to my mind was terrible.
>
> That mugshot of Myra Hindley portrayed her as she really was. She was a brassy blonde with staring eyes and an impassive expression on her face.

In an effort to garner sympathy for herself, whenever she later told anyone (other than the police) about the infamous photographs of her, she would say that as soon as she was charged she was dragged down to the basement of the station and was pushed down into a chair where she thought she was going to be interrogated, and clenched her teeth defiantly expecting to be given a slap – hence her harsh look. The next thing she knew was a blinding flash of light – the police had taken her photograph.

But the truth can clearly be seen; she wasn't sitting, more than the one photograph was taken, and she had to move for them to be taken.

Myra Hindley's mugshots.

David and Maureen Smith were then taken up to the moors to point out other areas that they had been taken to by Ian and Myra, but they found it difficult to remember exactly where they had been. David recalled:

> Joe Mounsey … explained as we drove out through the old mill villages that they'd managed to identify the place in the photographs as Hollin Brown Knoll. The name meant nothing to me, but as we rounded a sharp, high bend and the boulders came into view on the horizon – great black ugly rocks, like rotten teeth – I felt a sudden jolt of recognition. We parked below the boulders and crossed the road together, just me and Mr Mounsey at first, then with an army of coppers following us, clipboards at the ready. We stopped at the place I thought must have been where I'd stood with Ian the night before Angela died. It looked different in the watery daylight – the reservoir seemed wider, less of a silver streak bordered by high banks of land. I tried to answer Mr Mounsey's questions, concentrating hard. *Was the reservoir far away when you stopped, David? Was it this far or a bit further? Did it seem bigger or smaller than this? Would it be this angle or slightly to the side? Was the ground spongy beneath your feet like this, sinking in, or was it firmer, more rocky?* I felt painfully inadequate, as I stumbled out the truth: *it was dark when I was up there with Brady, and I hadn't even realised it was a reservoir until he told me so – I thought it was a river. I was wearing cowboy boots that night and the heels sink into anything that isn't concrete….* Mr Mounsey, to his eternal credit, didn't mock or become impatient: he nodded thoughtfully and paced about, occasionally waving me across to him and asking if *this* was actually the place I'd stood with Brady that night, or this … I wanted to help more than ever, to be able to point at the exact spot, but I couldn't. As we walked back to his car, I felt as if the whole thing had been a waste of time, because without knowing for certain which was the precise area, nothing could come of it.

Detective Chief Inspectors Tyrrell and Mounsey interviewed Brady at Hyde police station at 12.15 pm and told him that they were enquiring about the disappearance of John Kilbride.

> **Mounsey:** I have reason to believe that you have discussed the subject of doing bank jobs, killing people and burying them on the moors with David Smith.
>
> **Brady:** There are no others.
>
> **Mounsey:** I believe you spend a lot of time on the moors?

Brady: Yes, I do.

Mounsey: I believe you have also discussed with Smith which is the most satisfactory way of killing a person and as far as you are concerned there are two ways. One is to meet a victim and kill them there and then and the other, the method you consider more efficient and satisfactory, to meet someone by arrangement and entice them to a convenient place and kill them there.

Brady: I have discussed many things with Smith. It's all to do with the bank jobs. I have been planning these for a long time.

Mounsey: Have you discussed killing people and burying their bodies on the moor?

Brady: Yes, I talked about it in a vague sort of way. It was all part of the fiction to impress him.

Mounsey: Have you discussed burying people on the moors?

Brady: Yes

Later in the interview:

Mounsey: David Smith has told us that on the night Evans was killed you said it was the messiest yet, it normally only takes one hit. Did you say that?

Brady: I said something like it, it was just to do with the situation we were in.

Mounsey: Why did you say that, if there were no others? That remark could only indicate that you have committed other murders which didn't cause so much mess. I know that it took more than one hit to kill Evans.

Brady: There are no others.

Mounsey: Why say it normally only takes one hit?

Brady: It was just the situation we were in.

Mounsey: You have boasted to Smith of killing three or four people.

Brady: I may have given him a vague impression, but it was just part of the fiction I was promoting to impress him regarding the bank jobs.

Mounsey: Is that what the guns were for?

Brady: Yes.

Mounsey: Smith has also told us that on the Saturday night before Evans was killed you were questioning him, whether or not he believed you capable of committing murder and that you told him that you had and could and that the next one wouldn't count as you were not due for another for three months yet.

Brady did not reply, so Mounsey repeated the question:

Brady: I don't remember that.

Mounsey: You do remember talking to Smith about killing people and burying them on the moors, don't you?

Brady: I spoke in general terms.

Mounsey: You and Myra spent a lot of time on the moors, sometimes late at night with wine – having drinking parties.

Brady: I like the moors. It's quiet and peaceful.

Mounsey: Why did you go mainly at night?

Brady: We like privacy.

Mounsey: I think you went there at night to dispose of the victims you had killed, just as you told Smith.

Brady: That's not true. What I told Smith was just to build up an image.

Mounsey: You mean to impress him should it be necessary to kill again on the bank job?

Brady: Something like that. I'm only interested in profit. Killing is a last resort.

The interview was suspended at around 3.00 pm so Brady could have something to eat. He was then interviewed again half an hour later:

Tyrrell: It has been suggested that you and Myra have spent a lot of time on the moors, very often late at night, and that you had wine drinking parties up there.

Brady: I like the moors. It's quiet and peaceful.

Tyrrell: Have you been on the moors at night drinking wine?

Brady: Yes.

Tyrrell: At night?

203

Brady: Yes.

Tyrrell: Whereabouts did you go on the moor?

Brady: All over.

Tyrrell: Tell us where about.

Brady: We have been over the Snake [Snake Pass], and round Whaley Bridge.

Tyrrell: Anywhere else?

Brady: I can't remember.

Tyrrell: Why do you go on the moors at night?

Brady: It's quiet and we like privacy.

Tyrrell: Who do you mean by 'we'?

Brady: Me and Myra.

Tyrrell: I think you went on the moors at night to dispose of the bodies of the victims you have killed just as you have told Smith.

Brady: No, that is not true. What I told Smith was only to build up an image.

Tyrrell: You have boasted to Smith about killing people, was it in order to impress him should it be necessary to kill again when you did the bank jobs?

Brady: Something like that, I am only interested in profit, killing is a last resort.

Mounsey: Smith says that after Evans had been killed, Myra told him that on one occasion on the moors she was stopped at the roadside in the Mini with a body in the back while you were digging a grave some distance away and a policeman came up and asked if anything was the matter and she said she was drying her sparking plugs.

Brady: I remember something about an incident, but I wasn't burying any body. I would be practising with my revolvers.

Mounsey: In the dark and in the rain?

Brady: It was daylight.

Mounsey: Where was it?

Brady: I don't know.

Mounsey: When was it?

Brady: About six months ago.

Other matters were then discussed, such as the Nazi party. Brady told them that there was a lot of merit in their ideas and held a lot of admiration for some of their leaders. When asked how he felt about the massacre of 6 million Jews, he replied: 'It is a matter which causes me no concern', and that it was justified in the interests of the State.

He was then asked about David Smith's involvement with the murder of Edward Evans and what he thought about the Nazi's and Jews, but Brady would not say – insisting that it would all come out at the trial. He said that he did not know Pauline Reade, but Myra did. He was then given tea at 5.30 pm.

The interview restarted at 6.20 pm and DCI Mounsey, DCI Tyrrell and DCS Benfield asked him about the 'Disposal Plan':

Mounsey: There is an item on this list 'Check Periodically Unmoved'. Does this refer to the bodies you have buried on the moors? And is it a reminder to check that the graves are still intact?

Brady: It was only to do with Evans.

Mounsey: You were going to check that Evans' body had not been moved, were you?

Brady: Yes.

Mounsey: P/B – What does that mean?

Brady didn't respond so DCI Mounsey repeated the question

Brady: It means Penistone Burn.

Mounsey: Does it mean that you were going to bury a body in the region of Penistone Burn?

Brady: In that general area.

Mounsey: That seems to verify what Smith says you told him about burying bodies on the moors.

Brady: It was only to impress him.

Mounsey: Smith says that in conversation with him you once said that he and his wife had almost been sitting on the grave where you and Myra had buried a body. He has pointed out a place to us off the Penistone road where the river Etherow runs near the road, some distance from Woodhead Station. Is that the place you are talking about?

Brady: In that general area.

Mounsey: Have you buried bodies on the moor?

Brady: It was just part of the fiction I was promoting with him.

Other matters were discussed before the interview was ended and he was given a cup of tea. After his break he was questioned about John Kilbride:

Mounsey: We are making enquiries about the disappearance of a young boy, John Kilbride, aged 12 years who has been missing from Ashton-under-Lyne since 17.30 on 23 November 1963. Kilbride was last seen on Ashton Market.

Brady: I've read about him but I don't know anything about him.

He was then asked about the exercise book found with the name John Kilbride written in:

Mounsey: I have in my possession an exercise book which has been found at your home. Is this yours?

Brady: Yes.

Mounsey: Have you written these names in the book?

Brady: Yes.

Mounsey: Among these names is the name 'John Kilbride'. Can you tell me why you have written it in this book?

Brady: I don't know.

Mounsey: Does it refer to the young boy John Kilbride missing from Ashton-under-Lyne?

Brady: No, it's a lad I knew inside at Hull.

Mounsey: What was this lad's first name?

Brady: I don't know.

Mounsey: Who do the other names refer to?

Brady: Just people.

ARREST

At the trial, Thomas Byrne, a prison officer at HM Prison Hull, told how he 'searched the nominal register and can state that no one of the name, John Kilbride, was an inmate' at the time Brady was there.

A little later in the interview Brady was shown a photograph of John Kilbride:

Mounsey: John Kilbride was last seen on Ashton Market at 17.30 on Saturday, 23 November 1963. Where were you then?

Brady: I don't know.

Mounsey: How well do you know Ashton?

Brady: I hardly know the place.

Mounsey: How many times have you been there?

Brady: Not more than once or twice.

Mounsey: Did you and Myra do any shopping there?

Brady: No, we used to go to Hyde Market more often than not.

It was 8.00 pm before Brady was driven back to the remand centre. Hindley was taken there too and put in a room on the hospital wing.

In her remand cell the following morning, Hindley was handed a small brown envelope which contained Brady's 'reception' letter. In it, he told her that she would be out in no time, but that he knew he was going to get 'life'. He told her that he couldn't do 'life', as three months in HMP Strangeways had been enough, and that she would have to be brave. 'My influence will pall and you can begin a new life', he wrote. Upset by this, she asked the Governor for an 'inter-prison' visit before their next court appearance. In the meantime, she learned the tricks and trades of prison life: how to use cigarettes as currency, forge a cheque and carry out an abortion.

Meanwhile, three Detective Chief Superintendents, Arthur Benfield of Cheshire, Harold Prescott of Lancashire and Douglas Nimmo of Manchester, met at Ashton police station to study the files of missing persons. They started with a list of twelve and pruned it to eight. After a three-hour conference, DCS Benfield told the press: 'We were looking for a common factor but we did not find one. We were looking at the files of adults as well as children. They all came from the Greater Manchester area and they've all disappeared within the last three or four years.'

Detective Tom McVittie later recalled: 'Brady and Hindley wouldn't tell us where any bodies were. We did an awful lot of searching on the moors and I must say it was down to Mounsey that kept us going for weeks in the end – walking the hills and searching for graves.'

The *Manchester Evening News* had cottoned on to the story that was now unravelling and went with the headline: 'Police in Mystery Dig on Moors'. Denied access to the two central figures, journalists converged on the next best thing and within hours the entry phone to David Smith's flat was permanently ringing.

Initially, he was largely able to avoid the press, as his days were spent in an interview room, often for ten hours or more. He recalled:

> I'd be told to be down at Hyde station for nine. Maureen and Dad would come with me. They'd wait in the canteen and only left when I did. I ate in the interview room – someone would bring in a burger or chips for me and I'd be given half an hour to get that down before we were off again with the questions. I was always put in the same room at Hyde, but occasionally a bobby would appear and say, 'Right, there's going to be a couple of Manchester lads coming to speak to you today.' I was a bit bewildered the first time but soon got used to it. They'd take me down to Manchester regularly, where their coppers would ask me identical things from a slightly different angle. I hated that station. It was old and gloomy, and I was always interviewed by the same pair of 'heavies': Mattin and Tyrrell. Their boss, Nimmo, conducted the first interview I had there, but that was just a superficial thing before he handed me over to them. Nimmo stayed in the background after that.
>
> From the outset, Mattin and Tyrrell were always … very stern. It was another atmosphere altogether. The station itself was grim, with interview rooms that felt like prison cells and an ancient smell of misery about the place. Mattin and Tyrrell never gave me time to think about what they were asking – if I didn't reply immediately, one of them would bang down a fist and say 'Come on, you've got to give us an answer, we're waiting.' Sometimes I needed to think it through, but they wouldn't make any allowances. Hyde wasn't much better. I hated having to sit with Benfield and Talbot to go over things. I couldn't stick Talbot – we wound each other up – and I found Benfield faintly ridiculous. He looked like a womble, chubby, with little spectacles, and puffing away on his pipe until the room was so thick with smoke I could hardly see. At the end of every day I felt whacked out, drained of every emotion and incapable of thought. Then the next morning it would start up all over again.
>
> No one listened to me. They all wanted to speak to me, but everything I said fell on deaf ears. The Hyde brigade were only interested in Edward Evans and ignored what I tried to tell them about other murders – the ones Ian had boasted to me of having committed. I think Jock Carr wanted to know more, but the big brass weren't interested. Talbot and

his cronies saw me as someone out to save his own skin. They didn't believe what I had to say, that much was obvious. I couldn't understand it because all I wanted was someone to listen to me. But no one did – until Joe Mounsey came along.

I had a great deal of respect for Joe Mounsey. He was the first senior detective who took me seriously. He was like no one else. He didn't bark questions at me, he never raised his voice or came down heavy, and he listened acutely, to the point where I could actually *see* him taking it all on board. The relief I felt at knowing someone believed me at last was just incredible.

I kind of looked forward to going to Ashton for questioning. The police station there was modern and clean, all sparkling glass, and I was only ever seen – as far as I can recall – by Mr Mounsey. He had a couple of sidekicks, but he was in charge. Being told I was going to Ashton meant a good day ahead because his technique was laid-back and calm. That was the impression he gave and it worked to his advantage – no one else got me to speak at length like he did. The interviews I had with him were more like straightforward conversations. He would open with: 'OK, lad, how are you today? Got enough cigarettes? Right, then, in your own time. No rush. Just take it steady and we'll get there in the end.' He'd send out for extra ciggies if necessary and give me a proper tea break instead of just having a pot brought in. We'd go to the canteen together and he'd chat to me about rugby or football to make sure I had a rest from everything. When we returned to the interview room, he'd let me ease into it again and if there was a difficult question to answer, he'd tell me, 'Take as much time as you need, lad, on this next one. I have to ask it, but no panic. When you're ready.' He'd wait five or ten minutes if he had to, which is a long time to sit in silence. That was the big difference between Ashton and everywhere else: I was treated as a suspect at Hyde and Manchester, but at Ashton I was seen as a witness.

The following day, Wednesday 13 October, Edward Evans was buried in Southern Cemetery in Chorlton-Cum-Hardy, Manchester.

DCI Mounsey, head of Ashton CID, took three detectives and other policemen with him to Woodhead. They were armed with picks and spades and searched the bank of a ravine that fell sharply from the main road.

In places they dug holes and DCI Mounsey told reporters that they were working on 'a detective's hunch'. They found nothing and left for Ashton at lunchtime.

At Wardle Brook Avenue, forensic scientists from the Home Office Laboratory at Preston took over number 16 and behind drawn curtains started an extensive probe,

Police search the moors.

picking up dust and hair, blood samples from the floors and walls, and examining furniture, carpets and clothing.

In the Remand Centre, Hindley met with Brady for the first time since their arrest. They were separated by a sheet of glass and a guard stood at each of their shoulders. Brady told her that she'd go mad in prison if all she did was talk to other women and that she had to keep her mind on the 'outside' and to help with this he told her to order books from the prison library.

As the guards began to lose interest in the conversation, Brady suddenly asked her if she had managed to get to the 'left luggage' ticket before she was arrested, but she replied that she hadn't been let back in the house since his arrest. She told him that she had managed to get to the files at Millwards, however. He nodded his approval to her and they quickly changed the subject again.

The following day was thoroughly miserable weather-wise, and the search around Woodhead was soon suspended for the day.

Police search the moors.

Biologist Mr Colin Bancroft from the Preston Laboratory examined the blood stains found on the clothes of Ian Brady, Myra Hindley, David Smith and Edward Evans, worn on the night of Evans's murder. Brady's blood group, he knew, was OMN; David and Myra both belonged to blood group A; Edward's blood group was OM. Brady's jacket was blood-stained near the right-hand pocket, his shoes were spotted on the top and heavily stained on the sole. His shirt sleeve was smeared for eight inches above the right-hand cuff. All the blood samples Colin Bancroft took were similar to Evans' blood group. On Myra's black and white coat he found blood smears on the right sleeve over an area measuring 2½ inches by 1½. The front of her brown skirt was stained. Her casual shoes bore minute spots on the uppers of the right foot, a stain on the uppers of the left and smears on the sole. They were similar

211

to Evans's blood. There was a stain four inches in diameter on the back of David Smith's jacket and others on his jeans, his shoes and his socks. They too were similar to Evans's blood. He also found dog hairs on David's shoes and socks. Evans himself was covered in blood and the axe and David Smith's stick were stained.

A policewoman visited a school in Cheshire and spoke to 12-year-old neighbour Pat Hodges. Pat said she could identify the place that Ian and Myra used to take her to because she had also seen it on a television programme and recognised a white sign.

DCI Mounsey and DCI Tyrrell questioned Hindley at Risley Remand Centre at 11.25:

> **Mounsey:** We are making enquiries regarding John Kilbride aged 12 years, missing from Ashton-under-Lyne since 23 November 1963. I have reason to believe that you may be able to help us with our enquiries. I have been told you visited the Ashton-under-Lyne market regularly for over two years, particularly on Saturday afternoons, and it was on Ashton Market that John Kilbride was last seen at 17.30 on Saturday, 23 November 1963.
>
> **Hindley:** I have never been to Ashton Market.
>
> **Mounsey:** I have been told by your sister that you visited Ashton market regularly
>
> **Hindley:** It's not true.
>
> **Mounsey:** Where were you on 23 November 1963?
>
> **Hindley:** I don't know.

Later on questioning turned to Edward Evans

> **Mounsey:** I have been told that after Evans had been killed you told David Smith that on one occasion on the moors you were stopped at the road side in the Mini with a body in the back while Brady was digging a grave some distance away and a policeman came up and asked you if anything was the matter. You said you were drying your sparking plugs.
>
> **Hindley:** That's rubbish.
>
> **Mounsey:** Brady has agreed that he talked in general terms about robbing a bank, killing people and burying their bodies on the moors in conversations he had with David Smith.
>
> **Hindley:** It is not true, there have been no conversations like that.
>
> **Mounsey:** Not even about doing bank jobs?

Hindley: No! Smith's an idiotic moron!

Mounsey: Brady agrees that he said 'This is the messiest yet' after the Evans killing. What did he mean?

Hindley: He didn't say that.

Mounsey: Did he say 'it normally only takes one hit'?

Hindley: No.

Later in the interview DCI Tyrrell changed the subject.

Tyrrell: A girl called Lesley Ann Downey, who is 10, has been missing from her home since Boxing Day last year. She was last seen on a fairground off Hulme Hall Lane, Manchester about 5.30 pm.

Hindley: What are you suggesting?

Tyrrell: I merely want to know if you know anything about the disappearance of this girl.

Hindley: I don't know anything about her. I've never been near a fairground.

She also told the detectives that she didn't believe in religion or marriage any more. The interview came to a close at 2.15 pm.

DCS Mounsey and DCI Tyrrell then interviewed Brady, who told them about his books on torture and sex, and how everyone was selfish. The only people worth considering were those close to you. In regards to killing, he said that soldiers got a medal for it – civilians get charged with murder.

While at Risley, Brady spoke to other inmates about his crimes, as well as his views on Jews and black people. He told inmates, sometimes while playing chess with them, that 'I've done one or two', meaning murders. In regards to Jews, he said that he hated them because they were able to make money and he called them 'Scheming, cunning and sly.'

Myra wrote a letter to Elsie Masterton, the mother of Pat Hodges, who had agreed to look after her dog Puppet. She told her that she had left some money with her mother to give her for Puppet's food etc and that Ian was going to give his pension contribution money to her as well. The letter ends:

If you do write back, which I hope you do, don't mention anything of the case, etc., as I won't be allowed to read it. I hope the family are all right and if Pat's took Puppet for a walk, thank her for me.
Love, Myra xxx

Detectives lead the search.

Unknown to Myra, Elsie had already given Puppet to the RSPCA's Gorsey Farm Kennels in Ashton after her son Peter had had an allergic reaction to it.

On 15 October 1965, in swirling mist, a mass police search began at Woodhead; 160, twelve German Shepherds and a single policewoman, Detective Policewoman Pat Clayton, were drafted in to aid the search and they gathered at the entrance to a railway tunnel. The first group of searchers carried flag-topped canes which they used to mark anything that looked suspicious. The group who then followed them were armed with picks and shovels and used them to search the ground around the marker canes. The searchers found nothing but false alarms.

A mobile police station from Manchester was set up on the nearby A628 road to report back by radio to the headquarters at Ashton. Lesley Ann Downey's mother, Ann, arrived and told reporters: 'It's not very pleasant for me, but I had to come in case they found anything.'

At 1.30 pm that afternoon DC Peter Clegg drove slowly along the A635 road between Greenfield and Holmfirth with Pat Hodges at his side, giving him directions, and Policewoman Pat Slater in the rear. When Pat suddenly saw the white sign she was looking for, she told DC Clegg to stop. She pointed to the north side of the road and DC Clegg radioed back to Ashton. The information was passed back to DCS Benfield at Woodhead that Pat Hodges had located Hollin Brown Knoll. DC Clegg later showed the exact area to DS Eckersley at 4.30 pm.

The search was switched quickly and while arrangements were made to move the search parties six miles or so to Hollin Brown Knoll, Pat Hodges showed DS

Leslie Eckersley where Myra used to park the car. Other than the white sign that she remembered, the only way it could be pin-pointed was a little derelict building that used to be a pumping station, but darkness quickly fell on the moor.

While the searches were going on, David Smith was again interviewed, this time by DC Ian Fairley and DS Alex 'Jock' Carr. They had collected him from his home at Underwood Court and taken him to Hyde police station, but when they arrived the station was surrounded by journalists, so they returned to Underwood Court and interviewed David in the car. DC Fairley recalled:

> Smith was cooperative, he never hid anything, and he never changed his story. He was … not belligerent, but I think he was fed up. During the course of the interview, Jock asked him where they spent their time. Where did they go? David said he'd already gone through all of this – the moors, drinking, at home, drinking. Did they use guns? No, only for target practice. Then he talked about this robbery they'd plotted and at that point mentioned the fact that Brady had told him to bring anything he had that was incriminating back to him. Like what, we asked. He said books, and we knew what he meant, the sort of rubbish you could pick up from a dodgy place. He said he'd taken it all back to Brady and we asked him what had happened to it then. He said, 'Well, they put it in the suitcases.' Suitcases? *What suitcases?* Now, I don't know how many times this lad had been interviewed, and I don't know if he had mentioned the suitcases before or not, all I know is that it was the first time Jock Carr and I heard about the suitcases. We asked him again about these suitcases and he said, 'They were huge, packed with stuff, but I don't know what else, just the stuff I handed back.' We knew that no suitcases had been found because obviously there had been a search, and there was nothing. We started asking him again where they'd gone and he repeated what he'd said before. Then we asked where *they* went, Brady and Hindley, and he said sometimes they went into Manchester and Brady would go to the railway stations…

DC Fairley later recalled that when they returned to the police station at Hyde, DS 'Jock' Carr went ahead to the office, while he parked the car. When he walked into the station, he heard DCS Benfield shouting at DS Carr:

> When I say shouting, I mean *bawling*, telling Jock to get his arse in gear, wrap up the investigation. He turned on me and said, 'Where have *you* been?' I said, 'Manchester'. 'Oh aye? Well, don't go anywhere.' I went into the CID office. Jock's on the telephone. He said, 'Can you field the door for me? I've just got to make one or two calls. I'm trying

to get them to check the left luggage offices in Manchester.' So I go out and try to placate Benfield, act normal.

Later that evening, DCS Benfield asked for the file on Edward Evans. According to DC Fairley:

> He put the file, typed and finished, into his car. As far as Benfield was concerned, the inquiry was over. He buggered off. Talbot had washed his hands as well; he had other fish to fry. It was only Joe Mounsey who was interested, and because of him the search was due to last one more day – just one – and then the whole case would be closed. Jock said I could go home as well.

Back at 16 Wardle Brook Avenue the police search had continued and DCI Tyrrell found in the spine of a small white prayer book a left luggage ticket, which led the detectives to Central Station, Manchester. The abbreviation TICK and PB from Brady's list were now explained: 'Ticket' and 'Prayer Book'. DCI Tyrrell recalled:

> I examined this book carefully and found a counterfoil of a railway left luggage ticket. I found this rolled very, very tightly and pushed down the spine of the prayer book. The prayer book was inscribed: 'To Myra from Auntie Kath and Uncle Bert. November 16, 1958. Souvenir of your first Holy Communion.'

At 10.20 pm DS Carr took possession of one brown and one blue suitcase from DC Dennis Barrow of the British Transport Police, Victoria Station, Manchester. DC Barrow had found them at 7.50 pm. DC Ian Fairley recalled: 'I'd been home about an hour – hour-and-a-half when the phone rang. It was DS Alex Carr – they'd found the suitcases. They were big suitcases and they were jam packed full of stuff…. They were bloody heavy.'

The whole face of the investigation was about to change.

Chapter 14

Evidence

At 9.30 am the following morning, DS Carr handed the two suitcases over to Superintendent Bob Talbot. DC Ian Fairley recalled:

> Word had got out that we had got suitcases within the police network and the phones rang and by about 10.00 am every senior police officer in the North-West of England had descended on Hyde police station.
>
> We then started to go through the contents of the suitcases. It was like opening Pandora's Box. It was all there…. There was pornographic magazines, the Marquis de Sade, it really was the key that really identified what Brady and Hindley's involvement had been.

An unmarked police car was immediately sent to get David Smith and he was brought back to Hyde police station. He recalled how the police officers seemed to be acting differently towards him and how the station seemed full of detectives. As he was being led towards his usual interview room he noticed in the first office that he passed:

> The suitcases are on a table, the blue one and the brown. Both are open, their heaving contents spilling out like something wicked across the Formica surface. I'm rooted to the spot by what I see: a black wig, books with lurid covers – some of which I recognise – papers, photographs and several reels of tape. I remember the look that passed between Benfield and Talbot in the house when I mentioned Ian recording stuff on his eight-track and I feel a sudden chill without knowing why.

David was then taken to the interview room and left on his own for a while. A detective he hadn't met before then told him that they had found the suitcases he had mentioned and that he was free to go.

The blue suitcase contained books and magazines about sexual perversion, including, the books *The Anti-Sex, Sexual Anomalies and Perversions, Cradle of Erotica, The Sex Jungle, The Jewel in the Lotus, Confessions of a Mask, Death Rides a Camel, Werewolf in Paris, The Perfumed Garden, Sexus, Paris Vision 28, Satin Legs and Stilettos, High Heels and Stockings, The Life and Ideals of the Marquis de Sade* wrapped in the *Daily Mirror, The Kiss of the Whip, The Tropic of Cancer,* and a copy of *Mein Kampf* wrapped in the *News of the World.* There were soft porn magazines too, such as *Men's Digest, Penthouse, Swank, Cavalier* and *Wildcat.*

There was also a 1965 pocket diary belonging to Brady, notes, papers and photographs, an insurance form and a tax form belonging to him, two library tickets in the name of Jack Smith (David Smith's father), string, Sellotape, a bandolier belt for holding ammunition, bullets and a black wig.

Inside the brown suitcase were more pornographic books, including one called *Jailbait,* and a study of Jack the Ripper, fifty-four negatives and fifty-five photographic prints, key rings, a pamphlet on family planning addressed to Mrs A. Hope of 7 Bannock Street, a notebook belonging to Brady, his 1962 pocket diary, some papers, Myra's 1964 pocket diary, correspondence, an SS knife, a key on a shoelace, a sheath knife, a key wrapped in cloth, Brady's birth certificate, small truncheons, pieces of soap, a cutlery box containing a cosh and a black mask, another cosh with 'EUREKA' on it, some pieces of cloth, a Halibut oil tin – and two tapes.

Most disturbing of all, at first glance, was the Halibut Liver Oil tin with some photographs of a young child later identified as Lesley Ann Downey, naked. In some she was standing, in others lying on a bed. One was of her praying. There were others too, of her standing up, of her on a bed with her face to one side, and a back view of her with her arms spread wide, in the crucifix shape. One of two that the police felt were less disgusting to show Lesley Ann's mother for identification purposes was of her sitting on Hindley's bed wearing just her shoes and socks. Her arms were tied together with a black cord and she was gagged with a black cloth. DC Ian Fairley recalled:

> We came across a photograph of a little girl who was tied up. She was gagged with a scarf around about her face and she was laying naked on a bed…That really was something that immediately corroborated Smith's story.
>
> There was a tape and the tape was of a little girl being tortured and being abused. The tapes were played to senior and investigating officers and it was very hard for these officers to hide their emotions … but I can tell you there were a few tears in that room when it was played to these officers.

Detective Policewoman Pat Clayton recalled: 'I heard the tape many, many times and it was probably more horrendous the more you heard it.' This was the tape recording of Lesley Ann Downey's last moments and it completely changed the path of the investigation. Now there was proof that Brady and Hindley had been lying when questioned previously about Lesley Ann Downey.

EVIDENCE

DC Fairley recalled: 'People wept when they heard that tape. I heard it a week or so later and I cannot describe how horrific it is. Not just the content, but the preparation that had gone in to its creation.'

DCS Topping heard the tape during his reinvestigation in the 1980s and recalled:

> It is absolutely horrendous to listen to – it would move the hardest of people and it very much shows us the callousness of Brady and Hindley and the way that they actually went about committing the murders they were involved in and she was clearly there and was telling the child to be quiet and to 'shut up'. The child knows that something very serious is about to happen to her. She's begging. She's pleading. It didn't make any difference. They went ahead and did what they did.

On the other tape was some recorded radio programmes such as 'The Goon Show' and a programme about the rise of Adolf Hitler. Of the photographs found of Lesley Ann Downey, DS Roy Jarvis recalled:

> When we found the photographs of Lesley Ann Downey standing on a bed naked, legs apart, hands outstretched, clothed in nothing but a pair of socks and wearing a gag with a terrified look in her eyes, we realised that if we could link the bedhead in the bedroom at 16 Wardle Brook Avenue with the bedhead revealed in the photographs then this would be a major breakthrough. It would mean that Brady and Hindley knew of the whereabouts of Lesley Ann Downey.
>
> I had already found Myra Hindley's fingerprints on the photographs so we had to then do a comparison with the bedhead in the photograph and the bedhead in the bedroom. This was done in the same way as you would do a fingerprint comparison.
>
> Having found that similarity it meant that the fingerprints found on the photographs identified as those of Myra Hindley placed the photographs in Wardle Brook Avenue, placed the bed revealed in the photographs in Wardle Brook Avenue which showed that they must have had complete knowledge of the photographs, the room, and Lesley Ann Downey.

In fact, Hindley's fingerprints were found on three of the photographs, which showed that her interest in child pornography went at least to the extent of having a close look at Brady's work.

The camera used to take the photographs of Lesley Ann was not the one police found at Wardle Brook Avenue. They had found a Fujica camera which had been bought from a shop in Stamford Street, Ashton-under-Lyne. When they checked at the shop, detectives found that Hindley had traded in an Ensign camera for the Fujica. This was further proof that she had lied about never going to Ashton-under-Lyne. The shop manager, Brian Simpson, remembered taking the Ensign as a deposit for the Fujica, which she had bought on hire purchase. The Ensign was traced to its new owner, Mr Alfred Ashton of Dukinfield. DS Raymond Paton of the Home Office Forensic Science Laboratory at Preston used it in the house in Hattersley to prove that it was the same camera that had been used to take the pictures of Lesley Ann.

The police resumed their search on the moors at 9.35 am in an area around Hollin Brown Knoll, just as police back at Hyde were looking in the suitcases. DCI Mounsey, DI Mattin and DS Eckersley were in charge of a dozen men working on a patch about eighty yards north of the road when they decided to call it a day, as by 2.00 pm the rain had turned to mist which began to hamper the search. PC Bob Spiers recalled:

> The police had been searching the moors for several days without any success and on Saturday 16 October 1965 Joe Mounsey decided to bring the lads from the Ashton division up to make a search using the old-fashioned way that was done then of prodding metal rods and pushing them into the ground. No findings were made at all and it was decided to wrap the job up.

At 2.50, when the officers were getting ready to leave and started climbing into the van, PC Bob Spiers decided that he wanted to go to the toilet. He wandered over to an area away from where they had been searching and found himself standing in a clear patch on top of the ridge. Bob Spiers:

> On returning back down to the other officers my attention was drawn to a depression in the peat. This depression was filled with water. Protruding out of the water was what looked like a white weathered stick. On making an examination I saw it was a bone but I couldn't tell a bone of what – either a sheep or human. Due to the colour of the water you couldn't see anything but I could definitely feel something under the water and I decided then I would call the other officers up.
>
> The coach was loaded up and ready to go and they were shouting to me that it's time to go and I said: 'No, there's something up here, I'm staying.' I'd found something and I was not leaving the moor until it was uncovered, so we gradually moved the soil away gently and upon finding a piece of material realised it was clothing and we knew it was a human body and not a sheep.

DS Leslie Eckersley recalled:

I was called to a particular spot by Police Constable Spiers. He showed me a depression in the ground in a bank of peat. In that depression there was a pool of water, it was a depression in the bank of peat. There was a piece of bone sticking up from the water. I carefully removed a little soil from around the bone and I saw further bone. There was a strong smell of decomposing flesh and I removed a little further soil and I saw flesh and a human head. I then informed Chief Inspector Mounsey who came to the scene with Detective Inspector Mattin.

DC Tom McVittie, part of Mounsey's team, recalled: 'We could see that it was the body of a little girl, but where she had lain against the mud, that half of her was gone. It was destroyed, no features, nothing. But the other half had been perfectly preserved by the peat. Half of her face was intact.'

The police had found Lesley Ann Downey. Her clothes lay at her feet – a blue coat edged with white; a red dress with lace trimmings; a pink wool cardigan; a pink underskirt; white knickers with a flower on them; grey socks with white stripes; shoes; and a string of beads and matching bracelet – the ones Lesley Ann's brother had won at the fair and given to her a couple of days before she was murdered. The grave was seventy-one yards from the road.

Police discover the body of Lesley Ann Downey on Hollin Brown Knoll.

By 4.00 pm it was dark and the detectives continued to work by arc lamp. It wasn't until 9.20 pm that Professor Cyril Polson, head of Forensic Medicine at Leeds University, and Dr David Gee, a lecturer at Leeds, arrived to supervise the final excavation of Lesley Ann's body. At the subsequent trial, Dr Gee said:

> I was shown a partly excavated grave by Detective Chief Inspector Mounsey. My colleagues and I then set about exposing the remains in that grave. The body lay on its right side; the skeletal remains of the left arm were extended above the head, and the hand was missing. The right arm was beneath the body, the hand being near the right knee. Both legs were doubled up towards the abdomen, flexed at hips and knees. The head was in normal position. The body was naked. A number of articles of clothing were present in the soil near to the feet.

It was nearly midnight when the little girl's body was carried to the roadside on a stretcher covered with plastic sheeting by a sergeant and a superintendent in uniform and two detectives. It was taken by van to Uppermill Mortuary.

Lesley Ann's mother, Ann, heard a news flash on the television which announced that police in Manchester had discovered the body of a child in a shallow grave on Saddleworth Moor. Ann and her partner Alan, immediately ran around to a friend's house (as they had a telephone) and called the police, but Ann was told: 'No … the body is not Lesley Ann. It is the body of a boy…. Go home, get some sleep. Stop worrying. I can assure you that the body that has been found is that of a young lad.'

Police dig around the site where Lesley Ann Downey's body was found on Hollin Brown Knoll.

EVIDENCE

The following day intensive police activity was concentrated on Hollin Brown Knoll where detectives were now convinced they would find more bodies. The search began at first light. DC Gelder, a police photographer, took photographs near the grave and compared them with the enlargements he had made from the photographs seized from the house in Wardle Brook Avenue. He was satisfied that four of Brady's pictures were taken within fifty yards of where Lesley Ann's body was buried.

Two detectives called at Lesley Ann's mother's house and asked her to accompany them to Uppermill Mortuary to make a formal identification on the remains that had been discovered the previous night. She told the detectives that last night she had been told that the remains discovered were of a boy, but one of the detectives said to her: 'We need you to come and look at the clothes the little girl was wearing … to see if you can identify them. They might belong to someone else.'

As they got to the mortuary, there was a media scrum and Ann had to be ushered quickly inside, where she was informed that her partner Alan wasn't allowed inside the room where the body lay as he wasn't a blood relative. She was led through a door and on a table were some clothes – Lesley Ann's clothes. They had been washed that morning but the stench of decay still lingered. She identified them immediately and then began to vomit convulsively.

Unseen. The posts indicate where Lesley Ann's body was found.

Police and volunteers search the moorland.

Police search.

When she had recovered she was led deeper into the mortuary, where she later remembered the smell of rubber and formaldehyde was overwhelming. She entered a room where she saw a green sheet covering the little body from stomach to feet, and also covered the right-hand side of her torso and face. She began to wretch again as

DCI Joe Mounsey on the moor.

she realised the body that lay before her was her little girl. An officer gave her a glass of brandy, but she threw it straight back up again.

When they got home, Lesley Ann's brother, Terry, ran to his mum and hugged her. 'It's my fault, Mum. It's all my fault. I shouldn't have let Lesley go by herself. I should have been with her. I let her down. I should have protected her. I let her down!'

At 3.00 pm Dr Gee, with Professor Polson, Home Office pathologist Dr Manning, Dr Bartley and numerous police officers started the post-mortem examination on Lesley Ann's body. A police photographer, Detective Sergeant Thomas Rylatt, stood by to take photographs. He could not give the cause of death, but he could say that she did not die from any violent injury. His final report was eight pages long, but he summarised it during the later trial:

> The initial impression given by the injuries, notably two elliptical injuries of the right chest, was that the child had been stabbed; the clean-cut margins of the injury in the right groin had the appearance of a long incised wound. As soon as it was possible to examine these injuries more closely under low magnification, it was apparent that all the damage done to the body was unlike that due to human interference but entirely consisted of damage by animals. Stabbing was definitely

excluded by the fact that the damage in the region of these injuries was entirely superficial. The disappearance of the abdominal organs could have destroyed signs of the cause of death. The heart, lungs, air passages, gullet and brain were sufficiently preserved to permit the statement that no gross injury to which death could be ascribed was present. Signs of asphyxia were absent and therefore proof of suffocation was lacking. In summary, the post-mortem examination established that this was the body of a female child of an age between the years of seven and thirteen. Subsequent dental examination narrowed the age limit to that of approximately ten years. The post-mortem changes in the body were consistent with its having lain in peaty soil for a prolonged period: probably several months, but not several years. It was impossible to demonstrate the cause of death. The examination excluded certain possible causes, notably injury by blunt force, calculated to fracture bones. It also excluded strangulation by a ligature. It did not exclude other forms of mechanical asphyxia, notably smothering. I cannot, of course, exclude death by natural causes.

David Smith was again interviewed, this time about what he knew about Brady and his background. He told them of Brady's interest in Germany and of the books he read:

About once every five weeks Myra and Brady would come down to our house at 13 Wiles Street. I never knew when they were coming, more often than not they just arrived unexpectedly. Brady always brought drink with him, always cheap wine, he hardly ever drank anything else. On these occasions Brady and I would sit up talking until 4.00 am to 5.00 am. Myra and Maureen used to go to bed whenever they got tired round about 1.30 am. We all used to drink this wine Brady brought and invariably we all got drunk.

At first Brady used to talk about his interest in Germany and I must confess I got interested in it as well. Gradually as the months went on he began to take me into his confidence more often and he used to talk about books he had read on torture and sex. His favourite was called *Justine or the Misfortunes of Virtue* by the Marquis de Sade. This is a book about sexual perversions and torture. I think he had the original version of it which runs into seven volumes. He had strong feelings about the Nazi regime and he often used to say that the extermination of the Jews was right and that people who were useless to the state such as cripples and mentally backward people should be killed off, preferably at birth. As I got to know him it became obvious to me that he hated people in general, he had no friends that I know of, and his favourite way of describing people was as 'cabbages' and 'morons'. He told me he had read *Mein Kampf* and recommended that I read it too. I did borrow it some time later but I only read about half of it. I didn't understand it so I never finished reading it.

He then gave details about discussions with Brady and the events in the weeks leading up to Edward Evans's death, already covered in this book. He then continued:

About two days after Evans was killed I suddenly thought Brady might have taken the suitcases to a railway left luggage office because he seemed to be very fond of railway stations. He has told me several times that he liked to visit railway stations and that he had often walked to Piccadilly Station from Westmoreland Street in the early hours of the morning.

I reported the murder of Evans as soon as I felt safe to do so. I know I had discussed robbing a bank with him and I suppose I might have gone on it with him but killing is another matter, I couldn't live with that. After Evans was killed Myra and Brady showed no emotion at all, and I was satisfied then that what he had boasted about killing people before was true. He was so calm and composed that I realised it couldn't have been the first murder he had committed. I feel sure that Brady killed Evans to test my reaction.

Both he and Myra were fond of dogs but I cannot remember ever seeing Brady show any sentiment at all over any human being, nor can I remember him ever showing any affection towards Myra. Never once have I seen him put his arm round her or speak to her affectionately. She was just there and he just seemed to accept her. On the other hand, it was quite obvious that Myra was very fond of him. She used to call him 'Neddy'.

At daybreak the following day, Monday 18 October, police search officers set out in a circle surrounding the green tent that had been erected over Lesley Ann's grave. DCI Joe Mounsey was in charge and he spent the day consulting maps that had been marked with crosses where people had suggested that further graves might be found.

The searchers were still using their wooden sticks to poke into the ground and then sniffing the end to see if there was any smell of decomposition. Soon, Detective Inspector Douglas Smith, a Lancashire Police frogman, arrived with what was called a 'magic stick'. It was a 3ft-long electronic metal rod with a forked end which was used for finding cavities below ground.

David and Maureen Smith were again taken up to the moors by DCI Mounsey but were not much help. David was then driven back to Hyde police station where he faced his hardest day of questioning yet. He was asked about the books that had been found in the suitcases, along with the pornographic magazines, two library tickets belonging to his father, a bandolier and ammunition, a cutlery box containing a cosh and a black mask, and another cosh with 'EUREKA' written on it.

> The police didn't show me everything but they asked me what I'd taken round to Ian's the night before Edward Evans was killed and I told them: a notepad, books, a cosh, my starter pistol and the blank shells that went with it. That was it. Then they brought everything I'd listed as mine into the room and asked me if I could positively identify it all. I did – though I have no idea how those library tickets belonging to my dad came to be in there. That's a complete mystery to me. I didn't like admitting that the home-made cosh marked Eureka was mine, but I wasn't going to lie about anything.
>
> The notepad proved to be the biggest sticking point. It contained my interpretation of the books Ian had given me to read and the police pounced on it straight away. It was a major interrogation issue.

Inside the notepad David Smith had compiled a list of the novels recommended to him by Brady, with some extracts from the texts and his own understanding of the authors' intentions added alongside.

> I thought it was clear enough that the notepad was a sort of diary of what I'd read, but it became a real battle to try and prove that these were not necessarily my views, as such. I understood why the police needed to get to the bottom of what I'd written, but I really struggled to convince them that the notebook wasn't what it seemed. And I ended up becoming very defensive, which was the last thing I wanted. I'd never asked for a solicitor, not once, because I didn't want the obstruction and constant interjections of some legal bloke telling me I didn't have to answer this and that. Being upfront about the things that belonged to me in the suitcases might not have been the path a solicitor would have advised me to take, for example – he might have said that it wasn't in my best interests. But as far as I was concerned it was the only option. I knew which way I wanted to go and I knew it was something I had to do on my own.

Detectives then switched their attention to the photographs that had been found of Lesley Ann Downey. All nine of them were flipped over, one by one.

I couldn't take in what I was seeing. The detectives presented them in a certain way, and rightly so, to get an honest reaction from me. I freaked out and couldn't stand to look at them. The detectives started barking at me, as they turned the photographs over: 'What do you think of that? How does it make you feel? You know who that is, don't you? It's Lesley Ann Downey, isn't it? That little girl is Lesley Ann Downey and her body was found where you used to go for picnics with your sister-in-law and her boyfriend. What do you think happened to her after this was taken? Come on, let's have it – *what the fucking hell happened to her?*' That was their attitude.

I realised then what Brady had meant when he'd told me that he had 'photographic proof'. That burned itself into my mind. His words meant nothing until then. And it was obvious to anyone who saw those pictures that Lesley Ann Downey would never have been able to go home after they'd been taken.

The tape recorded by Brady and Hindley of Lesley Ann's last moments in Hindley's bedroom was then played to him.

The police acted fairly in how they played that tape. They needed an honest reaction from me. And that was, in this case, to cry. I cried, I got very upset, but they played the whole thing from beginning to end, and by the time the music came on I had my head in my hands, sobbing uncontrollably. It was completely horrific, that tape. Afterwards, I couldn't find my voice. But they had their questions: 'You know that was Lesley, don't you? What happened to her after the tape ran out? When it went quiet, what was going on then? Get it off your chest, lad. Admit to it – she wasn't going to bloody walk home, was she?'

I know that later on Myra Hindley claimed she never used that bedroom again after Lesley Ann Downey was killed. But I can say for a fact that she was lying. That's where she and Maureen would sleep when me and Ian were having one of our all-night drinking sessions. Time and again, she slept there. The murder committed in her bedroom didn't trouble her at all.

Brady, in a neat grey suit and a white open-necked shirt, appeared before the magistrates at Stalybridge. He remained silent throughout the proceedings. His solicitor, Mr Charles Fitzpatrick, renewed his complaint that he was unable to obtain a copy of Brady's original statement:

Seven days ago at this court I asked to be furnished with a copy of a written statement which the accused was alleged to have made to the police. I feel there must have been many copies made and one could have been available today. I feel the direction of the court seven days ago has not yet been complied with and I now renew my application for a copy of the statement to be furnished to me today so that I can go properly about my client's defence.

Superintendent Bob Talbot maintained that it was up to the Director of Public Prosecutions and assured Mr Fitzpatrick that nothing would be done to prejudice his client's defence. The magistrates accepted that it would be handed over as soon as possible. Brady was remanded for another three days. Shortly after he left the dock, Hindley, in a red coat, appeared, charged with being an accessory after the murder of Edward Evans.

Detective Chief Inspector John Tyrrell and other officers searched the house in Hattersley again. Home Office pathologist, Dr Bernard Manning, was also working in the house with the curtains drawn against prying sightseers.

Meanwhile, DCI Mounsey handed police photographer Mike Massheder three negatives of moorland scenes – one with Hindley in the foreground, one with her in the background and a general shot of the hills – with instructions to make 20 x 16 inch enlargements. Mike Massheder recalled:

> There were a large number of photographs found in the house and in the suitcases and photographic negatives. Some of the photographs

Ian Brady, 18th October 1965,
Pictured outside court.

were taken with Brady and Hindley and Moorland scenes in the background. It was very, very important that we started to identify all these scenes with a very strong possibility that areas in them were possibly graves.

At 2.35 pm DCI Haigh, DCS Benfield and Superintendent Talbot interviewed Brady at Hyde police station:

Benfield: Have you got a driving licence?

Brady: Yes.

Benfield: What is it for?

Brady: A motorcycle.

Benfield: Can you drive a motor car?

Brady: Yes, but I have never driven on a road, only on private land.

Benfield: There are two suitcases – a blue one and a brown one – which I believe are your property.

Brady: Yes, they are.

Benfield: I believe these were deposited by you at Central Station Manchester on 5 October 1965.

Brady: I can't remember the date.

Benfield: In these cases recovered from the station there are several articles bearing your name, do they belong to you?

Brady: Part of them do.

Benfield: These articles I am about to show you have been taken from these suitcases. Firstly, will you look at this envelope which bears the initials I.B. and contains photographs of a young girl with a scarf round her mouth? Did you take these?

Brady: Yes, I took them.

Benfield: Where?

Brady: At Hattersley. At Wardle Brook Avenue.

Brady was then asked questions about other photographs found and then about the books discovered in the suitcases. He was then shown a handle shaped instrument with string attached bearing the word 'Eureka'.

Benfield: What is this?

Brady: It's a cosh.

Benfield: Whose is it?

Brady: Smith's.

DCS Benfield then asked Brady about different items of clothing:

Benfield: I would like you to look at these articles of clothing and this set of beads. This child's blue coat, a tartan frock, a red woollen cardigan, a pair of shoes, a pair of socks, an underslip and this pair of knickers. These garments were recovered from the moor near Greenfield late last Saturday night, 16 October. This clothing has been identified as that of Lesley Ann Downey whose body was recovered at the same time and place.

Among photographs recovered from your suitcase were a number showing a little girl stripped naked with a scarf around her mouth. I have reason to believe that these are photographs of Lesley Ann Downey. You have already admitted taking these photographs, here are some enlargements of those photographs.

Brady: Yes.

Benfield: Would you like to say anything about these photographs?

Brady: Not at present.

Questioning then moved on to the tape recordings:

Benfield: I would like you now to listen to a tape recording. Two tapes were found in the blue suitcase belonging to you.

Brady: I know the tape.

The tape of Lesley Ann Downey being abused was then played to him.

Benfield: You say you know the tape, the voices appear to be those of yourself, Myra and I believe that of Lesley Ann Downey whose photograph you admit taking.

Brady: She didn't give the name Downey, it was something else.

Benfield: Do you wish to say anything else about this recording, about what took place?

Brady: Not at the moment.

Benfield: As I have said previously, this girl's body was recovered from the moors between Greenfield and Holmfirth last Saturday evening.

Brady: There is an explanation for it, I didn't kill Lesley but I took those photographs.

Benfield: The girl was missing from about 5.00 pm on Boxing Day 1964, where did you meet her?

Brady: I met her at the house, I don't know how she got there.

DCS Benfield then placed Lesley Ann's socks on the table in front of Brady, along with the photographs taken by him.

Benfield: Look at these photographs. Do you agree that the shoes and socks on the photographs are similar to these?

Brady: Yes.

Benfield: It is reasonable to assume that Lesley Ann Downey died at Wardle Brook Avenue.

Brady: No, I only took the photographs.

Benfield: Can you tell me how and where she met her death?

Brady: I don't know, there's only the photographs on my part.

Benfield: How did she arrive at the house at Hattersley?

Brady: She came in either a car or a van.

Benfield: Who brought her?

Brady: Two men. One stayed outside, I don't know him. The other man I do know, but I am not prepared to tell you at present.

Benfield: It appears that the photographs were taken in a bedroom. Who was present when they were taken?

Brady: Only Myra, myself and the little girl.

Benfield: Where was the man during this time?

Brady: Downstairs.

Benfield: Where was Myra's grandmother at this time?

Brady: I can't remember.

Benfield: When the man arrived at the house with the little girl what did he say about her?

Brady: He didn't need to say anything, I knew why he had brought her.

Benfield: During the recording of the tape it appears that you are trying to get the girl to put something in her mouth. What was it?

Brady: The scarf.

Benfield: After the photographs had been taken what happened to the little girl?

Brady: She left the house with the man who brought her.

Benfield: Was she alive when she left the house?

Brady: Yes. I was told later that she had been dropped off at Belle Vue.

Benfield: If you say the girl left Wardle Brook Avenue alive, surely you are prepared to tell us the name of the man who brought her and took her away?

Brady: …No. I will think about it and I may let you know later.

Benfield: Don't you think that in your own interests and in order that necessary enquiries may be made immediately that if there was such a man you should tell us now?

Brady: …No, I'm not saying who it is. I've met him in Manchester and he goes in Liston's bar.

Benfield: Do you know his name?

Brady: Yes, but I am not going to say who at present until I have had advice.

Benfield: In your own interests and everybody concerned it is important that if this man exists you tell us who he is.

Brady: I will mention this to Mr Fitzpatrick on Thursday and I will take his advice. When I saw him this morning he told me not to make any statement.

DCS Benfield then showed Brady a photograph of him standing on a rock against a moorland background.

Benfield: Alright, will you now look at this photograph of yourself standing on a moorland site. This appears to be the site where the body of Lesley Ann Downey was found.

Brady: I don't know the place. I have been all over the moors.

Benfield: Last week you said to other police officers in my presence that you had told David Smith that you had buried a body on the moors, but that you had said that to him only to impress him. We have now found the body of Lesley Ann Downey whose last known whereabouts was in the house at Wardle Brook Avenue with you and Myra.

Brady: I never said anything like that to Smith, and I deny what you say about telling other police officers that I had said it to Smith. I mean that I said I had buried a body.

Benfield: It is most important that you tell us who that man was who took that girl from the house and you tell us where we can find him.

Brady: When I have discussed the matter with Mr Fitzpatrick on Thursday I will take his advice.

Benfield: In that case, at this stage I have nothing further to say to you. You may sign the note taken by Mr Haigh.

Brady: Not at this stage.

The interview concluded at 8.05 pm. DCI Haigh and DCS Benfield then joined Superintendent Talbot and Detective Policewoman Campion in interviewing Hindley ten minutes later.

Benfield: I have reason to believe that on Tuesday 5 October 1965 you and Ian Brady went to Central Station at Manchester and deposited two suitcases there. We have recovered the two suitcases.

Hindley was asked about certain items found in the suitcases. The photographs were then shown to her.

Benfield: Now, will you look at these photographs. They are of a little girl stripped with a scarf around her mouth. These photographs of the little girl were also found in the suitcase. They are of a girl named Lesley Ann Downey.

Hindley looked at the photographs, looked down but said nothing.

Benfield: I have reason to believe that these photographs were taken in your bedroom at 16 Wardle Brook Avenue, Hattersley, by Ian Brady in your presence.

Hindley held her head in her hands but made no reply. She was sitting with her head down and had her handkerchief across her mouth with the knuckles of both hands against her cheeks.

> **Benfield:** Last Saturday night the body of Lesley Ann Downey was found buried on the moors on the Holmfirth Road together with this clothing. [Hindley was shown the clothing that had been found]. This little girl was reported missing from home at Manchester on Boxing Day last year and I believe that the photographs I have shown you of the little girl were taken on that day. Brady has told me that the little girl was brought to your home by two men. One of the men came into the house and remained downstairs while Brady was taking the photographs in your presence.
>
> **Hindley:** I'm saying nothing.
>
> **Benfield:** Also in one of the suitcases was a tape recording. I believe the voices are those of yourself, Brady and Lesley Ann Downey. I am going to play it.

While the tape was played Hindley sat with her head bowed and she started to sob and a vein at the left side of her throat was pulsating rapidly. He later said: 'She sat with a hankie pressed to her lips with her right hand. I noticed some pulsation in her neck and she began to look distressed. I wouldn't go so far as to say she wept, but tears welled up in her eyes.' Then the recording finished.

> **Benfield:** Did you hear that recording?
>
> **Hindley:** I am ashamed.

Hindley then started to cry, which lasted only a short while, and then:

> **Hindley:** I'm saying nothing.

The interviewed finished at 9.45 pm.

On Tuesday 19 October, at 10.00 am, the search around Hollin Brown Knoll resumed with eighty policemen now taking part.

DCI Tyrrell continued his search of the house at Wardle Brook Avenue, while four other detectives spent six hours at the BBC sound recording studio in Manchester where technician John Weekes tested and amplified the tapes found in the two suitcases to make the sound clearer.

At Ashton Police HQ, DCI Mounsey looked over the latest batch of Brady's moorland photographs that had been blown up by Mike Massheder and conferred with other senior officers about the possibility of using a helicopter to take aerial pictures of the area.

The following day was particularly cold and windy on the moor but the searchers fanned out again in an ever-increasing circle around the gravesite of Lesley Ann Downey. There were nearly 200 newspaper reporters, photographers and writers from across the world on the scene by now, including those from America, Scandinavia, France and Germany, all itching to get the latest news. Some stayed in the Clarence Hotel in Greenfield, where the police diggers went for their lunch, and sometimes information was exchanged for a free meal and drink.

At Ashton Police HQ the senior officers discussed the value of publishing some of Brady's moorland scenes in the hope that the public might be able to identify where they were taken.

On Thursday, 21 October, at 9.40 am, DCS Benfield charged Myra Hindley with the murder of Lesley Ann Downey and cautioned her. Fifteen minutes later he did the same to Brady. There was no precise date of Lesley Ann's murder on the charge, simply that they had murdered her sometime between 26 December 1964 and 16 October 1965, in the county of Cheshire.

Later that morning they both appeared in the dock at Hyde Magistrate's Court. Brady was again wearing his grey suit and the court dealt with him first. Superintendent Talbot described to the court how Lesley Ann had vanished from the fairground and how her body had been found on the moors. He told the court that Brady had replied 'Not Guilty' when he was charged. Brady's solicitor, Mr Fitzpatrick, mentioned that 'the prosecution has been good enough to provide me with the statement to which I have referred in earlier proceedings.'

Brady was granted legal aid and taken down to the cells beneath the court. On the way, he passed Hindley coming up with Detective Margaret Campion. She was again wearing her red coat. Superintendent Talbot repeated his evidence concerning Lesley Ann and said that when Hindley was charged, she replied: 'It's not true.' She was also granted legal aid.

At 11.00 am, DC Mike Massheder reported to DCI Mounsey at Hollin Brown Knoll. Mounsey had the three photographs, one the dramatic picture of Hindley kneeling with her dog Puppet in her coat, which he had enlarged from Brady's negatives. Mike Massheder:

Another photograph that was very, very interesting was of Myra Hindley, kneeling on a Moorland with a puppy dog in her coat, staring down at a patch of what looked like recently disturbed ground.

The trick was to find this scene. I got a telephone call at Ashton-under-Lyne police station – 'Get yourself and your camera up to the moors and don't be followed.'

When I got there I was given the photograph of Myra at Hollin Brow Knoll. 'Look at that and see if that means anything to you.' As I walked around I suddenly realised I had hit upon absolutely the same spot. That's when I took another photograph showing the foreground and background of Hollin Brow Knoll and matched it up with the photograph. Those two photographs are quite a picture, because the only thing missing from my photograph is Hindley and the puppy.

The background of the picture of Hindley, he saw, tallied with the hill scene as he looked north from the south side of the A635 road, the opposite side to where

Myra Hindley looking at John Kilbride's grave. This image was used to find his body.

The police photograph used to match that taken by Ian Brady of Myra Hindley over John Kilbride's grave.

Lesley Ann Downey's body was found. Detective Inspectors John Chaddock and Joe Mounsey studied the two photographs and the order was given to probe the spot. At midday, DI Chaddock prodded his stick a few inches into the ground. DC Massheder:

> There is a stone immediately to the left of the foot of the accused Hindley in the photograph. This is the spot at which preparations were made to start digging. Inspector Chaddock then pushed a stick into the ground about halfway between that stone and the stone immediately below it in the photograph. When he removed the stick there was a strong smell of decomposing flesh.

Detective Inspector John Chaddock recalled at the trial:

> We removed the top soil to a depth of about nine inches and uncovered
> a boy's left black shoe. Underneath the shoe I saw some socks and
> what appeared to be part of the heel of a body. At this stage digging
> operations were suspended and I cleared a little more soil and exposed
> the right lower leg.

DCI Mounsey sent for Professor Polson and Dr Gee, the forensic experts, and
policemen erected a canvas screen to hide the excavation from people on the road.
The grave was 88 yards south of the road and 373 yards from Lesley Ann's grave.

Most of the officers leading the investigation quickly arrived at the scene: Arthur
Benfield, head of Cheshire CID; Assistant Chief Constable Eric Cunningham,
head of the North West Regional Crime Squad; Chief Superintendent Harold
Prescott, Lancashire CID chief; Chief Constable Scott of the West Riding; Chief
Superintendent Douglas Nimmo, head of Manchester CID.

At 3.20 pm Professor Polson and Dr Gee arrived to complete the excavation of
the body. Dr Polson, Professor of Forensic Medicine at the University of Leeds, later
told the trial:

> I and Dr David Gee arrived at Saddleworth Moor at a spot which had
> been surrounded by screens on the south side of the A635 road. In the
> ground in this area where a superficial excavation had been carried
> out was a black shoe, approximately size 6 with a rubber sole that
> was worn relatively slightly; also visible in the excavation was part
> of a shirt. Dr Gee and I then began to excavate with hand tools. We
> soon came upon two rounded objects covered with cloth, later shown
> to be socks; the rounded objects were the heels of the deceased. By
> careful hand digging we traced the lower limbs, then the trunk, and
> head, and finally exposed the body and undercut it so that it could
> be removed intact. The orientation of the body was approximately
> at right angles to the main road; he had his feet towards the road,
> head away from the road and facing towards Holmfirth. The body lay
> at a depth of approximately 12 to 18 inches. The soil in the region
> was apparently more sandy than in the grave on the opposite side of
> the road already investigated. The body I was exposing on this day
> was fully extended with the front of the lower limbs and toes facing
> downwards. The upper part of the trunk was twisted somewhat to the
> left. The head also faced to the left. The right forearm was folded
> across the chest and was under the body. The left arm was straight
> and lay against the left side of the body. The features were now

obscured by post-mortem change. Short brown hair was still present. The small bones of the feet and hands had separated. Those of the feet were still held within the socks. After the body had been exposed and all appropriate photographs taken, it was carefully lifted from the grave, rolled onto a sheet of galvanised iron, and transported to the post-mortem room.

At 5pm Mr Tim Coffey, a West Riding pathologist, arrived with two stretcher bearers and the two forensic scientists left. Twenty-five minutes later two detectives came from behind the screen carrying a sack which they put in the back of a police car.

At 5.50 pm the body, covered with plastic sheeting, was carried on a stretcher to a waiting van and driven to Uppermill mortuary.

John Kilbride's body is removed from Saddleworth Moor.

The site of John Kilbride's grave.

The police were unsure as to who the body was as it had been buried in a stream bed, and as such it was unidentifiable. The estimate at the time was that it was a boy of around 12 years of age and they had two missing children matching this description on their books at the time – Keith Bennett and John Kilbride.

Officers went to visit Winnie Johnson first, mother of Keith Bennett, and they showed her the mugshots of Brady and Hindley and asked: 'Have you ever seen these two people?' Winnie and her husband Jimmy both shook their heads. Winnie recalled:

> The police told us they thought they had something to do with it. Then the more we heard, the more we knew that was right. They only lived quarter of a mile from us, and it was horrifying to think we probably passed them in the street dozens of times after Keith had gone, and never

EVIDENCE

The view from a helicopter of John Kilbride's gravesite on Saddleworth Moor.

knew. One day a couple of chaps from CID came and asked to speak to Jimmy on his own. They took him into the front room. When they came out, the detectives left. I asked Jimmy what it was about, but he didn't say a word. He just lifted Joey, the baby at the time, out of his pram and sat there with him on his knee, and the tears streamed down his face.

Eventually, after an age, he said, 'Winnie, I've got something to tell you. They've found a lad's body on the moors, but they think it's John

243

Kilbride because it's quite a lot taller than Keith.' I didn't say anything. The police brought the clothing they'd found, in a plastic bag, but it wasn't Keith's. The funny thing was that the t-shirt John Kilbride had been wearing was very similar to one Keith had on. For a moment my hopes were raised that they'd found the body, but then they were dashed again.

In the evening Chief Inspector Mounsey took the left shoe to show Mrs Sheila Kilbride. She recalled: 'They brought a shoe to me to identify and I knew right away that it was John's. I had to go up to the mortuary. I knew it was John's shoe – Super Duke. Just been mended, chisel toe. I knew it was his.'

The following day, Friday 22 October, the West Riding Coroner, Bernard W. Little, opened the inquest on Lesley Ann Downey. It was quickly adjourned for two months after hearing that two people had been arrested for her murder.

At 10.30 am, back at 16 Wardle Brook Avenue, DCI Tyrrell set a team up to dig the front and back gardens. They started with the front, prodding canes into the earth and sniffing the end that came out for any signs of decomposition. They then shovelled samples of earth into polythene bags which were tagged and taken away for analysis. They dug down to a depth of 3ft and probed again, but found nothing.

Meanwhile, Sheila Kilbride was taken to Uppermill Mortuary to identify her son John Kilbride by DCI Mounsey. Detective Policewoman Pat Clayton recalled:

> The remains were there, but she obviously couldn't identify a body. She had to identify him by the clothing. She was upset. We were all upset. We just hung on to one another in the back of the car and hugged. It was terrible. It was her child that was being identified wasn't it? But there was no child to identify. It was only clothing.

Sheila Kilbride:

> They cleaned it up as best they could, but I'll never forget it. I'd altered his jacket, I'd altered his underwear, his father's underwear, because I wasn't rich and I couldn't always buy him new. I knew it was his.
>
> The buttons on the jacket were footballs that I'd stitched on myself. There was no doubt at all. It's not nice to look back on that.

Mrs Kilbride looked at the articles of clothing which had been removed from the body and cleaned. She saw the jacket he was wearing when he vanished, with the plastic buttons made to look like footballs that she had sewn on herself (she had one over and gave it to the police as an exhibit for the trial), and she pointed out where she had turned up the hem of the sleeves. An elderly neighbour, Mrs Margaret Doran, had passed the jacket on to Mrs Kilbride for John. It had been her grandson's. The vest he was wearing had been one of his father's and she had sewn on odd-coloured buttons.

Sheila recalled: 'I know how he was found. Not in a grave. In a hole head first with his feet 9 inches from the top and his head 3 inches. I'll never forget that.'

At Uppermill Mortuary, Professor Polson and Dr Gee began the post-mortem examination on the body of John Kilbride. His testimony is taken from the eventual trial:

> The body was still clothed, and the following garments were removed by me: a jacket of greyish blue bearing a football type of button on the cuff; a woollen pullover in royal blue; a shirt; a woollen vest; trousers of jean type; underpants; socks – these I had to cut to effect removal.
>
> The trousers were pulled down to about mid-thigh position. They were nearer to the knee than to the top of the thigh. The underpants were also rolled down in a band about 1.5in broad at about mid-thigh level, and appeared to be knotted at the back. The coiled underpants were removed so as to leave them in the form found on the body.
>
> The principal feature of the unclothed body was a general transformation of the body fat into adiopocere – that is a white, soft, soapy material. No obvious injury was found. Loss of surface tissue was minimal and entirely consisted of the disintegration and loss during burial and recovery of the body. The skin of the neck was intact; no ligature was round the neck nor were there any marks to indicate strangulation or throttling. There were no signs of asphyxia visible, and these, if present, would have been completely obscured by advanced post-mortem changes. Extensive search failed to detect any fracture of long bones or the skull.
>
> The brain was shrunken and now a semi-liquid tissue. No trace of bleeding was found inside the skull, nor was there any obvious damage to the brain. The neck structure showed advanced post-mortem change; no obvious signs of bruising were present. The pleura, lungs and wind pipe showed severe post-mortem change; there was no obvious disease or injury. The heart showed severe post-mortem change; there was no obvious disease or injury, and no congenital malformation. The liver and kidneys showed severe post-mortem change. The stomach and intestines showed post-mortem change but were still identifiable, especially the appendix. The anus was patent but I found no obvious injury to the passage; the expression 'patent' means that it was open. The external genitalia were now of indefinite shape owing to severe

post-mortem change; the skin between the front of the body and the back passage was intact; there was no vaginal orifice, nor did I find any female genitalia inside the pelvis, where preservation was relatively good.

In the presence of this severe post-mortem change, it was not possible to ascertain the cause of death. It was possible to exclude certain causes of death. First of all, there was no gross injury of a kind which would lead to the breakage of bones, and there was no major wounding. There was no gross disease. If the death had been due to suffocation, no proof of this was obtained, but it was not excluded as a possible cause of death. The position of the trousers – more particularly, the position and arrangement of the underpants – appeared to be unusual and was not consistent with the lowering of the garments on a visit to the toilet.

Police continue to search the moorland.

The stature during life was approximately 4ft 9in. It appeared to be the body of a boy of between 10 and 14 years. The extent of the post-mortem change indicated that burial was of several months rather than several weeks.

Maxwell Saunders, Lecturer in Conservative Dentistry at the University of Leeds Dental School, told the trial:

I received from Professor Polson a specimen of upper and lower jaws bearing teeth, and made an examination of them on the same day. The middle teeth in the upper jaw had a space between them. These teeth were squarish in shape. Having examined all the teeth I came to the conclusion that the age of the body was between 12 and 14 years.

The bodies of two children, for whom evidence had been found that could link Brady and Hindley to them, had now been found, but the search went on. There was no concrete evidence at this point linking Brady and Hindley to Keith Bennett, and only the fact that Hindley knew of Pauline Reade to link them to her disappearance. The top brass were growing concerned at the manpower being used and the escalating cost of the investigations, and pressure to end them was increasing. But those in charge of the investigations remained convinced that there would be more bodies found. DCS Benfield told the gathered journalists: 'We have not fixed a time limit for the search, although perhaps the weather might stop us. We will go on until it starts to snow or the ground freezes.'

The following day, Saturday 23 October, the search of the moors was stepped up in a final push in five separate areas. Over 200 people had reported seeing suspicious movements on the moors over the past few years and the police were intent on following up all possible leads.

Edward Arnfield of Maple Bridge, Cheshire, motored out to the railway halt and led a police car over rough roads and tracks to a place where he had seen someone digging at night. A Robert Ashworth also pointed out a spot where he had seen a van parked in a field. The police marked it with yellow dye for future investigation. Areas close to Uppermill and Holmfirth were also pointed out to the police.

Near the railway tunnel at Woodhead, officers returned in greater number near the Etherow Valley. They took with them German Shepherds and marked areas picked out by the dogs for excavating. At Hollin Brown Knoll, DCI Mounsey led a team of twenty searchers in prodding the peat yard by yard on both sides of the A635 road.

Searchers sniff the ends of their prodding prongs for the smell of decaying flesh.

Volunteers search the moorland.

Photographs taken of Hindley at the Snake Hill Pass road from Manchester to Sheffield, near Glossop, led the police to search there too. One hundred hikers and forty members of mountain rescue teams started out in a 500-yard line on both sides of the road armed with marker canes and whistles.

Volunteers walk onto the moor to begin searching for more bodies.

Myra Hindley on the Snake Pass.

At Hattersley, DCI Tyrrell and his team, searching Hindley's home, took away twenty cardboard boxes of evidence.

The following day, the search continued in much the same fashion. Outside Glossop, Derbyshire Police had set up a mobile headquarters to deal with the information that was pouring in from the public. As it was a Sunday, many hikers and motorists took the opportunity to go out on the moors to try to help the police.

Brady's moorland scenes were printed in large numbers and distributed to rambling, hiking and cycling clubs and taken to shepherds who roamed those parts of the moors, in the hope that they might recognise the views.

Left: Unseen photograph of Myra Hindley from Ian Brady's 'Tartan album'.

Below: Unseen photograph from Ian Brady's 'Tartan album' of moorland. It was this type of photograph that detectives had to try to locate during the investigation.

EVIDENCE

As well as the above photograph, printed here for the first time ever are pictures taken by Brady and Hindley of various moorland scenes that were found in their tartan album, that the author has had released:

Forensic work finished at Wardle Brook Avenue on Monday 25 October, and Dr Bernard Manning, the Home Office Pathologist, and his team of five experts from his Preston laboratory, moved on to an empty house in Gorton. Crowds quickly

Unseen photograph from Ian Brady's 'Tartan album' of moorland. It was this type of photograph that detectives had to try to locate during the investigation.

gathered to see what was going on and in the afternoon part of a door painted red and green, a dining-room chair and a wooden bed end were sent to the laboratory. At 5.00 pm, Dr Manning told waiting reporters that he would not be returning and, after a number of labelled, white plastic bags were carried out to a van, another scientist said: 'We have looked under the floorboards and taken away a lot of samples, but we have not done any digging.'

Unseen photograph from Ian Brady's 'Tartan album' of moorland. It was this type of photograph that detectives had to try to locate during the investigation.

Unseen photograph from Ian Brady's 'Tartan album' of moorland. It was this type of photograph that detectives had to try to locate during the investigation.

Unseen photograph from Ian Brady's 'Tartan album' of moorland. It was this type of photograph that detectives had to try to locate during the investigation.

Unseen photograph from Ian Brady's 'Tartan album' of moorland. It was this type of photograph that detectives had to try to locate during the investigation.

Unseen photograph from Ian Brady's 'Tartan album' of moorland. It was this type of photograph that detectives had to try to locate during the investigation.

Unseen photograph from Ian Brady's 'Tartan album' of moorland. It was this type of photograph that detectives had to try to locate during the investigation.

The search was continuing on the moors, but it was quickly narrowed down to three areas – Hollin Brown Knoll, Woodhead and the Snake Pass road.

Lesley Ann Downey was laid to rest on Tuesday, 26 October at the Trinity Methodist Church in Butler Street, Ancoats. Her plain white coffin with a cross of red roses was carried in to the church by her father, her stepfather Alan, and other pall-bearers, while the other members of her family walked behind.

More than 2,000 people had gathered in silence outside the church and over 300 were inside. The Reverend W. Harold Ford remembered Lesley Ann as a 'bright child' and told how she had been in church for the Christmas morning service the day before she vanished. He told those inside the church:

> The justice, wrath and punishment of God will, I fear, be terrible – terrible indeed. It is not only a terrible crime, but an awful sin and the person or persons responsible will one day have to face God. Lesley

Downey was a bright, intelligent, affectionate little child and, like most children, was trustful. Unfortunately that quality in her was a means whereby some evil person led her away.

When the service was over the cortege moved across Manchester, in the rain, to Southern Cemetery in Fallowfield. Lesley Ann was laid to rest just yards from Edward Evans.

Meanwhile, the search on the moors continued and an RAF Canberra jet was used. It had infra-red film on board that was capable of taking a minute survey of the terrain. The film was to be compared with recent surveys of the area in the hope that any differences spotted would be searched.

The following day, Wednesday 27 October, the police began a more systematic search around Hollin Brown Knoll. They decided to conduct another search without

Lesley Ann Downey's funeral.

Huge crowds gather for Lesley Ann Downey's funeral.

using the photographs or tips from the public and wanted to cover every square yard of the hundreds of acres in sight. It was freezing cold with gale-force winds as the seventy diggers advanced step-by-step at arm's length over the terrain.

In an interview given by DCS Benfield to the press near Hollin Brown knoll, he praised the response of the public to police appeals for information and again told them that the search would go on until they were stopped by the weather. Everyone who was there knew that it would be over in just a matter of days.

The forensic team continued investigating at two more houses in Manchester, by now reoccupied by people who had nothing whatsoever to do with the case – for this reason the information was withheld. The scientists removed samples for analysis only.

Detectives trying to trace Hindley's first car, the old green Morris, found it on a farm on the outskirts of Nottingham. They learned from the motor taxation office that it had been bought and sold a number of times; when they found it it was being used to house hens on a chicken run.

At 4.15 pm DC Derek Leighton accompanied Detective Policewoman Campion to Gorsey Farm Kennels in Ashton-under-Lyne where he took four photographs of Hindley's dog, Puppet.

At 8.45 am on Thursday 28 October, Brady was driven into Hyde Town Hall to appear before the magistrates. Hindley was taken in half an hour later in a separate vehicle. Only a few people and press were there to see them arrive, but by 10.00 am more than 100 had turned up in Water Street in the pouring rain to see what the commotion was about, as the press had arrived along with a television outside-broadcast unit.

Inside the court there were thirty press reporters crammed in at the press bench, while in the public gallery, which was no more than raised benches behind the dock, mainly women with young children and shopping bags had filled the court room to capacity. There were also a few men – most notably Lesley Ann's father and his brother, Patrick.

At 10.05 Brady was led into the dock by two policemen and was immediately followed by Hindley who was led into the dock between two police women. Six more policemen surrounded the dock. The hearing only lasted a couple of minutes as Brady was charged again with the murders of Edward Evans and Lesley Ann Downey, and Hindley was charged with the murder of Lesley Ann Downey and harbouring Brady knowing he had killed Edward Evans. Brady took a look around the court and then stared straight ahead at the magistrates, while Hindley just stood with her head bowed. As they were remanded back into custody there was a loud noise from the gallery and words such as 'shame' and 'monsters' could clearly be heard.

Lesley Ann's uncle, Patrick, had spent his time in the gallery trying to loosen an oak block which was already loose below his feet. He recalled: 'I would have smashed their heads in if only I could have snatched it up in time. But I daren't reach down. The police were watching everywhere.'

Above left: Ian Brady arrives at court.

Above right: David and Maureen Smith running through the market.

As the court emptied, Patrick and other members of the family were escorted out peacefully by police officers, where they joined the crowd outside which had grown considerably. They were angry and wanted to get their hands on the murderous couple. A small Mini then emerged and the crowd assumed that it contained Brady as someone with a coat over their head was sat in the back between two policemen. They shouted and threw things at the car and one man, his face screwed up with rage and with tears in his eyes, ran forward and managed to slightly open the door as the car sped past. Policemen managed to grab him and pull him to one side, away from the road. That man was Patrick Downey. As the commotion was unfolding, another car sped out on to the road, this time containing a figure with a coat over their head and surrounded by two policewomen. The crowd thought that this was Hindley, but were too distracted by what was going on with the police and Patrick Downey to be able to react. The police had anticipated the obvious threat and the two cars in fact contained decoys. Brady and Hindley were held back in the court until the press and crowds had fully dispersed, before being taken to Ashton-under-Lyne police station for more questioning.

David and Maureen Smith, who had been in the public gallery, were chased from the court and across Hyde Market by a group of angry women. A report in the *North Cheshire Herald* said:

> A young couple who had been spectators in the public gallery were later chased across Hyde market by a group of shouting women. As cameramen's flashbulbs popped, the couple dodged in and out of the stalls. The girl, in high heels and a grey suit, had difficulty keeping up with the man accompanying her.

At 1.30 pm DCI Mounsey interviewed Brady at Ashton-under-Lyne police station. This time, the detective showed Brady some of the photographs that had been found of the moorland, and in particular one of himself standing on a rock. The picture included the site of John Kilbride's grave in the distance and was taken close to where Lesley Ann Downey's remains were found on Hollin Brown Knoll. It also showed Hindley's Mini van.

Brady: It was taken on the Moors somewhere. Myra took it.

Brady was then shown the picture of Hindley kneeling and looking down at John Kilbride's grave.

Brady: That was taken somewhere on the moors, too. It was about eighteen months ago. I can tell by the age of the dog.

Mounsey: This photograph was taken by you showing your girlfriend crouching over John Kilbride's grave. How could you possibly say you know nothing about his death?

Brady: I've only got your word that it is a grave.

Mounsey: Do you imagine for one moment I would tell you lies about a matter as serious as this?

Brady: If my solicitor gets another photograph from somewhere….

Mounsey: What do you mean?

Brady did not reply. DCI Mounsey asked Brady further questions before coming back to the subject of these photographs again.

Brady: It's just a snap shot. I didn't have anything to do with John Kilbride. I didn't kill him.

He was then pressed further and started to trip himself up:

Brady: There's no explanation for Myra crouching there. If that grave is near there, there is an explanation.

Mounsey: You took the photograph – you must know who killed John Kilbride!

Brady: Yes, I know. It is one of two men. I have given their names to my solicitor.

He then refused to give the officers the names.

Mounsey: You say you know who killed him. You must have known that the photograph of Myra showed John Kilbride's grave. You knew that when you took it, you knew it was John Kilbride's grave, didn't you?

Brady: Yes.

While he was being interviewed, DCI Tyrrell and DI Mattin teamed up to interview Hindley regarding what exactly happened to Lesley Ann Downey and John Kilbride.

Tyrrell: There is strong evidence against you and Brady. If you have any evidence against anybody else, it is in your interests to tell me now and I plead with you to do so.

Hindley: You know that Lesley Ann Downey was at the house. She was brought by Smith and taken away by Smith.

Tyrrell: Can you prove it?

Hindley: I cannot say.

Tyrrell: When we saw you previously you said you didn't know among other people, Lesley Ann Downey. I think you know all about this unfortunate child being killed and being buried on the moors.

Hindley: [Annoyed] As far as I know, there was nobody killed and nobody buried and, as far as Lesley Ann Downey is concerned, Smith took her out of the house and I have not the slightest idea who did it.

DCI Tyrrell then moved on to John Kilbride.

Tyrrell: Since I saw you last there have been some further developments in this enquiry and I must now ask you some further questions…. When did Ian Brady come to live at 16 Wardle brook Avenue?

Hindley: Five or six weeks ago.

Tyrrell: Did he live with you at Beasley Street? [Bannock Street was the more recent name for what was formerly known as Beasley Street]

Hindley: No, but he spent a lot of time there.

Tyrrell: He was spending most of his time at Beasley Street with you before you moved to Hattersley wasn't he?

Hindley: He spent most of his time with me.

Tyrrell: When did you first meet him?

Hindley: About six years ago, I met him at Millwards.

Tyrrell: How long was it before you started going out with him?

Hindley: I don't know. Not long.

Tyrrell: How long have you lived with him as man and wife?

Hindley: We haven't lived as man and wife.

Tyrrell: You have been sharing the same bed?

Hindley: Yes.

Tyrrell: How long for?

Hindley: Two or three years, yes more, several years I have been sleeping with him.

Tyrrell: How long have you known David Smith?

Hindley: Personally?

Tyrrell: When did you first meet him?

Hindley: He lived in the same neighbourhood since he was about 6 years of age.

Tyrrell: Have you known him personally since then?

Hindley: No, only since he started going out with Maureen. They were married a year last August.

Later in the interview:

Tyrrell: You probably know that the body of John Kilbride has been found. It was recovered from a shallow grave near to where the body of Lesley Ann Downey was found, whose murder you have already been charged with.

Hindley: Yes.

Tyrrell: It is known that Lesley Ann Downey was at your house.

Hindley: I have already been charged with that. I don't want to say anything about that charge.

Tyrrell: I am not going to discuss that charge, and I do not propose to ask you any questions in relation to it. I merely mentioned that little girl's name to indicate the location where the body of John Kilbride has been found.

He asked her about the Ford Anglia she had hired on the day he disappeared. She told him that she remembered hiring it but she did not know when or where she went in it.

Tyrrell: When you returned it, it was very muddy and the hire company commented on it. Where had you been?
Hindley: I told you, I don't know.

He showed her the photograph of her kneeling over John Kilbride's grave. Hindley told him that she did not know when or where it was taken, but she suspected that it was taken by Brady. She said that she was not looking at a grave, but either at the snow or at her dog.

Tyrrell: Who chose the place where you would kneel?

Hindley: No one. We just took a photograph where we felt like it.

He then showed her the photograph of her standing on Hollin Brown Knoll with her car in the background:

Tyrrell: Where was this photograph taken of you standing on the rocks?

Hindley: I don't know. It could have been one of a dozen places.

Tyrrell: Who took it?

Hindley: Ian.

Tyrrell: Was that your vehicle there?

Hindley: Yes.

Tyrrell: When was it taken?

Hindley: No idea.

Tyrrell: Did Ian take all the photographs.

Hindley: Not all, but quite a lot.

At this point, she seemed to play for time and act dumb, as she realised that she might have said something that Brady hadn't.

Tyrrell: Who else would take photographs of you?

Hindley: Just depends who I was with.

Tyrrell: Who else has taken a photograph of you on the moors?

Hindley: Who do you mean?

Tyrrell: Who has taken a photograph of you on the moors, other than Brady?

Hindley: Who do you mean?

Tyrrell: It's quite simple. Who else has taken a photograph of you on the moors?

Hindley: You say these are on the moors do you?

Tyrrell: Yes, they were both taken on Saddleworth Moor above Greenfield.

Hindley: Possible.

She then tried to implicate David Smith again: 'Well, Smith could have taken this. I can't remember.' Tyrrell told her that it was taken near where Lesley Ann Downey was buried and that she was looking down at the grave of John Kilbride.

DCI Tyrrell then handed her another photograph, taken by Mike Masscheder, from the same angle as that taken by Brady of Hindley.

Tyrrell: Do you notice the similarity in the skyline and the position of the stones in the photos?

Hindley: They could be similar, yes.

Tyrrell: You can see they are, can't you?

Hindley: Yes, they could be.

Tyrrell: The second photograph was taken by the police. It is the same ground where you were crouching down in the first photograph. After this particular photo was taken, the police dug up the ground and found the body of John Kilbride.

Hindley: I don't know anything about that. You have asked me already about bodies on the moors and I have told you I don't know the slightest thing about them. I don't.

Tyrrell: Do you think this is a coincidence?

Hindley: I don't know what it is.

Tyrrell: It seems an ideal place to bury a body.

Hindley: I've nothing at all to do with that and I don't know what you're talking about. I can't remember the circumstances about hundreds of photos I've had taken.

Tyrrell: I think you know what happened to John Kilbride.

Hindley: I don't know anything about it. I don't know anything about people's graves. Are you going to charge me with a third?

Tyrrell: It is not my duty to charge you with anything at this stage. I understand you have intimated that someone else is mixed up in this. You have told a relative, an aunt, I believe that someone else is mixed up in it.

Hindley: Regarding the charges I told my solicitor about it.

Tyrrell: You have every right not to answer questions if you don't want to, but if anyone else is mixed up in this, now is the time to say so.

Hindley: I can't offer any explanation because I don't know what you are talking about.

Tyrrell: I'm talking about John Kilbride whose body was found on the moors where you were crouching down in this photograph. It's just a short distance from where Lesley Ann Downey was found. If someone else has done them to death, now is the time to offer an explanation.

Hindley: I was not asked to pose for the photograph and as far as I was concerned it was just a normal photograph.

Tyrrell: It's almost two years since John Kilbride disappeared and all that time his mother didn't know what had happened to him.

Hindley: Neither did I!

Tyrrell: It seems rather strange that you had a photograph taken on the spot where the child was buried. Either you or the person who took this photograph must have known what you were doing. You say Brady took the photograph so you or he must know the purpose for it.

Hindley: Which child do you mean?

Tyrrell: John Kilbride

Hindley: I don't know anything about John Kilbride.

Annoyed that Tyrrell kept going on about the photographs matching with where two bodies had been discovered:

Hindley: [Sarcastically] So there could be bodies all over where I have stood then?

Tyrrell: Look, we know Lesley Ann was in your bedroom shortly before she died and here is a photograph of you standing very near the grave.

Hindley: Must be a coincidence.

Tyrrell: It's a coincidence we found a photograph of you standing on John Kilbride's grave?

Hindley: As far as I'm concerned they are two normal photographs I have had taken. I don't know when or where.

Tyrrell: I know they were taken on the moors where the bodies of two children were found.

Hindley: Well, I wouldn't know that.

Tyrrell: It seems that you and Brady take a great delight in taking photographs of graves, or perhaps you had other reasons. That spot is on a stretch of moorland some distance from the road and a most unlikely place to take a photograph. I suggest that their purpose is so that you can locate the graves and satisfy yourselves that they haven't been disturbed.

Hindley: They have no significance for me.

DCI Tyrrell then showed her photographs of the dug-up grave and the remains of John Kilbride. They were so gruesome that at the magistrates' hearing Mr Mars-Jones advised the lady chairman, Mrs Dorothy Adamson MBE, not to look at them. The photographs were part of a book put together by Mike Massheder.

> The night before I'd been up till about two o'clock in the morning under Joe's instructions. 'Make up a book of photographs,' he said, 'of all these moorland scenes, and in among them I want Lesley's grave and the photographs of Lesley's body being exhumed, I want John's grave and the photos of John's body being exhumed. Muddle them up, so we don't know what's coming when we turn the pages.' Now, I frightened myself to bits making this book up. It shook me, and there's not a lot I haven't seen. But the idea was to present them with one of their landscape photos and ask, 'Do you recognise this scene?', then on the next page present them with a grisly photograph of the victim in order to get Myra, especially, to break down. Even just a look of revulsion would have been something.

Hindley looked at some of them, then turned her head and said: 'I don't want to see any more.'

Tyrrell: What about Pat Hodges?

Hindley: What about her?

Tyrrell: You have taken her on the moors at night time, drinking wine close to where Kilbride's body was buried.

Hindley: She's been with us on the moors but I keep telling you I don't know anything about any bodies.

When DCI Tyrrell had finished questioning her, Detective Inspector Norman Mattin of Manchester Police took over. Hindley's sister Maureen had told the police how much Myra had changed since she met Brady, and Mattin asked her if it was he who had altered her outlook.

Hindley: I made all my own decisions. People go through several stages in their life – after discussions they change their mind. Ian never made me do anything I didn't want to do. All that about killing is bloody rubbish.

What time did Smith say he left our house that night?

Mattin: I don't know, but it was very late.

Hindley: It was about 3.00 am or just after, and, what time did he go to the police? They told me it was sometime after he left the house…. Well, obviously, he was getting his story straight.

Mattin: If you say he is responsible for these deaths let's be knowing just what it is that you know.

Hindley: I'm not saying any more except that he brought her to the house with another man and Smith took her away with the other man. So far as John Kilbride is concerned I don't know anything, nor does Ian.

By now it was 6.30 pm and Hindley was given a break. She was given a cup of tea, bread and butter and a plate of ham. At 7.20 DCI Tyrrell took over questioning again, but the interview lasted just ten minutes.

Tyrrell: I must ask you again, have you ever been to Ashton market?

Hindley: I've only been twice in my life. The last time was a month before I moved to Hattersley. I went with two girls to buy a tea set. The other was when I was working at Lawrence Scott's, when I was 15 and I went with three or four girls to buy an outfit.

Tyrrell: Did you go to Ashton on 23 November 1963?

Hindley: No.

Tyrrell: Have you bought anything else from Ashton besides the camera and the fireside chairs?

Hindley: I bought a radio from Curry's.

Tyrrell: Where were the chairs from?

Hindley: Woodhouses.

Tyrrell: How long is it since you bought these things?

Hindley: I've not had the radio long, less than six months. I went for the chairs at the same time as I went for the tea set. That was a month before I moved to Hattersley. Winifred and Mary Hill were with me, but I didn't get the tea set.

Tyrrell: When did you first know that John Kilbride was missing?

Hindley: I don't know anything about John Kilbride.

Tyrrell: I must tell you that Brady has told other officers who were interviewing him that he didn't kill John Kilbride, but he knows it was one of two men who did and he has given their names to his solicitor.

Hindley: He didn't kill Kilbride and I didn't kill Kilbride. I never set eyes on Kilbride before.

Tyrrell: Has Brady ever spoken about Kilbride?

Hindley: I refuse to answer any more questions.

Tyrrell: Since you and Brady have been associating together has he, so far as you know, ever been out on his own?

Hindley: Never! Wherever he has gone, I have gone.

Tyrrell: Brady admits writing the name of John Kilbride in a notebook. Do you know anything about this?

Hindley: I refuse to answer any more questions. I don't know anything about John Kilbride. As far as Lesley Ann Downey is concerned…

Tyrrell: Think carefully before you say anything further. If you say you are innocent we will do everything possible to prove it. You are being given the opportunity now to tell the truth. A thorough investigation will be made into any explanation you give.

Hindley: As far as Lesley Ann Downey is concerned, Ian didn't kill her. I didn't kill her. I suggest you see Smith! You know she was at the house. She was brought there by Smith and taken away by Smith.

Tyrrell: How can you prove that?

Hindley: I can't say.

Tyrrell: When we saw you previously, you said you didn't know Downey.

Hindley: [no reply]

Tyrrell: I think you know about this unfortunate child being killed and buried on the moors.

EVIDENCE

Hindley: As far as I know, there was nobody killed, nobody buried, and as far as Lesley Ann Downey is concerned, Smith took her out of the house and I haven't the slightest idea who did them.

These words were to condemn David Smith to a lifetime of suspicion and hate.

Hindley stuck to her word and said no more. At 7.30 she was left in a waiting room with a policeman and policewoman guarding her while DCI Tyrrell and DI Mattin went to question Brady at 7.50. They questioned him about the car Hindley had hired and then about the visits to the spot on the A635 over the moors, near where the two graves were found.

Tyrrell: On 23 November 1963 Myra Hindley hired an Anglia motor car for two days. Do you recall that?

Brady: We hired a few cars.

Tyrrell: Do you remember her hiring the Ford Anglia in November 1963.

Brady: I can't remember the kind of cars, they are all the same to me.

Tyrrell: Do you remember the Anglia in November 1963?

Brady: I can't remember.

Tyrrell: Where did she hire the cars from?

Brady: I think it was George Bakers.

Tyrrell: Can you tell me why she hired a car?

Brady: Because we didn't have one of our own I suppose.

Tyrrell: What did you do with the cars?

Brady: Go for a run.

Tyrrell: Where?

Brady: Leek, yes Leek.

Tyrrell: How many times have you been over the A635 road?

Brady: I don't know it by name.

Tyrrell: You know the Greenfield to Holmfirth Road?

Brady: I have been shown photographs of Myra with the dog.

Tyrrell: Were they taken near that road?

Brady: Yes, we've been over there several times. I like it up there.

Tyrrell: You have taken a young girl called Pat Hodges on to the moor at night?

Brady: I know a girl called Pat Hodges, she's got black hair and a fringe. She lives near Myra.

Tyrrell: This girl says that she used to come and pick you up with Myra in the car when you lived at Westmorland Street, Longsight, and that they used to wait in the street until you came out, sometimes for an hour. Why didn't Myra come to the house for you?

Brady: I told her never to come to the house. I like to keep the two environments separate. Relax at home and drink at Myra's. It's just a question of keeping things separate.

Tyrrell: Are you fond of children?

Brady: I like children, I never thought of it.

Tyrrell: Pat Hodges has told us that you and Myra took her to one particular spot on the moors more than any other, in fact seven or eight times at night, drinking wine. She told us that you took her up there on Christmas Eve last year, late at night, and that you were drinking wine and she says that you told her you were going back to spend the night there.

Brady: She has taken wine, yes, with Myra and me.

Tyrrell: How?

Brady: She asked for it.

Tyrrell: Do you know the stretch of road you took her to?

Brady: She has been all over the place.

Tyrrell: One spot she has pointed out is on the A635 from Greenfield to Holmfirth.

Brady: Yes, it would be. If it's the road where you can hear shots from Crowden Rifle range.

Tyrrell: What attraction has this place for you?

Brady: No attraction as far as I'm concerned. We used to go to Glossop as well.

Tyrrell: Isn't it a coincidence that the spot should be where the bodies of the two young children have been recovered?

Brady: I don't know – it's just fantastic. I've made a statement about that to my solicitor. I also talked to Mr Benfield about it and I'm not going to discuss these matters any more now.

Hindley was then interviewed by DCI Mounsey and DI Leach at 7.50 pm. It did not last long.

Mounsey: Please look at these photographs

Hindley refused to look.

Mounsey: I am making enquiries into the death of John Kilbride whose body was found buried on moorland on the A635 road between Greenfield and Holmfirth on Thursday, 21 October 1965. I have been told you used to frequent Ashton market on Saturday afternoons. This photograph shows you looking down on the ground at John Kilbride's grave. Why are you crouched above his grave? I have reason to believe that you and Ian Brady killed John Kilbride.
Hindley: It's not true.
Mounsey: I do not believe you.
Hindley: I refuse to answer any questions.

Pat Clayton:

Myra was a hard, arrogant woman. She had no compassion for children. She had nothing. She wouldn't say anything. She would not talk. She wouldn't answer a question.

During an interview someone put on the table in the interview room a poster of John Kilbride and her lunch was brought in on a tray. It was put in front of her so she could see the John Kilbride poster and that didn't have any effect on Myra. She was just an emotionless female.

DC Tom McVittie: 'She could've opened her heart and told us the whole story of what had gone on from start to finish, but she didn't and she wouldn't. The breakthrough was finding the body of Lesley Ann Downey.'

It was the following day, Friday 29 October, when DCI Haigh, who was responsible for the cooperation with the RAF photo-reconnaissance team, was told that the survey carried out by the Canberra had revealed many disturbances to the ground. Arrangements then went ahead to translate the locations of these 'disturbances' onto Ordnance Survey maps so that each place could be investigated.

The following day, Lesley Ann's mother, Ann, was asked by detectives to look at some of the photographs they had found of her daughter and taken by Brady. The detectives selected the two least offensive pictures that they had found and Ann was able to confirm that they did show her daughter. She later recalled this harrowing experience:

> I can see them now. They had Lesley naked tied over a chair, gagged and her hands bound behind her back, naked and the next one was on Hindley's bed and she had her mouth stuffed and gagged and she was bound – her hands together as though she was praying on Hindley's bed.

A team of detectives were issued with a questionnaire which contained questions covering the timetable of missing young persons and it was designed to get the slightest scrap of useful information from the residents in the immediate areas concerned. They went door to door around the 5,000 houses in the Hattersley overspill estate and to houses in a number of areas of East Manchester. DCS Benfield described the response from those questioned as 'excellent'.

Mountain Rescue teams volunteered again that weekend with the detailed search around Hollin Brown Knoll, Woodhead and the Snake's Pass areas, but by the middle of the afternoon on Sunday 31 October the searches were called off due to the driving rain, gale-force winds and poor visibility, which would last for the next two days.

On Monday 1 November, the detectives took the opportunity to investigate the age of Hindley's dog, Puppet. Brady had told them in interviews that the dog was around 18 months old, but the police needed to establish proof of a more exact age to prove that the photograph of Hindley kneeling over the grave of John Kilbride was taken after he had gone missing. Detective Policewoman Margaret Campion collected the dog from the animal pound and they both took it to Veterinary Surgeon James Gourlay in order for him to give his professional opinion as to the age of the dog.

At 1.00 pm he examined the dog and estimated that it was between 18 months and 3 years old. He explained at the committal hearing:

> It was suggested to me that confirmatory evidence should be obtained by X-raying the dog's teeth. To X-ray a dog, it must be absolutely still, and to achieve this it had to be anaesthetised. A general anaesthetic was administered and while I was carrying out the X-rays I noticed that the dog was not breathing as it should have been. In fact, it was not breathing at all. Immediate steps were taken to apply artificial respiration and this was continued for about three-quarters of an hour, but the dog failed to revive.

Unknown to anyone, the dog suffered from a kidney complaint. When the police informed Hindley of the death of her dog she cried and screamed that the police were 'Murderers'.

As this was going on, John Kilbride was buried at Hurst Cemetery near his home, after a well-attended service in St Christopher's Church.

Searching began again on Wednesday 3 November. 110 diggers, spread out in a line, were working 200 yards from Lesley Ann Downey's grave at Hollin Brown Knoll, but soon had to stop as it began to snow. From this day on, the search was spasmodic and it completely ground to a halt later in the month due to the weather conditions.

The following day, Brady and Hindley made a brief appearance in the court at Hyde and the public gallery was full to the brim with interested spectators determined to see the murderous couple for themselves.

As this was happening, DCS Benfield, DCI Haigh and DCI Mounsey flew down to London for consultations with the Director of Public Prosecutions. It had become known that the investigating officers had sent a list to all Chief Constables across Britain of thirty missing persons whom they wished to trace. The names, sex and age of these persons was never publicly divulged.

On Friday, 5 November, Hindley wrote her first letter to her mother since her arrest. There was no mention at all about the charges she faced. She simply told her mother that she wanted to look her best for the committal hearing: 'If you could send to the station a decent pair of high heels, I'd feel a lot better than I do in these mules. I feel like a tramp in your clothes (only because they don't fit me properly),' and she criticised the police for the death of her dog, Puppet: 'I feel as though my heart's been torn to pieces. I don't think anything else could hurt me more than this has. The only consolation is that some moron might have got hold of Puppet and hurt him.' She then told her mother to retrieve Puppet's neck-tag and store it with the rest of her and Brady's possessions before warning her: 'This letter will probably be censored. If you should write at all, do not mention anything regarding the cases.

While at the Remand Centre, Brady and Hindley had insisted on their rights: all un-convicted, cohabiting prisoners were allowed to see each other. They met in the visiting room, separated by a sheet of glass, talked and exchanged their letters. Hindley admitted later that she carried all of Brady's letters to her on her person because it made her feel close to him. In conversations, they would reminisce about films they had seen and trips they had taken, which to the guards stood at their shoulders seemed boring, but reminded Brady and Hindley of other things they had done on those days – namely the murders. They enjoyed the thought of being so close to danger, thinking 'if only they knew what we were *really* talking about'.

During one of these meetings, Brady told Hindley that it would be a good idea to get her mother to look after *all* of their photographs, not knowing that the police had seized them all in the investigation. Hindley agreed, saying that it would be a good way of remembering the good old times.

She wrote home to her mother: 'Dear mam … keep all the photos for us, <u>for reasons</u>, the ones of dogs, scenery etc.'

They had also discussed marriage and on the 9 November she enquired as to the possibility of her being allowed to marry Ian. Despite neither of them believing in marriage, becoming husband and wife before they were convicted would allow them to visit each other, even if they were sent to prisons at opposite ends of the country.

On Wednesday, 10 November, Saddleworth Moor was searched for the final time. The cost of the investigation and the state of the weather had both taken their toll on the searching officers. Ice had formed each morning on pools of water over the depressions in the peat and, as it thawed, the whole area turned to patches of thick, black sludge between the rocks. The gullies began to run with rapidly flowing rivulets washing away the top soil on either side. The remains of Pauline Reade and Keith Bennett were not found. Margaret Mounsey, wife of DCI Joe Mounsey, later commented:

> Joe didn't want the search to end. He felt sure that they would find the other missing children. He never forgot – he often went up to the moors, even many years later, just to stand at the roadside…he knew – we *all* knew – that there were other victims up there. Unfound.

The following day, at a hearing at Hyde Magistrates Court, Mr Fitzpatrick, solicitor for Brady and Hindley, asked that the prosecution should name the date for the full evidence to be given in public: 'I have tried to explain to them why they are coming here every week for a brief appearance and then being taken back to the remand centre. If that date were known, their anxiety would be eased.' Superintendent Talbot, who had been the butt of defence complaints previously, replied:

> The preparation of the file of evidence is delicate and difficult. The Director of Public Prosecutions is fully aware of the details of that preparation and the file is being prepared with all possible speed. We hope that in the near future we can decide on the date on which committal proceedings will continue.

Exactly one week later, Brady and Hindley again arrived at Hyde Magistrate's Court. People had started to queue outside for two hours before the session started, desperate to get a view of the accused from the public gallery.

Brady, wearing the same grey suit he had worn on previous occasions, but with a collar and blue tie this time, was handcuffed to Sergeant Hinks and PC Dyson when he was brought in to the dock. Hindley was then brought up straight after him, handcuffed to both Policewoman Carrie Slater and Policewoman Hazel Simpson. The public gallery gasped as she emerged, still trying to get their heads around how a woman could murder young children. Hindley had previously worn a cherry red coat to the proceedings, but this time was wearing a speckled black and white tweed suit with a canary yellow polo-necked jumper.

They now knew that they could no longer face the death penalty if convicted of murder, as the Murder (Abolition of Death Penalty) Act had become law on 9 November.

They were back in court again on Thursday, 2 December, where Superintendent Talbot asked for them to be remanded into custody until the following Monday when, he said, the committal proceedings would begin.

By this time Brady had been charged with three murders: Edward Evans, John Kilbride and Lesley Ann Downey. Myra Hindley had been charged with the murders of Edward Evans and Lesley Ann Downey, and with harbouring Ian Brady after the murder of John Kilbride. David Smith's evidence and that of the tape was felt sufficient to charge her with two murders, but in the case of John Kilbride there was nothing to link her to the killing, except that she had driven Brady to the Moor and had a photograph of herself kneeling above his grave. By the time the case went to trial, though, the prosecution had added the charge of murdering John Kilbride to her tally.

When they were driven back to Warrington's Risley Remand Centre, Hindley wrote a letter to Brady's mother to thank her for visiting them both:

Dear Mrs Brady,
I was glad to see you this morning and hope you got home without any trouble. I hope you understand the discussion we all had, and, as Mr Fitzpatrick said, you can refer to him with any queries etc. My mother will do the same.

It's about 4 pm now, locked in for the night. We arrived back here at about 3.30. It's strange to think of being locked in for the night at 4 pm, when, if we were at work, we would have finished the bundle of work and would no doubt be drinking tea and impatiently waiting for five o'clock, to go home. Another annoying thing is this. You'll know we used to have to work every other Saturday morning. About ten weeks before all this started, I got a petition up at work asking the managers to terminate Saturday work. On the very day this trouble began the boss came in and said Saturday work would be terminated if we agreed to work until 6.30 each night. This was accepted by all the staff, Ian and I included, and then this happened, and now everybody at work is reaping the benefit of a five day week after I went to all the trouble of obtaining it. I could kick myself.

I haven't yet received the 'report' on the dog. They were quick enough to kill him, but are taking their time about giving me the report. One thing I can't put out of my mind, if only those women at the wine shop had taken Puppet (which I know they definitely would have done, willingly) they would have insisted on the police getting permission to touch Puppet, and might even have arranged for their own vet, which is the same one you had for Bruce … to make an examination of puppet's teeth, without having to kill him to do so. However, I can't dwell on this subject for very long, it hurts too much to even think about Puppet without crying … Ian was terribly upset about Bruce when she died, although of course he wouldn't show it.

She then talked about taking the dogs for walks with Ian, and finishes the letter:

I hope if you have any news from Glasgow (pleasant news that is) that you'll pass it on to Ian. He doesn't want to write, under these circumstances. Please excuse my writing, I am doing this letter in a hurry, before the lights go out. – When we were at Pollok in September I weighed myself on the bathroom scales and was 150lbs. Now I weigh 138lbs in spite of the chocolate you bought me…

Ian and I have been courting for 6 years on the 23 December. We didn't get married yet as we both had good jobs and were earning over £24 a week between us.

It's just one rotten thing after another. Still, not to worry we're not dead yet.

Love, Myra xx

Chapter 15

The Committal

A committal is heard in a lower court to decide whether there is a case to go forward to trial. Pre-1967 the law said that the full prosecution case had to be produced before magistrates, so they could decide whether there was enough of a case to send it to trial. The press also had the right to report the case, unless specifically ordered not to by the magistrates.

Unfortunately, there was not enough evidence to charge Brady or Hindley with the murders of Pauline Reade or Keith Bennett. The police had been unable to find their bodies. As Chief Superintendent Douglas Nimmo was to say later: 'I am certain they were murdered by those two bastards. But knowing is one thing, proving it is another.'

He had given special orders that Winnie Johnson be made to feel welcome if she ever came into her local Longsight police station. She said at the time,

> I call in when I'm out shopping and just walk to the CID room. Sometimes I take my younger children in with me. I chat to the detectives for about half an hour each visit. It helps a little to talk about Keith. Sometimes I break down and cry, but they are very understanding, always so kind to me.

On Monday 6 December, at Hyde police station, the torture for Lesley Ann's mother continued, as she was told by Superintendent Talbot about the tape they had discovered of part of her daughter's assault by Brady and Hindley. He told her that he wanted her to hear it as it was going to be played in court as part of the evidence against them and that, 'It is not pleasant but I must ask you if you can identify Lesley's voice … I'm going to turn this on and then ask you if you recognise the voice, OK?'

He played her a small exert from it and then switched it off. As he asked her if she could confirm that it was Lesley Ann's voice, her mother remembered that Talbot was choking back tears. She confirmed that it was her daughter's voice.

At 10.00 am the committal proceedings began. As brady and then Hindley were led into the dock, a line of twelve policemen formed across the back of the dock, facing the public gallery and ready for any trouble. Mr David Lloyd-Jones, counsel for Brady, asked the magistrates to hear the case in private.

I would respectfully remind you at this stage that the Tucker Committee, under the chairmanship of Lord Tucker, made a recommendation that there should be a prohibition upon the press from reporting any details of committal proceedings. That was done in 1958. The position at the present time, I understand, is that parliament has this very much in mind. I understand the Home Secretary is concerned and exercised at the present time in his mind about bringing forward legislation.

After referring to a different case as an example, he went on:

In this case, the matters to be investigated will inevitably rouse, and have roused, the greatest and most powerful reaction ... I do not think I am putting it too highly when I say that probably never before has there been more need for an approach by the jury to such a grave issue to be unbiased and unprejudiced and, above all, unhampered by pre-conceived ideas. Such is public interest in this matter that it is seldom that such a great number of professional disseminators of news in our country has assembled in a magistrate's court.

One must accept that the public are interested in these matters, but equally it is necessary to take every possible measure to obviate prejudice to the defendants. With the best will in the world where, as here, emotions are aroused, rumour has been rife and speculation rampant, it would be virtually impossible for those who may have to consider issues in the case to do their duty uninhibited and to come to the right conclusion if there is still further discussion of this case.

Hindley's counsel, Mr Philip Curtis, supported the application for a hearing 'in camera', and told the magistrates about one of the effects of the rumours and speculation in the area.

A report has appeared in the press that in one of the towns where one of the alleged victims lived, a petition has been organised and I think the result was the obtaining of twenty-four thousand signatures; the purport of the petition being an application for the reintroduction of the death penalty.

Prosecutor Mr Mars-Jones said he did not oppose the application, but suggested that the magistrates should hear his opening statement outlining the case before they made up their minds, so the public were ushered out of the court and Brady muttered to

Hindley before they turned to watch everyone filing out of the court. Mr Mars-Jones outlined the case against the defendants with only officials and policemen in the court until lunch the following day.

Brady's counsel, Mr Lloyd-Jones, then countered with his argument:

> However careful a report of these proceedings may be, because of the extent and nature of the evidence, it is inevitable that part of it cannot be properly reported. And because of the gravity of the allegations and the nature of some of the evidence, it must follow that part of the evidence, perhaps of a more sensational appeal, would have prominence … from that, in my submission, it would follow that those ultimately concerned with the issue – the jury – must be taken as having read the reports which would follow. Accordingly, there would be in the minds of any jurors in the North of England, if not in the whole country, an impression formed and gathered from what they would read.

Hindley's counsel, Mr Curtis, agreed, saying that the newspaper reports would make it impossible to find a jury who would not already go to a trial with fairly detailed knowledge of one side of the case.

Without any speeches in opposition, it seemed that the magistrates would agree to hear the case 'in camera', when they retired to consider the submissions. When they returned to the bench after only thirteen minutes, it seemed even more certain – and it was a shock when the magistrates announced they would hear the whole case in open court. Mr Mars-Jones then started to outline his case again in a shortened version for the benefit of the press. It took him until the following day.

On Wednesday, 8 December, David Smith recalled two policemen coming to his flat first thing in the morning. They were to take him and Maureen to the court. They met other officers on the way down to the waiting police car and were warned, 'There's a load of press outside and a fair-sized crowd. Go careful.'

The press already knew where he and Maureen lived, and had gained access to the flats weeks before. They left their business cards, usually wrapped in a £5 note, asking him to contact them if he wanted to go for a drink and discuss the case. He later recalled how he and Maureen put on sunglasses before they left Underwood Court and as soon as the front door opened, they were met by a torrent of abuse and profanities. The police encircled them and tried to herd them towards the waiting police car, all the while trying to avoid objects being thrown at them and women spiting at Maureen. The press were also there and were shouting questions to the couple, one being, 'Any news from your sister?' Annoyed at this, David tried to break through the police line to get to the reporter but was manhandled by them into the back of the police car. As the car doors shut, the fists of the waiting crowd pounded the windows of the car before the driver managed to put his foot down and drive away.

The police car was followed by the press and when they stopped at traffic lights the press pulled up beside and behind them, eager for a picture of David and Maureen. When they reached the court, the street was crowded and they suffered more people banging on the car with their fists and screams of 'murderers'.

The committal began properly, and the first of eighty-six witnesses and the first of 179 exhibits was produced in a hearing that was to last for the next eleven days. Throughout, Brady and Hindley appeared each day, not handcuffed as they were at the remand appearances, and in the same clothes. They both made notes from time to time and occasionally Hindley glanced around the gallery, but Brady kept his eyes firmly on the magistrates and hardly ever glanced at the witnesses. PC John Bayliff of the Cheshire Constabulary gave a statement which read:

> I was on Court duty at Hyde, Cheshire in connection with the Court proceedings regarding Myra Hindley and Ian Brady. I was sat in the dock just behind Ian Brady.
>
> During the course of Mr Mars-Jones's outline of the case to the Justices I knew that the prisoners were talking in low tones to each other. They seemed to be conversing and discussing various points which were brought up and from time to time Myra Hindley made notes.
>
> Shortly before the adjournment, Mr Mars-Jones had explained the evidence of Detective Chief Inspector Mounsey describing the finding of the body of John Kilbride. He went on to describe Chief Inspector Mounsey's description of finding what appeared to be clothing and feeling flesh underneath the clothing.
>
> The body was clothed and the trousers and underpants were down below the knees. At this time Brady leaned across to Hindley and said, 'I thought he didn't have his trousers on.'
>
> They continued to talk but I could not hear any more of what was said.

Throughout the committal, Hindley and Brady looked bored and thoroughly uninterested in the proceedings. Hindley occasionally held her head up in her hands and Brady chewed gum to keep himself alert.

Before David Smith gave his evidence, the Court Clerk, Mr Kenneth Pickup, warned him that: 'You will be asked to answer several questions. If, by answering these questions, you feel that you might incriminate yourself you are not obliged to answer them.' Then Mr Mars-Jones told the committal: 'My instructions are

David and Maureen
Smith leaving the
committal

that the Director of Public Prosecutions does not intend to institute proceedings against Mr Smith in respect of the matters discussed and in his statement made to the police.'

Brady and Hindley were not interested even when David took to the witness box and stood there for close to seven hours telling the court about the murder of Edward Evans, night-time trips up to the moors and Brady's boasts of killing. There wasn't even any show of emotion when Maureen stood in the witness box for over two hours. Instead, they made the occasional note on what was being said and they drew caricatures of the magistrates.

The next letter Hindley wrote to her mother came after Maureen and David had given their evidence:

> This committal may last until January, as it may be adjourned next Friday … so the muck raking will continue for a while. Don't worry about it … I hope you aren't suffering on account of this. I hope none of the family are.
>
> I hope you will soon transfer our things to Mrs Brady. I hate them being in an empty house. What's happened to our house? Have they bricked it up? We were saving for a fitted carpet and 3 piece suite for the living room after Xmas. I cry every time I think of everything that we've lost, but have now accepted that Puppet is better off where he is, he would only be fretting. It's fantastic to think a heap of dirt could break so many hearts. You'll find out later just why he's done all this. (His repulsive father was sat in the police canteen with him and Maureen drinking tea. They'll all have given up work I suppose).

Now comes the 'asking' part of the letter. I want you to get me some things and parcel them up for me. Do you think you can come down to Risley next Saturday? If you can't manage it, don't worry just post the parcel…

Did you see the lies Maureen told the court, about me hating babies and children…. She said I kept things under lock and key, she didn't say the only thing I locked away were my clothes because she was always 'borrowing' them without telling me. Do you remember the time she put on my brand new flared underskirt under her dress so I wouldn't know, and I saw it as she walked downstairs.

She wouldn't look at me once in the dock mam. She couldn't, she kept her face turned away. I noticed she was wearing a new coat and boots etc., and that Smith had a new watch on and new overcoat and suit. I suppose he's had an advance on his 'dirty money' from the press. I'm dying for the trial, to see him ripped to pieces and exposed as the — (you know the correct description) that he is. Throw this letter away after, if it gets into the wrong hands (that can mean anyone) the natural expression of bitterness can be twisted into threats etc.

The 'dirty money' Hindley was referring to was in reference to the fact that David Smith had entered into an agreement with *The News of The World* newspaper, an arrangement that caused serious concern at the subsequent trial. David's father and his Uncle Bert set the deal up between them and sold it to him by saying: 'You've been through hell, the public hate you, you're crippled with debt, you've no chance of a job while this is hanging over you, and there's Maureen and the baby to consider … why shouldn't you make some money out of telling your story?' *The People* newspaper offered him £6,000 up front for his exclusive story, while *The News of The World* offered him £1,000, but made it sound like he would earn much more through syndication and serial rights. He and Maureen met journalists George Mackintosh and Jack Knot from *The News of The World* for lunch to discuss the deal and at the end they gave David and Maureen £40 each.

They all met up again a few days later, this time with the newspaper's editor Jack Taylor and with David's father and uncle. David recalled that they met in a members-only club and everything was paid for by the newspaper. They signed the contract that day.

Under the terms of the contract, David and Maureen Smith were paid £15 per week until the trial. Upon Brady and Hindley's conviction, *The News of The World* would run a series of articles about the couple from David's perspective, and he and Maureen would receive a lump sum of £1,000. They also paid for the Smiths to go on holiday to France and would pay for their hotel accommodation during the trial. None of this was disclosed to the detectives on the case.

On 9 December Hindley wrote a letter to her mother:

Dear Mam,

This is just a few lines before I go to court, Thursday.

I just want to say that all you read in the papers, and hear from TV and radio, is <u>only</u> (and I repeat <u>only</u>) the evidence from the prosecution, and approximately 75% of that evidence is based on Smith's statements. I need say no more but the name Smith. At this hearing there cannot be any denials etc, made by defence on Ian's and my behalf, we have to wait until the trial. I'm only telling you this as such a lot of filth and lies will be printed during this committal. What you read may upset you. Before it does so, remember what I've said, it is mostly based on what Smith has said.

I wouldn't bother writing this, but I just want you to know that what you will read etc, is only one half of a story. We will (Ian and I) have to 'stay put' for want of a better expression until our time comes.

Out of all the rubbish I've listened to for the last 3 days in court, the one thing that came as the biggest bombshell was to hear some of the things Maureen will say when she goes in the witness box against me. I never thought, in a thousand years, that anyone would willingly (or is it willingly?) stand and say what she is going to say, and she isn't just an acquaintance, she is my sister.

However, I won't continue now, the consolation that the truth will out, will have to suffice for the moment.

Don't worry about me, I feel fine, a little tired, a little heath sick, I am keeping well. I told you I was in the hospital not because I am ill, but because of the nature of the charges. I have a small room with chair, locker, and a clean, warm bed. I have plenty to read so don't worry about anything, I'm fine. What people say and think at present, has no effect on me whatsoever. You know I couldn't care less what people say unless they mean anything to me. This is why I'm explaining this early part of the letter to you. You know how I feel about Ian and he about me. Nothing matters in the world as long as Ian is alright. You know what I mean. I'll write again soon.

Love, Myra

XXXX

On 11 December, Hindley again wrote to her mother:

Dear Mam,

I hope you're not letting the press reports etc. of the committal get you down. Remember what I told you, you know Ian and I better than what the papers say. I showed Ian your letter which he was glad to read and he asks to be remembered to you and gran…. No wonder, the filthy lies Smith is saying about him and me, it's agony having to sit listening to them without being able to say a word in defence at the moment. The prosecution are supposed to have 80 witnesses against us, so when the committal is over, Mr Fitzpatrick and the defending counsel will begin building the defence, and will look for witnesses.

If you could come one day, Saturday if possible, I'd be glad. I'll be at court again all next week, so don't come then. The week after that, commencing 20, I won't be at court (I hope). As many as 3 people can come at once, and the visiting is between 1.30 and 3.30, not on Sundays though. This is what I want: tangerines, oranges, some cashew nuts (the proper ones, like Woolworth's ones, not peanuts) some liquorice tablets, some coffee creams, glacier mints, some bananas, and a couple of paperback books. I don't mind when I receive the parcel, as long as it's for Xmas. If you would pop Ian a short note and a box of Maltesers, I'd be glad. He said he doesn't want anything sending in, even from his mam, but I know he'll be glad you've sent them. He rarely eats sweets but if they're there he'll eat them (if you know what I mean). Maybe eating chocolate will make his neck fit his shirt collar. (Joke).

Believe me mam, when I say that 99% of Smith's evidence against Ian and I, particularly Ian, is lies, nothing else. Mr Fitzpatrick says the prosecution are painting the blackest picture of us as possible. Our turn will come.

Love Myra
XXXX

She also asked to be allowed to take exercise on her own at Risley. Her notes state that she was worried about the reaction to her by the other inmates and didn't wish to become involved if there was any trouble.

On Tuesday 14 December, in one of the most powerful moments of the whole case, Lesley Ann Downey's mother gave evidence. Her eyes were red from where she had been crying even before entering the witness box, and the tears flowed as she told the court about hearing her daughter's voice on the tape recorded by Brady and Hindley. A policewoman put her arm around Ann as she tried to steady herself from collapsing and questioning was halted for a few moments.

Her head then turned towards Hindley, who was staring at her from the dock, and she shouted: 'I'll kill you, I'll kill you … an innocent baby….'

Mr Mars-Jones asked her to try not to distress herself, but Ann went on: 'She can sit there staring at me and she took a little baby's life. The beast….' as she wept into her handkerchief.

Hindley, however, was unmoved and continued to stare straight at her. Brady, acting as though the whole procedure was boring him, just sat chewing his gum. Once Ann had managed to gain her composure back, she looked straight at Hindley and in a level voice said to her: 'You tramp!'

She then sat down and told the court about Lesley Ann's movements on the day she disappeared and what Ann herself did when her daughter didn't come home. She was shown the photograph of Lesley Ann that she had given to the police at the time, one that had been taken a few days before with Father Christmas, and she began to cry loudly. She grabbed at the rail of the box again and the policewoman, Margaret Campion, moved forward to help her. She was in the witness box for twenty-nine minutes.

On Friday, 17 December, DC Donald Tempest of Ashton-under-Lyne police went to Ashton-under-Lyne market and showed a folder of photographs to people working on the stalls. There were twelve photographs in the folder and no names were given. Each photograph was instead given a letter of identification from A–L. A photograph of Myra Hindley was given the letter 'G'. He asked each person to look at all the photographs and tell him if they recognised any of the women portrayed.

Her photograph was picked out by Denise Pierson, who said that she was very familiar from seeing her on the market and by Charanjit Lal Bhaseen, as being a woman he had seen on the market. The following day DC Tempest returned to Ashton-under-Lyne market and again showed the photographs to people running stalls who had not been there the previous day. Hindley's picture was picked out by Betty Morley as being that of a woman who had been to her stall on occasions and by Walter Smith as someone he recognised.

A decision was reached on Monday 20 December. After hearing again from Mr Mars-Jones, the three magistrates retired at 3.05 pm. Just eleven minutes later, the Chairman of the magistrates committed Brady and Hindley to stand trial on all charges against them.

Given a chance to make a 'guilty' or 'not guilty' plea again, knowing that there was now going to be a trial, Brady bowed his head slightly forwards and pleaded 'Not guilty to all three.' Hindley, leaning her elbows on the edge of the dock and with her hands clasped over the side, repeated what Brady had just said. Following the decision for her and Brady to stand trial, Hindley wrote to her mother the following day:

Dear Mam,
Thanks for the parcel, it's just what I wanted. I hope you were alright yesterday and that you feel better now. I notice you look ill and pale. I know it's no use saying don't worry, and forget everything, because I know you can't, but remember, you've got yourself to think about, and it's no use making yourself ill and tired, try and forget it as much as possible, don't brood over things…

It's no use trying to express in words what I mean, I just hope you understand.

The nurses have been putting up Xmas decorations here. It looks quite nice. It's funny how many people don't even think about people in prison at Christmas. I certainly never did. They gave us new mattresses today, they're lovely and soft and springy. I'm sitting by the radiators writing this, they're always red hot. I'll be getting in to bed shortly, I've got a good book to read. Mr Fitzpatrick gave me a book of poems by Wordsworth for a Christmas present and Ian a book of poems ... I like Wordsworth.... Most of his poetry is about the Lake District. Ian and I went there last year on our way back from Glasgow (not the time we took those two tramps) and Ian took a photo of me standing outside the school room. Next to Scotland, I think the Lake District is one of the most beautiful places I've seen.

We were going by train to Glasgow for the New Year. We arranged it in September.... We weren't going to travel by car in case of bad weather. I was looking forward to going. Ian says the celebrations last for days. Too bad we never went up for New Year before now.

I do hope you'll soon be able to sort the things out at Hattersley. The sooner they're at Mrs Brady's, the better I'll feel. Especially knowing who's crawling around the estate.

Mrs Brady is coming tomorrow (Wednesday) with two lots of chicken sandwiches and Harvey's Port for Ian and I. We'll probably have it for tea tomorrow. It'll be a welcome change. I had to laugh at her last month. She brought a box full of groceries, including cheese, eggs, bacon, butter, biscuits and cakes etc, to Hyde for Ian and I to take back to Risley with us. She had to take them all back again as we're not allowed groceries unless it's in the form of a complete meal. Last week she brought Ian a new shirt and tie and change of underclothes to Hyde, and they sent her home with them, saying that he'd already had a change. He hadn't, but one of the hundreds of officers floating about there made a mistake. (Or so they said).

I don't know why my letters take so long to reach you. The Xmas post could have something to do with the delay. However, I can't do anything about it. I'll just have to write and hope you receive it eventually. If anything important crops up, which is unlikely, I'll wait until Mr F. comes on a defence visit and leave it with him to tell you. Even if he only comes once a week, it'll be as quick to tell him as it will be to write.

Don't forget to cash that policy, it won't be more than £5, but you may as well have it as them. Mr Fitzpatrick will give you the money for the removal van. As I said, keep those two bronze hanging baskets and other things, it's only personal things of ours that I want you to send to Heywood. There is a lot of things that the police still have of ours, besides the things they are using as exhibits, and M. F. is writing to the Director of Public Prosecutions to ask that everything other than exhibits can be given back, so he'll let you know about that.

I hope the Town Hall can fix you up with an exchange after all the trouble I went to get no.16, I wish I'd never have bothered. Everything is 'if only', it's hopeless talking about it.

Ian's XXXXX. He's smoking too much really, but can you blame him? No wonder, under the circumstances. The letters we write each other every day are a great measure of comfort. There's so many of them I can't carry them around with me, I have to leave them in my room. When I first came here, I kept calling my room 'my office', it was just force of habit. Also, when the phone rang, I kept going to answer it. I'd have said 'Hello, Millward Merchandise' and given the caller a shock (and myself one too).

After this I'll just drop a short note to Mrs Brady, and then write my usual letter to Neddy (I still call him that) Then it will be supper time 8.0 pm and then I'll get into bed and read. (I'm awfully busy aren't I).

Look after yourself

Love, Myra XXXX

Brady and Hindley exchanged letters on an almost daily basis while they were kept in separate cells in Risley Remand Centre. While at the committal, and in meetings where they had both been present while talking to their solicitor Mr Fitzpatrick, they had written in their notebooks and worked out codes so that they could still discuss the crimes they had committed together, without anyone else knowing, even if they read the letters.

The first code was simple enough, with the first letter of each line spelling out a message when read vertically. When the authorities cottoned on to this code, it revealed their plans to get married … before the trial started if possible, and an even more sinister message – 'Smith will die and Maureen too.'

Another of Brady's coded letters to Hindley was deciphered and read: 'I knew that once we brought your family into it they would blow the gaff.' After they were imprisoned and Hindley broke off all contact with Brady, she insisted that it was his idea to get David Smith involved, and she was completely against the idea. This coded letter would seem to suggest that at the very least, if it wasn't at her insistence, then she was very agreeable to the idea.

Another code they used was called the '6-7-8' code. If the date on the letter was underlined, there was a hidden message in the sentences that followed. The code began six lines into the letter, taking the seventh and eighth words as the start of the message. There was no code in the next line, but the seventh and eight words of the following line continued the message. Hindley later explained: 'It carried on in this way on every other line until the message was over [and] was written in such a way as to make complete sense as a normal letter to whoever read it…'

Just before Christmas their solicitor, Robert Fitzpatrick, went to Risley. He gave Hindley a book of poems by Wordsworth and Brady got a book of Ovid. While Fitzpatrick's head was down getting out his papers, Brady slipped Hindley a notebook. It was filled with stories about harming children, written in a secret code. He also handed her a slip of paper on which he'd written the key. (This was the '6-7-8' code described above). When she got back to her cell she began copying these 'messages' into an exercise book. She disguised them as verse and interspersed them with real poems. She used the same code to write back to Brady, and when decoded, one of her letters read:

> I've been thinking for a while, WHY DON'T you ask if you can go
>
> to church on Sundays so we can at least see each other there? YOU
>
> GET someone to help with this.
>
> See the Governor if necessary. There are places in the chapel for
>
> people in your situation, Ian, so ask SOMEONE TO look into it for
>
> you. There's someone here who goes with two officers. She is in here
>
> for killing her own children and also for attempting to THROW
>
> ACID in her boyfriend's face. No one likes her; she's on Rule 43, of
>
> course. Re: your mention of facial expressions in your last letter…
>
> I could have seen the one ON BRETT. His face was a picture when
> you stared him out!

The words in capitals (authors) spell out 'Why don't you get someone to throw acid on Brett?' using the '6-7-8' code. Clearly Lesley Ann's mother had upset Hindley to the point that she wanted revenge for being called a 'tramp' at the committal. Hindley said that the messages made her feel that they were still as one. She later wrote:

> Brett was at that time the youngest son, aged about four or six, of Ann West. This was in the papers at the time of Lesley Ann's disappearance; details of the family as part of the reporting of the disappearance. That's not the whole message, but those ten words were the crux, so to speak…

This also showed how Brady and Hindley would read newspaper reports about the children they had abducted and murdered, in stark contrast to what they claimed in their police interviews of never having heard of the missing children.

Up until the trial the following April, David and Maureen Smith were easy targets for those who believed Brady's and Hindley's stories that he was involved in the murders of the children and because Maureen was Myra's sister and David's wife, that she must have known what had happened too. David later recalled:

> We'd go to the pub and people would fall silent and stare, then start whispering and calling us names. That would lead to lots of 'accidental' pushes and shoves, then proper physical aggression. I tried to stay away from pub toilets because in any closed environment I'd be followed and beaten up. The New Inn on the estate was out of bounds. Even if I went into Hyde … eventually it would descend into violence, whether it was before I'd got inside the pub, at the bar, in the toilets or as I was leaving. It usually started verbally but always led to a good hiding. No one – not *one* person – ever tried to intervene or told me I'd done the right thing by going to the police. No one would have a drink with me either, apart from Maureen and Dad. He had to get rounds in because no one would serve me. Standing at the bar was too risky anyway – if I wasn't careful, someone would approach me from behind, grab me by the neck or hair and hold me down until there was a whole crowd involved, kicking and punching the crap out of me.

Maureen was equally targeted.

> She couldn't go down to the shops without being attacked. Women especially would call her names, spit at her, pull her hair, shove her in the back, and lash out at her every day. She started retreating into her shell, not wanting to go out. I reacted differently – the abuse made me defiant. I wasn't going to sit at home cowering … Maureen wasn't as frightened if she was with me – we'd often go to a social club on Underwood Court, even though we knew we'd come home with black eyes and busted lips. Together we stood our ground. I never ran from anything, because I had nothing to run from, and it was as simple as that.

Back at Risley, Brady wrote a letter to his mother on 28 December:

> Mam,
> Please excuse rudeness on my part during last Friday's visit.
> But also note that the cause of some was due to your repetitive use of the phrase, 'the trouble I've gone to, etc.'.

I realise you did your best, which fell short of my simple requirements.

The mass of food you bought was, as I have told you in the past, unnecessary.

I asked for chicken, wine and books, nothing else. I can buy most other things here. However, to avoid future trouble, which seems unavoidable each time we meet, I suggest you pay me no further visits. You can write if you so wish, that being a happier medium for us both I think.

I have not written to anyone in Glasgow, I do not intend to write at any future date either.

I would have liked to have written to Mrs Sloan but it is pointless, there is nothing to say.

I hope the food and wine you brought for Myra was delivered to her alright, as she was looking forward to it.

You recall the conversation we had with Mr Fitzpatrick at Hyde, regarding what you must do after the trial?

Please do not forget the requests I made on that occasion, as the benefits from same will all go to Myra.

Do not mention the above matter in any letters you write to me here. Mr Fitzpatrick will answer any questions you have on that subject. I should have asked you when you came on the visit but it slipped my mind, will you send, either by post or Mr Fitzpatrick, a clean blue shirt and underwear etc. I have only the clothes I am wearing at the moment.

You can also send a few books along with them. I will now sign off wishing you and Pat a Happy New Year, my own shall be quiet I'm afraid (joke).

Yours affectionately
Ian.

P.S. If you still intend to store both Myra's and my own property, clothes etc., please enquire at Mr Fitzpatrick's office to find out exactly where the things are. You can have a van to collect them, Mr F will supply funds for same.

Ian

Epilogue

The trial of Ian Brady and Myra Hindley took place at Chester Spring Assizes on 19 April 1966. At 4.56 pm on the 6 May 1966, Brady was found guilty of the murders of John Kilbride, Lesley Ann Downey and Edward Evans and was sentenced to three concurrent life sentences. Hindley was then found guilty of the murders of Lesley Ann Downey and Edward Evans and harbouring Ian Brady knowing that he had killed John Kilbride. She was sentenced to two concurrent life sentences for the murders and seven years for harbouring.

While Brady was sent to HMP Durham to begin his sentence, Hindley was sent to HMP Holloway at the opposite end of the country. Over the next six years they continued to write to each other and, using codes devised while they were on remand, relived their crimes and sexual kicks.

However, by 1972, Hindley wanted out of prison and so re-embraced the Catholic faith she had left behind when she started to date Brady. She also took lesbian lovers and got them to do jobs for her. Brady didn't mind the lovers so much, in fact he told her that she needed to do what she needed to do to in order to survive, but he was angered by her returning to the Catholic faith and made this obvious in his letters to her. This eventually led Hindley to finish with Brady and begin an affair with a female prison guard named Patricia Cairns. By this point, Hindley felt that she had served her sentence for the harbouring of Brady for the murder of John Kilbride and both she and Brady had stated from the day they were arrested that she was not involved in any of the murders.

Hindley knew that she would not be coming out of prison anytime soon and after starting the affair with Cairns they quickly devised a plan to break Hindley out of prison using moulds from Cairns's keys. They planned to go to Brazil and get jobs as Missionary workers. However, they couldn't do it alone and recruited a trustee on Hindley's wing to make the moulds and take photographs of Hindley in her cell. When the moulds were made they were smuggled out of the prison and sent to a contact of the trustee, and it was only then that the trustee realised how close Hindley was to escaping. As she finally broke down and told of the plot, the parcel had been intercepted by an off-duty policeman who quickly realised what the moulds were and alerted the authorities. Hindley was sentenced to a further twelve months and the judge made a recommendation that the escape attempt should be noted when it came to any review for parole for her. Cairns was sentenced to six years imprisonment, but both remained devoted to each other (despite them both having other relationships) to the end.

David and Maureen Smith's lives were made hell after the trial, where both Brady and Hindley insisted that David had helped to kill Edward Evans, had brought Lesley Ann Downey to Wardle Brook Avenue to be photographed and had then taken her away again (implying that it was he who had killed her), and had then denied it all and sold his story to the newspapers. That mud stuck, and David and Maureen were both regularly beaten up, had their flat vandalised, and were spat at in the streets. Eventually, the couple split up when David went to prison for attacking a man with a knife. Both eventually remarried and Maureen made up with both Hindley and her mother before Maureen passed away in July 1980.

It was during the 1980s that Hindley continually stated that she had served her sentence and wanted to be paroled. Brady had grown tired of this and eventually told a journalist who was visiting him that Hindley played a much larger role in the murders than he had ever stated and that they were both responsible for the disappearance and murders of Pauline Reade and Keith Bennett. This led Greater Manchester Police to reinvestigate the murders, but when they visited Brady he didn't want to talk about it. They then visited Hindley and she decided to tell them her version of what had happened. She stated that it was Brady who had killed them both and that she wasn't present when he did this. At Pauline Reade's murder she said she was waiting in the car, and at Keith Bennett's murder she said that she was elsewhere on Saddleworth Moor keeping a lookout while Brady killed him.

Both Hindley and Brady were eventually taken up to Saddleworth Moor twice to help in the search for the missing bodies, with Hindley stating that she didn't know where they were buried, but she would point out 'areas of interest' to Brady.

Eventually, the body of Pauline Reade was recovered from Saddleworth Moor, just 100 yards from where Lesley Ann Downey had been buried. Somehow it had been missed during the original investigation and Brady took great pleasure in this fact.

Hindley never did get out of prison, and died of bronchial pneumonia due to heart disease on 15 November 2002.

Brady, who had stated that he never wanted to come out of prison, but who was known to be having sex with underage boys while housed in the hospital wing of HMP Strangeways in 1976, died on 15 May 2017 at Ashworth Psychiatric Hospital from heart disease.

Bibliography

Topping, Peter. *Topping* Angus & Robertson Publishers 1989.

Keightley, Dr Alan. *Ian Brady: The Untold Story of the Moors Murders.* Robson, 2017.

West, Terry. *If Only.* Wild Wolf Publishing, 2018.

Various Authors. *Moving Targets – Women, Murder and Representation.* University of California Press, 1994.

Marchbanks, David. *The Moor Murderers.* Leslie Frewin, 1966.

Goodman, Jonathan. *The Moors Murders* David & Charles, 1973.

Lee, Carol Ann. *One of Your Own.* Mainstream Publishing, 2010.

Smith, David with Lee, Carol Ann. *Evil Relations.* Mainstream Publishing, 2011.

Rhattigan, Tommy. *1963 A Slice of Bread and Jam.* Mirror Books, 2017.

Potter, John Deane. *The Monsters of The Moors.* Elek Books Ltd, 1966.

Staff, Duncan. *The Lost Boy.* Transworld Publishers, 2007.

Garrett, Geoffrey and Nott, Andrew. *Cause of Death.* Robinson, 2001.

Wilson, Robert. *Devil's Disciples.* Express Newspapers, 1986.

Wilson, Robert. *Return to Hell.* Javelin Books, 1988.

West, Ann. *For the Love of Lesley.* Warner Books, 1989.

Harrison, Fred. *Brady & Hindley.* Harper Collins, 1987.

Ritchie, Jean. *Inside the Mind of a Murderess.* Angus & Robertson, 1988.

Coming in Part 2 –
'Convicting The Moors Murderers'

The story doesn't end here. *Convicting The Moors Murderers* gives details of the full trial and will show you how the after-effects of the crimes and trial on David and Maureen Smith finally split the couple up, and how they both struggled to find happiness.

You will read how Brady and Hindley stayed devoted to each other from their separate prisons for many years and how, eventually, Hindley finished the relationship with Brady and turned to lesbianism and drugs in order to survive inside.

You will see mugshots of Hindley that have never been printed before from her time inside and, for the very first time, you will read the FULL account of how Hindley charmed and manipulated a prison officer into helping her attempt to escape from prison, only failing at the very last minute due to an extraordinary piece of luck.

You will also discover how Brady grew frustrated with Hindley's attempts to distance herself from the crimes and win her freedom. He then confessed to a journalist that both he and Hindley were responsible for the deaths of Pauline Reade and Keith Bennett and, over the course of the mid-1980s, told police of Hindley's true involvement in the murders.

Due to this news, police reopened the files on the two missing children and Hindley finally offered her full and frank confession (that was later proved to be anything but) and you will read how both Hindley and Brady managed to be taken back to Saddleworth Moor twice to help police in their search for the graves.

Pauline Reade's body was eventually recovered, but questions remained as to how the original search failed to find her, and who exactly owned a necklace that was found in her grave.

As the story progresses through to the eventual deaths of these depraved monsters, including what really happened when Myra Hindley met fellow child-killer Rose West, the over-riding question still remains… Where exactly is Keith Bennett?